When Buffalo Free the Mountains

Books by Nancy Wood

WHEN BUFFALO FREE THE MOUNTAINS

WRITTEN AND PHOTOGRAPHED BY

Nancy Wood

DOUBLEDAY & COMPANY, INC.

Garden City, New York

1980

DESIGNED BY LAURENCE ALEXANDER

Library of Congress Catalog Card Number 76–42412
ISBN: 0-385-01474-0
Copyright © 1980 by Nancy Wood

For Donald, Melanie, Fawnda, Eric, Clyde,
Valerie, and MaDonna Whyte;
and for Theresa and Norman Harlan and Sadie Frost.
They will endure.

I don't feel we did wrong in taking this great country away from them [the Indians]. . . . Our so-called stealing of this country from them was just a matter of survival. There were great numbers of people who needed new land, and the Indians were selfishly trying to keep it for themselves. What happened a hundred years ago in our country can't be blamed on us today. We'll all be on a reservation soon if the socialists keep subsidizing groups like them with our tax money.

—JOHN WAYNE

Acknowledgments

When Buffalo Free the Mountains would not have been possible without the co-operation of the Utes themselves. I have enjoyed their friendship and hospitality for many years and have shared with them a spiritual bond that has made this book especially significant.

The idea for a major work on the Utes originated with my longtime editor, Janet Chenery, who was with me that day in the mountains when I felt the strange presence of the Indians. Her encouragement and sensitive editing on this, the fifth Indian book we have done together, have made it seem as much her project as mine.

Initial funding for the photographs was provided by the Colorado Centennial/Bicentennial Commission, which in 1976 awarded me a grant to photograph the rural people of the state. This evolved to include the Utes, who had not been extensively photographed since 1908. Over a four-year period I shot more than two thousand photographs of them, all with a 35 mm camera. The Colorado State Historical Society Foundation awarded me a grant when the CCBC funds ran out.

Colorado Springs photographer Andrew Taylor processed all of my film and made over six hundred prints for this book. The quality of his work has added another dimension to my own.

Special acknowledgment is made to investigative reporter Jeanne Englert of Durango, who supplied much of the political, economic, and social data; without her talent, insight, and careful reading of the finished manuscript, the book would not have been the same.

Colorado historians and old friends Janet Lecompte and Marshall Sprague have corrected the historical passages. To Mr. Sprague I give special thanks, since it was his excellent Ute book *Massacre: Tragedy at White River* that supplied the background for this one.

Virginia Wright, my friend and neighbor, helped with the photo editing and also arranged for my interview with Alvin Root. Thanks also to the Western History Department of the Denver Public Library for allowing me to use the rare old Ute creation legend.

Copy editor Timmilou Rixon applied her genius and her pencil where needed. I thank her.

I could never have finished this project without the support and love of my husband, John Brittingham, and my two "at home" children, Kate and India Wood. Thanks also to my patient typist Helen Lynch and my faithful housekeeper, Edna Walker. The road was easier because of them.

Ute Creation Legend

IN THE BEGINNING there was nothing but the blue sky, clouds, sunshine, and rain. No mountains, plains, forest, or desert, no men either, red or white. The Manitou or great He-She spirit lived alone in the middle of the sky and was the ruler of all that was. There were no other powers or gods. He was alone.

After a while he became lonesome and wanted something new. He got tired of telling the sun to shine, the wind to blow, and the rain to fall. So he made a big stone drill and made a big hole through the heavens and kept on making it bigger and bigger until he could look down through onto the nothingness that was below. He was pleased with his work.

When the hole was as big as he wanted it, he took snow and rain and poured it through the hole into the void below. Then he took the dirt and stones that came out of the hole in the floor of heaven and poured them through. After he had poured all these things for a long time, he looked through the hole and saw a big mountain that he had made and all around the mountain there were other mountains, and to the east a great plain.

After looking at the top of the mountain the He-She thought he would like to see more, so he made the hole bigger and crawled through it and stepped down to the top of the mountain. When he finally got down, he found that all the stones, dirt, snow, and rain had formed an immense thing that was ugly and bald and that did not look nice. So he touched the earth with his fingers and there the trees and forests appeared. He swept his flat hand over the plains and there were grass and small plants. Then he told the sun to shine through the hole in the sky and as the snow melted, it made lakes and rivers and creeks. These flowed east and west and afterward went into great holes that formed the Sky Blue Waters, the Oceans. They stole their colors from the sky, which accounts for their name. It was all very pretty and every day the gentle rain fell and the earth blossomed.

The He-She came down every day from heaven and enjoyed the great creations. At that time there were no animals or men, only trees, grass, and water. After a while he got tired of it and wanted something else.

When the He-She came down from heaven he always carried his magic cane and as he sat and pondered, he broke off the small end of it. Out of this he made fishes, big ones and little ones, and of all sizes and shapes. Then he stroked them with his hands and breathed on them and they came alive. So he looked around to see what he would do with them and finally he put them in a stream and they swam away. That's how we have fishes in the streams now, but we don't eat them because some wicked people threw dead bodies in the water and they became fish. We don't know now who are real fish and who are dead people. Of course that was a long time afterward.

Then the He-She went to the forests and he found lots of leaves that were on the ground and had pretty colors. These he took into his hands and making magic, blew on them and they grew wings and feathers and became birds. From the oak leaves he made eagles, ravens and hawks; from the red sumac the red bird and from the green aspen leaves the blue jay. Each leaf made its own kind of bird and the birds all sang nice songs.

From the middle of his magic cane the He-She made the antelope, buffalo, rabbits, squirrels, the coyote and all the other animals. They lived together in peace for a long time until the coyote got bad and caused a lot of mischief and then they began to fight. The strong killed the weak and soon there was lots of blood all over everything. The He-She looked on and was disgusted with his creations.

After a while he decided that he would make one big captain or wise animal who was to be chief and rule the rest of the animals with wisdom and strength. So he made the great grizzly bear. To him he gave all wisdom and power to govern the world and that's why the grizzly is such a wise old man today. He is the big chief of all the animals. He also explained to the animals that they must stop fighting and live at peace as those were the orders of the great He-She and that if they did not do it he would punish them. Most of them obey him excepting when the coyote makes mischief.

Then the He-She went back to the heavens to rest awhile and he left the bear to rule for him.

Chief Buckskin Charley and Chief Nanice
As told to Jean Allard Jeancon
Ignacio, Colorado 1904

Introduction

THE COLORADO STATE PENITENTIARY is an unlikely place to work on a book about the Ute Indians, but that is where I found myself one gray December afternoon. The fortress-like institution in Canon City, a waspish town along the Arkansas River, was more forbidding than usual that day. Two months before, six hundred inmates had gone on strike, refusing to make any more license plates. They wanted their pay raised from sixty cents to three dollars a day and demanded "touch" visits with their families. As the threat of violence increased, the inmates were confined to their cells in the maximum security section. No Christmas decorations were allowed except for a token tree in the prison barbershop. Even so, the prisoners had shown no sign of giving in. As rumors of an impending riot spread, extra guards were posted along the deserted halls, while in their cells the prisoners slept and sulked. Alvin Root, a Ute Mountain Ute, was one of them.

Throughout the festering prison that day, the atmosphere was strangely tense and, as one automatic gate snapped shut and another opened, I felt hostility being generated from the unseen cells of that maximum-security section. The prison barber, standing beside a tinsel-draped, bauble-studded fir tree, peered anxiously down the corridor, seeing only the wary guards and his own distorted reflection in one of those round, warped mirrors designed to catch shoplifters.

In the ominous glare of fluorescent lights, I waited in a shabby, sewer-lagoon green room that used to be the prison's radio station, listening to what sounded like CB jargon coming over the loudspeaker system and the annoying squeak of rubber-soled shoes plodding along the spotless corridor. I strained my ears for another sound—of a human voice coming from somewhere within that garish abyss of ultralight and anonymity. But the Christmas spirit had stopped dead outside the prison walls and there was only silence to confirm it.

When Alvin Root, an Indian from the tribe known as the Ute Mountain Utes, came into the room he was wearing blue jeans and a gray prison work shirt, a traditional eagle-bone choker, and his black hair in long braids. His solemn, reddish face was severely pockmarked like a lunar landscape and had not the faintest suggestion of kindness to it.

The prisoner took a seat behind the shabby metal desk, his reflexes taut, his body agile with an insinuation of violence to it. His black, expressionless eyes were filmed over as if from cataracts and he kept them fixed on the lacerated desktop, never shifting his bleak, exhausted gaze. The guard—portly, imperious—glance once at the inmate, then left the room; his presence remained just outside the door. I sat three feet away from Alvin Root, my heart beating wildly, wondering why I had gone to so much trouble to interview this potentially dangerous man, sentenced to nine to fifteen years on a second-degree burglary conviction.

At first Alvin Root refused to speak about the unsolicited letter he had sent me several weeks before, describing in clear though ungrammatical writing how he had grown up at Towaoc, the Ute Mountain Ute reservation in southwestern Colorado. He had written about his mother and his nine brothers and sisters, of the thirty sheep his stepfather owned, and of the first time a girl had chosen him to dance at his tribe's Bear Dance. He also wrote about his "artistic endeavors, which one of these days my tribe will commend me for," and of his desire to attend an Indian college and start a new life. He had heard that I was doing a book about his people and was willing to share his recollections if I could come visit him at the penitentiary, a task that proved difficult, since Root was in solitary confinement along with 599 others.

Finally the prisoner began to talk, slowly and with difficulty, his dead eyes still glued to the desktop, his hands with their long, squarely trimmed nails tightly clasped in front of him. In a low and almost inaudible voice he spoke, first about how he had recently gotten his GED (Graduate Equivalent Degree—the equivalent of a high-school diploma), going from the seventh to the twelfth grade in just three months and how he had been painting in his cell, using oils and charcoal. Before his involvement in the strike, he had had 150 days counted as "good time," required before his transfer to the medium-security prison in the sandhill country southeast of the prison. Now it looked as though he would remain where he was, in the maximum-security section in a cell between two murderers. Root, considered a high-risk prisoner because of his leadership in the strike, was also considered, according to a prison chaplain, "off in another world" because he was an Indian and "you know how they are."

"In school they make it clear that you're nobody if you're an Indian," Alvin Root said impassively. "The only way is to be white like them. Some of us said, we want to be what we are. We'd go home but there was no one there to help us, no elders anymore and anyway, everybody is drunk all the time. The old people forget what they know from long ago, so there is no one to teach us Indian ways. I learned a lot in Cub Scouts when I was thirteen, from a Cheyenne Indian who is married to one of my relations. I was taught how to dance as we Indians call it, a War Dance. But we don't dance for war anymore.

"I went into the Sun Dance because I had a great dream first and I told my grandmother about it, like a vision of what I was going to go through and the outfit I was supposed to wear. She said, 'are you sure?' and 'the great dream came to you already and you're so young?' She couldn't believe it. I was seventeen when I went in the first time and my grandmother was seventy. I danced for her, up in the mountains there at Towaoc where we used to have our dances. I went to Ignacio sometimes and up to Fort Duchesne, to Fort Washakie, everyplace. I went twelve years in a row until the trouble last year, then I'm here.

"Sun Dance is supposed to give you strength, make you see it's good to be just Indian, not white like everyone tells you to be. But there's this pressure all the time pulling you away from it and sometimes you want to lay down and go with it. You want to forget Sun Dance, forget everything. There's nobody to pull you through."

He paused and shook his head slowly, then went on, his eyes like two dull stones. His lips barely moved.

"I don't remember what I did but I guess I got drunk. And I guess I decided to rob this house and just broke in. Well, I was in the Cortez jail along with some other guys from Towaoc and we didn't like it there—we wanted to go home. So we broke out and went to Albuquerque and got caught with expired plates. We all ended up down here but I don't see those other guys much except in the yard. There's a lot that goes on here but the white guys and the Mexicans, they don't like to mess with Indians too much."

A hint of a smile flickered across his face. "Indian guys are tough, even in here. A lot of people think we have some sort of power, like a lot of Indians do. Me and those other two Indian guys, we don't say nothing. Just let them think it, you know."

The prisoner paused and swallowed a couple of times. His face had begun to relax a little and even the harsh, insidious overhead lights could not diminish the greater face behind it, the one that his ancestors wore and that time and disappointment had covered up. It was a face I had seen before.

"When I get out of here I'm going home," Alvin Root announced. "I want to paint the things I see in my mind—birds, horses, people, the white buffalo coming to the mountains to free them. People laugh but my grandmother told me that. She said when the white buffalo free the mountains, then we'll be free too. Like we used to be when we lived there."

Alvin Root looked up for the first time and stared at the bars on the windows and at the armed men in the next room, separated from us by a glass panel, who monitored each cell block and gave orders over a radio. He started to speak again but the guard entered abruptly and took him away, stopping first to frisk him before the electrified door opened automatically and then clanged shut. The Indian did not turn back, he just moved along the corridor toward his cell with catlike steps, a few paces ahead of the guard, whose right hand hovered over the automatic weapon in his gun belt. I never heard Alvin Root say another word.

From somewhere in that starkly inhuman world, a radio suddenly began to play "Silent Night," followed by a commercial for Rolaids. In five days, the maximum-security prisoners, along with the rest of the inmates, would receive a roast beef Christmas dinner, followed by their present from the state: two pounds of candy, an apple, orange, and banana, and a package of cigarettes. Not long after that, the entire prison would be condemned by a federal judge who ordered it closed.

"Merry Christmas," said the guard politely as he crossed my name off the daily visitors' list. Then he uttered the standard American cliché: "Have a nice day."

Not even his smile could ease the overwhelming hopelessness of the place.

By the time I saw Alvin Root in the penitentiary I had already spent more than three years researching a book about the Ute Mountain Utes and their cousins, the Southern Utes. The third Ute tribe—the Northern Utes—was located in Utah and I had decided, because of the enormous amount of time involved in researching yet another Ute tribe, not to include them in any great detail. The story behind the two Colorado tribes was more than enough for the purpose.

I was intrigued by Ute history and the dichotomy of their twentieth-century lives; I was also distressed that little had been written about them and I set out to make a record, in words and pictures, of their existence. The challenge has been greater than anything I could have anticipated that late-summer afternoon in 1975, when hiking in a high mountain pass above Aspen I felt the eerie presence of ancient Utes who used to hunt there, saw guarded faces in the weathered rock, and heard old songs on the cold and shrieking wind. It was then that I committed myself to this book. I wanted to find out what had happened to this once-great tribe that had tried vainly to stand up to the whites over a century ago, that was closer to the mountains than any other, and that in the end had inherited little of the fighting spirit of their ancestors. What made them lose everything they had?

While I was drawn individually to the Utes, as tribes they did not add up. They were fragmented, estranged, unpredictable; they did not seem to know which way they wanted to go. With each successive trip to Ignacio, the culturally split Southern Ute town, and Towaoc, the isolated headquarters of the Ute Mountain Utes, I realized that these tribes defy generalization while at the same time they seem not at all unique. Their story is the story of nearly every other tribe in America, the remnants of a once-whole people forced into the yoke of civilization. What had the history books omitted? Why did these people have, like all displaced people, a permanent hunger etched into their faces? And why did they have little in common and seem proud of their striking differences?

The outgoing, semisophisticated Southern Utes live in a fertile valley with seven rivers running through it; the introverted, suspicious Ute Mountain Utes live in the desert at the foot of a low mountain that has no water at all.

The Southern Utes have hustled millions of dollars in federal funds to build themselves a whole new set of buildings; the Ute Mountain Utes hustle no one except each other and cannot account for between twenty million and forty million dollars in tribal funds.

The Southern Utes have an almost incestuous relationship with the BIA; the Ute Mountain Utes despise the bureaucracy but are entirely at its mercy.

The Southern Utes welcome tourist dollars, have built a motel, convention center, and racetrack; the Ute Mountain Utes welcome no one, not even their Indian brothers, except once a year at Bear Dance time, and offer nothing to the hundreds of tourists who venture up to Towaoc.

The Southern Utes have a public-relations department to project a noble Indian image to the public; the Ute Mountain Utes project their image themselves, and it is one of corruption and despair.

On top of all that, hardly anyone has ever heard of the Utes, virtually ignored by Colorado's staid educational system, conservative politics, and slick tourist ballyhoo.

Caught in the middle, the Utes struggle to sort out the conflicting messages of their convoluted lives. Society may tell them to adapt and regress both at the same time, yet the Ute hears another voice as well, this one from his heart, coming out of a distant past that echoes down through his misfortunes and his fears, the voice of ancestors and eagles, of a nature so strong that even Alvin Root in the Colorado State Penitentiary is aware of its power behind bars.

It is this primordial message that advises the Ute that even now as the world stumbles toward the twenty-first century, there is a depth to his collective experience that no other American can match, there is a history to him that our immigrant population cannot duplicate, there is an ancient closeness to earth and seasons that the rest of the country can only longingly emulate through solitude and contemplation, two largely unpracticed arts.

The Utes still have a lesson to offer even if it is stratified under layers of cultural debris dumped on them by the American system. Something stubbornly Indian remains—in their quiet, gentle faces, in their exuberant, inquisitive children; even in their alien reservations, which have now been home to at least four generations. They are Indian in their determination to survive there.

We are a nation of achievers interested mainly in results; we have no time to linger over meaning, since experience is all that counts. The Utes, perhaps because their ancestry has not yet been totally beaten out of them, still know how to savor details, small patches of sunlight on an ever-darkening field; they have still a wry humor, a singular ability to recognize if not resist the mediocrity that presses in from all sides. Theirs has always been a losing battle, yet they may go down holding onto their own particular grace, if they can secure a future for themselves.

I have tried to grasp the essence of these people over the years, ever since I first met a few families in 1967 and was struck by the shadows of the mountains still remaining in their eyes. A handful of them have given me a new frame of reference, a fresh definition of life that has nothing to do with success. If the white buffalo will someday free the mountains as Alvin Root's grand-mother said, then they will also free the rest of us.

One day a few months before she died, an old Ute Mountain Ute friend, Harriet Whyte, told me a similar story but this one had the survivors of the earth sealed in the mountains following the destruction of the world by fire. The white buffalo came and with his sharp, powerful hoofs split the mountain open and, like lava, the people flowed out.

"The people will form a river," Harriet Whyte said. "All kinds of people—red, white, black, yellow, and brown. They will take up the ashes of the old world and make a new one. Everything will be new and different and everyone will have an Indian name."

She called me Chicken Papoose.

NANCY WOOD
Colorado Springs, Colorado
May, 1980

When Buffalo Free the Mountains

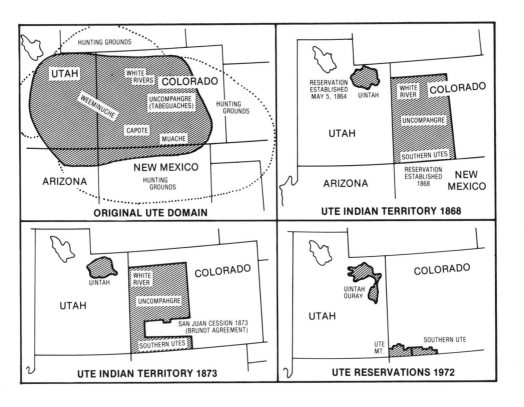

ORIGINAL UTE DOMAIN

HUNTING GROUNDS

UTAH

WHITE RIVERS

COLORADO

WEEMINUCHE

UNCOMPAHGRE (TABEGUACHES)

HUNTING GROUNDS

CAPOTE

MUACHE

NEW MEXICO

ARIZONA

HUNTING GROUNDS

UTE INDIAN TERRITORY 1868

RESERVATION ESTABLISHED MAY 5, 1864

UINTAH

WHITE RIVER

COLORADO

UNCOMPAHGRE

UTAH

SOUTHERN UTES

RESERVATION ESTABLISHED 1868

ARIZONA

NEW MEXICO

UTE INDIAN TERRITORY 1873

UINTAH

WHITE RIVER

COLORADO

UTAH

UNCOMPAHGRE

SAN JUAN CESSION 1873 (BRUNOT AGREEMENT)

SOUTHERN UTES

UTE RESERVATIONS 1972

COLORADO

UINTAH OURAY

UTAH

UTE MT.

SOUTHERN UTE

THE
UTE MOUNTAIN
UTES

1

THE UTE MOUNTAIN UTE reservation in southwestern Colorado is a hungry land—blistered and cracked, a semidesert drenched in blinding sun, perpetually scoured by a dry wind blowing out of the Four Corners country. A few gnarled old junipers and stunted piñons grow stubbornly out of the sand and rock; along the waterless creekbeds, billowy stands of cottonwoods murmur in summer winds. Much of the reservation is covered by a stubbly carpet of short brown grass, punctuated with clumps of sage and yucca whose bayonetlike stalks pierce the thin, dry air. In spring, wildflowers gently· push forth, calming the earth; native grasses, long, sensuous, and green, sway with the suggestion of abundance. Yet here it is not to be found; like everything else on this 567,377-acre reservation, abundance lies beneath the surface.

A great expanse of searing blue sky dominates the land like a giant teacup turned upside down on a saucer a hundred miles wide. The sky is home to the eagle, red-tailed hawk, and peregrine falcon, but the Indians no longer notice. Forged now by desert and not the mountains, the illusion of distance has gone from their eyes; theirs is the look of limitation and short experience.

Sometimes the sky grows dirty along the southwestern edge of the reservation when the wind blows the pollution up from Farmington's new, gigantic power plants; in the eye-stinging haze the Indians can scarcely make out Shiprock anymore, that ghostly landmark that has dominated the horizon forever. All around, craggy mesas rise like chopped-off waves, crashing toward a pale

Chimney Rock, Ute Mountain Ute reservation.

horizon stretching away into the deeper reaches of the desert in New Mexico, Arizona, and Utah, a horizon that does not even offer dreams to the Ute Mountain Utes anymore. Instead, the land is a mirror to their own desolation, as parched and exhausted as their own interior landscape.

Like their land, the Ute Mountain Utes are a sparse, unsettled people. Less than three fourths of their official numbers live on the reservation; the rest are scattered all over the country, in cities and on other reservations. Of the nearly nine hundred Indians who call the dusty, waterless mountain where they live home, most seem to spend their lives in vehicles—campers, trucks, automobiles—always going somewhere, to Cortez or Farmington and beyond. As one Colorado Department of Health official observed while studying an influenza epidemic there, "The Utes are nomads. They are always on the move, just for something to do. Nobody wants to stay home because it's so damn depressing here."

Their ancestors once inhabited the huge chain of Rockies eighty miles to the east where they were nomads of a different sort. Perhaps such roots are the reason why for successive generations of Utes adjustment has not come, even after a century of confinement on a land they never asked for. Part of their spirit remains in the mountains, more attuned to forests and herds of elk than to sand and rattlesnakes. Even though today's Ute is forced to accept his canyons, mesas, and desert as home, an appearance of displacement marks him, as a sailor removed from the sea. This alienation from mountain that not even one of them remembers, coupled with a hundred years of gradually eroding values, is probably at the very core of what is wrong with this tribe today. But they cannot have their mountains back, nor is the large sum they received for them enough to assuage the pain of a betrayed and betraying people.

On the back roads of the reservation, where big black pumps shaped like kiwi birds suck out Indian oil, where whole mesatop forests have been chained (by hooking a chain between two tractors), cut, and burned to provide more grass for Indian cattle, where white men in hard hats ride in tribal trucks to search out

Ute Mountain Ute, Blanding, Utah.

more Indian uranium, a sadness rises along with the dust. After more than a century of exploitation, the Ute Mountain Utes have become passive to the point of unconsciousness and only a deep and abiding distrust of all white people keeps them from forfeiting their resources entirely.

According to a Calder Coal Company estimate, approximately 226 billion tons of coal lie between the Dolores County line and Gallup, with a significant part of this vast deposit on Ute Mountain Ute lands. Not only does lack of water inhibit development, but the noncommittal attitude of the Indians inhibits it as well. The Pacific International Development Corporation of Texas tried vainly to persuade the tribal council—backed by the BIA (Bureau of Indian Affairs)—to give them a coal lease only to be driven off by the Indians' chronic apathy and a steadfast refusal to entertain the company's proposal. Mobil recently dropped its $2.4 million uranium lease with the Ute Mountain Utes, claiming it had paid too much for mineral speculation. Now the tribe receives most of its million-dollar annual income from oil and gas leases, but even these are handled with typical Indian indifference.

While they occasionally marry within the other two Ute tribes, the Ute Mountain Utes seldom join forces with them socially or economically unless it is to push for a water project, a land-claims settlement, or more money from the government. They prefer to remain aloof from the world, whites and brother Indians included, ignoring their responsibility within the tribe, seldom even assisting one another in times of need. At Towaoc, it is every Indian for himself, a situation that has resulted in the most aggressive ones driving expensive cars, owning large herds of cattle, and freely spending tribal funds on whatever suits their whim, while the weaker ones succumb to alcohol, unemployment, and suicide. Indeed, at Towaoc despair is endemic: The average life expectancy is only fifty-six and cause of death is almost always alcohol-related. Social workers from Cortez estimate that half of the 887 tribal members who live at Towaoc are alcoholics; average age—sixteen. At Towaoc the suicide rate is 22 per cent higher than anywhere else in the world, including Scandinavia, and double the

Ute Mountain Ute, Towaoc.

rate for all U. S. Indians combined. Unemployment stands at 70 per cent.

But statistics alone do not tell the story. Beneath the astounding figures is a deeper story that began when Chief Ignacio, like Moses, fled into the desert with his people; unlike Moses he did not find a promised land but a veritable prison where survival was possible only through the sheerest endeavor. If the Ute Mountain Utes have survived at all, it is because the desert has hardened and shaped them while denying them the luxury of memory.

From the beginning, the Ute Mountain Utes did not belong anywhere except in that great hard fist of mountains, drawing strength from masses of granite looming above a land that even today transcends the tangle of roads and fences and towns. The land was big but the people were bigger, believing themselves to be one with eagles and bears and buffalo, possessing sureness derived from rivers and energy passed on by the sun. They were, according to one old legend, like the tree that stands by itself, looking out in all directions at once, enduring every kind of weather and misfortune, yet strong enough to crack the rock beneath it.

The Ute Mountain Utes, or Weminuche as they were once called, lived in the San Juan drainage of Colorado for about two hundred years, not far from their brothers, the Tabeguache (Uncompahgres); the Grand River band lived in the Colorado River area, while the Yampa band roamed near the northwestern Colorado River, which bears their name, and the Uintah group settled the Utah-Colorado border. The Muaches ranged south along the Sangre de Cristos as far as Taos; the Capotes inhabited the San Luis Valley and the upper Rio Grande, where they raised sheep and corn. All seven bands shared the same Shoshonean lineage and linguistic stock; all shared a common love of horses and often traded women and children to the Spanish for them; all were gifted hunters and warriors, roaming an area of more than a hundred thousand square miles. The Utes were said to have been a part of the wilderness for so long that they wore mountains in their eyes and chased the wind to hear a lesson in its song.

Pinecrest Ranch near Gunnison is owned by the Ute Mountain Utes.

Sometimes the wind rushes out of the mountains far to the east of where the Weminuche live now, carrying with it memory and old songs. The east is the direction of invasion and remorse.

Sometimes the wind blows hot and dry from the desert, gathering words from sand. The west is the direction of the Hopi and the Navajo, of sacred earth ripped open to get at a commodity called coal. The west wind is a wind of ghosts and warnings.

Sometimes the wind comes with a gasp from the south, the direction of Coronado and de Vargas, of friars carrying salvation in flasks of water verified as holy. The south is the direction of Chief Quiziachigiate signing the first Ute treaty with the whites in 1849. The south wind is a wind of expectation and deceit.

Sometimes the wind comes from the north, the direction of eagles caught in darkness, of bears who do not awaken in spring, of ancient forests falling and mountains bleeding dust. The north wind is a wind of virginity lost in commerce.

The cries of the old Weminuche, Capote, and Muache bands are on the wind and the cries of the animals who came with them also. In the night you can hear the lion pacing up and down and the eagle beating his wings against the air. You can hear the hoofbeats of the buffalo echoing across land that was stolen, then sold, and sold again. It is not imagination that is necessary to hear history on the wind but an ear that accepts a different version of the facts.

The motivating force behind the theft of Indian lands and identity was originally trumpeted by the New York *Democratic Review* in 1845, which wrote about "our manifest destiny to overspread the continent allotted by Providence for the free development of our yearly multiplying millions." That editorial, written about the proposed annexation of Texas, served as the rationalization for the seizure of millions of acres of Indian lands wanted by capitalists and adventurers anxious to escape the social and economic barriers back East. Manifest Destiny meant simply that the white race was ordained by God to rule all of America and that included the Indians, believed to be an inferior race deserving of extinction. The Utes, along with all other tribes of the time, were to fall victims to this abstract tool of imperialism.

No sooner was gold discovered near Denver in 1859, than tens of thousands of gold seekers poured in from the East, staking claim to property that the Utes already owned, shooting the hapless Indians as they sought to protect themselves, and demanding that the natives relinquish the eastern half of the new Colorado Territory and all of their New Mexico lands.

All seven bands of Utes refused to yield their lands for nearly a decade. Then in 1868 their white-appointed chief, Ouray, signed the third Ute treaty, remarking bitterly as he did so, "The agreement that an Indian makes to a United States treaty is like the agreement a buffalo makes with his hunters when pierced with arrows. All he can do is lie down and give in." Although Ouray, under the circumstances, did the best he could for his people, he was never accepted by them because he was part Spanish, part Apache, and only a quarter Ute, and because he had not been selected chief by a council of elders, as was the custom. His white appointment as chief was because of his ability to speak fluent English, Spanish, and Ute.

Ouray reluctantly agreed that the Utes would retreat to the western side of the Continental Divide, an area of sixteen million acres guaranteed to them "forever," a time span that lasted just eleven years, long enough for the gold seekers to scramble over the mountains and make strike after strike in the Utes' vast homeland. The Utes, the fierce, reclusive Weminuche among them, resisted to the end, pitting their simple wisdom against the cunning duplicity of United States negotiators who tried to convince them that land could be sold, work was desirable, schools were necessary, and that the government in Washington was their best friend. The Indians, claiming that all they wanted to do was hunt buffalo, live quietly, and keep their children at home, realized their situation was hopeless. The San Juan Cession of 1873, most commonly known as the Brunot Agreement, stripped the Utes of another four million acres, which was to yield, in years to come, over two hundred million dollars in mineral wealth.

In return, the Utes received hunting rights on the ceded lands and the sum of twenty-five thousand dollars a year "for their use and benefit forever." Another clause gave Ouray a salary of a thousand dollars a year, a payment that most Utes considered a bribe, especially when Ouray was further placated with a new house near the present town of Montrose, furnished with the latest in Victorian splendor, including china, silver, and curtains.

But Ouray, sickened by the hopeless state of his people and the triumph of the Americans firmly entrenched on twenty million acres of Ute lands after only an eleven-year struggle, made no attempt to hide his grief as he remarked a few months before signing the treaty: "I realize the destiny of my people. We shall fall as the leaves of the trees when winter comes and the land we have roamed for countless generations will be given up to the miner and the plowshare and we shall be buried out of sight. My part is to protect my people and yours, as far as I can, from violence and bloodshed and bring them into friendly relations."

Such was never to be. Removed to the new Southern Ute reservation, a ribbon of land 110 miles long and 15 miles wide, slashed transversely by 7 river canyons and further cut up by numerous cattle driveways used by ranchers, the Capotes, Muaches, and Weminuche tried to adapt as best they could to their new environment. The Muaches and Capotes, goaded and threatened by self-righteous Indian agents, succumbed to farming in one of the most productive agricultural areas in the Southwest.

But the restless, stubborn Weminuche, under the leadership of their gentle Chief Ignacio, were not happy in the lush Pine River Valley, where they were expected to take up farming. They longed for the mountains that miners were already blasting apart to get at vast treasures of gold and silver, they mourned for the rivers now filled with tailings from the mines, they missed the great yawn of sky now filled with smoke from the mills that had gone up overnight. Sometimes, when they could sneak past the Indian agents assigned to "protect" them, the Weminuche left the Southern Ute reservation and traveled by foot a hundred miles back to their old homeland, there to stare in disbelief at thousands of men destroying mountains that had been theirs for centuries, there to be driven off by settlers who now owned the land, there

Jacalyn Tom, Ute Mountain Ute, is granddaughter of Jack House, last great Ute chief.

THE FIRST GIANT STEP
WOUNDED KNEE "73"

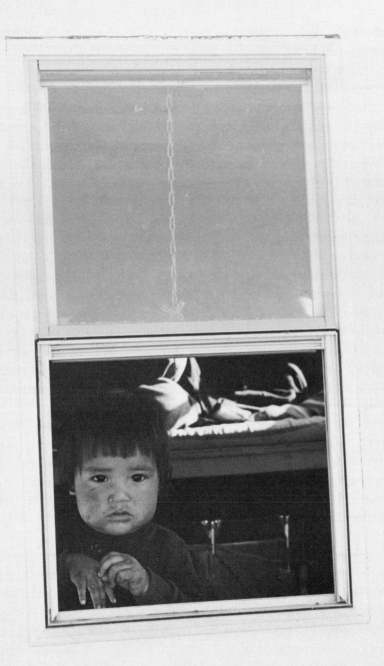

also to lie down with the earth for one last time and die within its familiar embrace.

For ten years the brooding Weminuche tried to live on the reservation with the rest of the Southern Utes, but the Weminuche became more and more estranged from them, refusing to plant so much as a bean in the dark, rich soil of the valley. They kept to themselves among rocks and piñons, roamed the canyons that the seven rivers made, ached for the mountains they had left behind, and finally, hearing of a plot to ship all the Utes into the Utah desert, simply vanished into that wasteland themselves.

Some historians say that this was a final act of defiance by Chief Ignacio and his band, who had still believed as late as 1888 that they would be returned to the mountains; others say that Ignacio had simply given up and taken his people into the desert to die; still others claim that the Weminuche fled west into Utah in hopes of finding their lost freedom among the dry washes and endlessly blowing sand. By that time pressure from Colorado citizens was mounting, and the Utes themselves detested their narrow, cut-up reservation, overrun as it was by cattle, sheep, and greedy whites who ignored reservation boundaries and simply moved in, wagons, livestock, belongings, and all.

The memory of mountains went with the Weminuche in 1888 and the exploits of warriors, only a generation or two removed from their own limited yet remarkable experiences, were recounted again and again. The strength of an estimated three hundred Weminuche seemed to come from someplace deep within as they endured the parched and alien desert, the hostile Mormons, and the ever-marauding Navajos; their resiliency was all that remained from happier days in the mountains just twenty-five years before. Marooned in the desert, living in mud and stick hogans or under a hide stretched between two rocks or stunted trees, the Weminuche subsisted on roots, rabbits, birds, bugs, and lizards; nearly half of them died from hunger, thirst, and exposure. As hunters and warriors, they were finished; as human beings, they were barely even acknowledged.

Finally, in 1895, the Weminuche were forced back into Colorado by government agents anxious to assign them each a 160-acre allotment, a political scheme designed to decrease Indian holdings even more, since once allotments were made, the rest of the reservation was to be thrown open to white settlement.

The tattered, half-dead Weminuche refused allotments and instead established a camp at the western edge of the Southern Ute reservation. Some historians say that the Weminuche refused allotments on the principle that land could not be divided; others insist that crafty whites hurried over to the small settlement and for a few gold pieces persuaded the aging Ignacio to sign papers giving up whatever land he had along the fertile Pine River Valley. Whatever the case, the Weminuche did relinquish their share of the Southern Ute reservation and remained where they were, at the base of a waterless, barren mountain shaped like a woman lying down, her face turned west, away from the mountains as though in sorrow.

Some of Ignacio's group fled into the wasteland after the Bureau of Indian Affairs established a subagency at Navajo Springs, now Cortez, in 1897; the Weminuche preferred the deep canyons and brush-covered mesas of what was to become Mesa Verde National Park in 1906. Still others moved into the desolate Mancos Canyon area where Navajos already lived. No one lived at what is now Towaoc until 1914, when the BIA moved its offices there.

At night, eerie, forgotten voices of ancient cliff dwellers moaned on the wind rushing down the canyon. It was ironic that the Utes, thought to be the tribe that displaced the Anasazi in the late thirteenth century, had now, six hundred years later, come to live among their ghosts. In the crumbling ruins of small cliff dwellings in the farthest reaches of Mancos Canyon, the Weminuche carefully hid what few possessions they had left, a few pieces of beadwork, some ragged buckskin, even the remains of a set of china dishes somehow acquired from the whites. Years later, when archaeologists combed the area, they would wonder at these strange findings; then, however, there were just the displaced Indians trying desperately to survive.

The Ute Mountain Utes, isolated, suspicious, and half wild,

continued religious practices as they had before. The Sun Dance attracted numerous men, the peyote ritual was practiced regularly, and a vigorous group of shamans and elders came under the leadership of their great chiefs, Mariano and Redrock. Certain rituals left over from their old days under Chief Ignacio were said to be still performed.

At the death of a relative, the Ute Mountain Ute would open the eyes of the corpse and stand before it, weeping a last farewell.

Freshly dead bodies were dug up from primitive graves and the sexual organs, both male and female, were cut off along with the tips of tongues, fingers, lips, and toes. All these were carefully cured and dried by the shaman, then dispensed to the young in little pouches to aid in their courtship.

Fingernails and toenails were cut only at night, then offered to a benevolent being called *Inu'sakats* with the prayer: "Give me long life and help me, *Inu'sakats!*"

But such an incantation appeared to do little good at Towaoc, the most primitive, backward, and threatened Ute reservation of all. The BIA, in an effort to force farming upon the Indians, cut their rations almost to the starvation point in 1913, dispensing only flour, baking powder, sugar, salt, soap, beans, and salt pork to them. Beef rations were kept by the agent himself, who handed out only such undesirable cuts as intestines to his charges. Virtually imprisoned on the reservation, with hunting declining as the Cortez area became settled, the Weminuche managed to raise a few goats and sheep on the hard, unyielding soil, tended their beloved herds of horses, and huddled in pole shelters and tepees. Neglect, poor diet, and a harsh environment took their toll.

By the 1930s, syphilis had claimed one fourth of the population, reduced then to 450 ragged, half-starved souls. Other diseases were rampant—gonorrheal arthritis, trachoma, and tuberculosis; in one family alone five deaths occurred from TB during one three-year period. By the start of the Depression, only six Ute Mountain Utes spoke English and only two or three had gone to school, despite BIA efforts to educate them. Indeed, twenty-seven Ute children were sent to boarding school in Albuquerque in 1883 and before they were allowed to come home, more than half of them died, reason enough for the Ute Mountain Utes to refuse education for their children for the next fifty years, even after the agency built a school at Towaoc in 1915. So acute was Indian hatred for the BIA that, following attempts to kill two officials, the agency closed its office at Towaoc shortly after World War I and moved to Ignacio. For more than thirty years, the destitute Ute Mountain Utes had to go by foot, wagon, or horseback to the Southern Ute headquarters, eighty-five miles away, to request even the smallest assistance.

Day after day, embittered youths hung around the trading post, reduced to begging for food and such essentials as shoes as they stood barefoot in the cold, often with nothing more than a ragged, filthy blanket around their shoulders. One fifteen-year-old boy who had never been to school said at the time: "The old people had better brains. We youngsters have nothing and we do nothing." Another claimed he was too poor to have a name.

Studied by curious anthropologists and sociologists who issued dire reports and brought in fresh teams to study and save them, the Ute Mountain Utes withdrew into a cocoon of indifference. The lack of a bureaucracy at their Gaza Strip bothered them not a bit as they struggled to survive on their own, becoming an easy target for zealous missionaries who promised salvation in exchange for custody of their souls. The "lost" Indians, hungry, humiliated, and clutching the remnants of their old pantheistic religion to them, spurned salvation and once more withdrew into the wilds of their reservation, where they could not be found in the vastness of desert, rock, and mesa.

During the fifties, when the rest of the country was riding the crest of the postwar economy, hunting for communists, and buying their first television sets, the Ute Mountain Utes had heard of none of these things and cared less. As far as most citizens knew, the Utes did not exist either. Then suddenly in 1954, the collective guilt of America over its nineteenth-century sins against the Indians was assuaged by a thirty-two-million-dollar land-claims settlement awarded to all three tribes of Utes. The Ute

Mountain Ute cut amounted to six million dollars, a windfall from which they have never fully recovered.

The change was abrupt and crushing. Ill prepared for their sudden wealth, the Ute Mountain Utes responded with a sense of disbelief and frenzy. They wandered into Cortez, twenty miles away, and bought furniture, appliances, and cars, handing over thousands of dollars to merchants who reportedly overcharged the Indians by as much as 100 per cent. The Utes were oblivious. Unaccustomed to money, they would offer a twenty-dollar bill to pay for three dollars' worth of groceries, then walk off without their change. On most nights in Cortez, the favorite sport was "rolling the Indians."

Automobile dealers, wise to the fact that they could not legally enter federal land to repossess Indian cars, simply charged more than the list price for vehicles at high interest rates, covering their actions with phony bills of sale and undated receipts. The Ute Mountain Utes, who had been outcasts in the knife-wielding, motel-packed, curio-shop town of Cortez for sixty years, now found themselves courted by businessmen who lured them in with promises of deals and discounts. With their pockets bulging, the Indians unwittingly fell into the hands of Cortez merchants who up to then had considered them unwelcome in their stores. Now, for Indians who could read, signs were posted to encourage their business; salesmen and bankers suddenly were eager to take them to lunch. According to a former tribal attorney, one Cortez bank frequently charged the Ute Mountain Utes as high as 13 per cent interest per month and over 100 per cent per year. Cortez, once a sleepy crossroads town on the way to somewhere else, blossomed overnight with the sweet smell of lump sums and promissory notes.

The Ute Mountain Utes, giddy from all the attention, raised more than financial expectations in Cortez. For the first time in their lives legally able to buy liquor, they indulged themselves at local bars and package stores—and were usually arrested for drunkenness. In one year, the town of Cortez levied nearly $130,000 worth of drunk fines against the Indians—more than ten

Towaoc.

times that of other towns that size. Always there were at least three Ute Mountain Utes in the drunk tank overnight, sleeping off the effects of their late-night follies.

Meanwhile at Towaoc, the BIA reappeared after a thirty-year absence, swept out its old office, and went to work disbursing $3,000 to each tribal member to build a house or buy land; for a family of six this meant $18,000 for a modern, new house when most of them had spent their lives in tents and hogans. Asbestos-shingled bungalows went up all over Towaoc beside shade houses (a rectangle made entirely of cottonwood trees) that the Indians refused to take down, accustomed as they were to sleeping in them during warm summer nights. The BIA moved the Ute Mountain Utes into the new houses with promises of electricity and plumbing, which few knew how to cope with, often jamming garbage down the toilets, stuffing sinks with trash, and inserting their fingers in mysterious electrical outlets. The agency doled out another $1,000 for each family member to buy furnishings when few had ever slept in a bed, eaten at a table, or sat on anything except the ground.

Once again, the Indians went wild in Cortez, purchasing two and three refrigerators at a time, buying freezers that often stood empty, and laying out cash for a television set, which quickly replaced gambling—practiced daily for years in the tribal chairman's house—as the major diversion among them.

Within a few years, Towaoc took on the appearance of a ghetto. The new houses, abandoned when a tribal member died, were quickly vandalized and sometimes set on fire; the occupied houses became heaped, inside and out, with debris, most of it appliances that had quit working or furniture demolished by children. The BIA refused to pay for repairs or replacements, claiming that the Indians did not know how to take care of anything, ignoring the fact that they had never been instructed in the first place.

There is no welcoming sign at Towaoc, for no one is welcome; until recently tribal police turned back all strange cars coming onto the reservation, but now there are only spot checks and an inquiry as to business there. On either side of the sloping road is a new rash of HUD Mutual Help houses, 101 in all, ranging in price from $50,000 to $56,000. The Indians can buy them with no money down and payments as low as $29 a month. However, 51 of the houses are electrically heated, resulting in average winter utility bills of $250 a month, a distressing fact that has prompted the Utes to apply to HUD for more funds to refit the houses with a natural-gas heating system. Strangely, neither HUD nor the BIA ever suggested solar heating in an ideal environment where the sun shines an average of 325 days a year.

While the new houses, brown and impudent in the sun, stand out like monuments to a crazed bureaucracy, the old Ute Mountain Ute houses are sad reminders of failed efforts at conformity and instant responsibility. Like the old Mountain Ute houses, these too are neglected; many are abandoned and others show feeble attempts to individualize them. To the south, beside one of the new houses, a tepee has been erected in a field, to be used for regular peyote ceremonies, which have been part of Ute life for eighty years. Nearly all of the old houses have outhouses built behind them because the Ute Mountain Utes are in the habit of using their bathrooms for trash bins, storage closets, or garbage disposals. When the plumbing backs up, they simply use their dependable, old outhouses.

Except for the new houses, Towaoc has no new buildings, no motel, no restaurant, no stores, and no school. A recreation center, built in 1966 for $1.2 million, has an Olympic-sized swimming pool and basketball court but after a child drowned in the pool a few years ago, the Utes refused to go there, saying there was a spell on it. The center is closed most of the time despite a sign that says, "Welcome to the Ute Tribe Recreation Center and the facilities. Enjoy yourselves. Staff members on duty at all times."

There is one gas station in Towaoc, a small cafe where children like to gather after school, the police building, and until recently, a trading post and post office. A long, wide, tree-lined plaza has on either side rows of shabby old government buildings erected in 1917 with the Utes' own money, about $40,000, all that was left in the tribal treasury after their first land-claims settlement in 1910. In these are located the tribal offices, the BIA, the Boy Scouts, and such programs as Headstart, Community Action, Community Health, employment, housing, food stamps, and a small library, containing no books on Indians. The library doubles as a Catholic church on Saturday afternoons when a priest comes out from Cortez.

Except for the trading post, there is nothing to buy in Towaoc, no Indian craft shops, no souvenir stands, no curio items. There are no monuments to the past, no plaques and no parks, nothing except the decrepit buildings to suggest that anyone lives there. Towaoc is a place of ghosts and disaffection, of rancid dreams and strangled individuality. Most of the time the Indians are nowhere about and even in the middle of the day, the plaza is eerily deserted. The only activity is when a car or pickup lurches

OVERLEAF

Ute Mountain Ute house, built in 1978.

down one of the dusty, rutted roads past houses of dead tribal members; the houses are boarded up because of evil spells said to be on them. Most Indians, bound to this place in body, are elsewhere in spirit, restless and preoccupied, yet a certain joy now and then creeps through, particularly at Bear Dance time in spring, when the tribe turns out to dance, sing, and play endless card and hand games, betting away hundreds of dollars at a time. Then laughter echoes across the big field where the dance is held and the Ute Mountain Utes transcend all that is petty and confining, even inviting their old enemies, the Navajos.

North of the plaza is a row of sagging government houses where BIA employees live; some of the houses are boarded up, others are falling down, only three are occupied. The government houses, like the Indian houses, have the look of houses that are not homes; an atmosphere of desolation surrounds them. There are no lawns or gardens, no patios, porches, or picnic tables. Young Indian children roam the streets and vacant lots, buy candy, pop, and gum at the cafe; they have learned to live with boredom unrelieved by the television set and with the pressures of a school system that expects them to conform. Most of the tribe's high-school students go to BIA schools in Phoenix, Santa Fe, or Utah rather than attending the public high school in Cortez, where they often feel inferior.

Towaoc is a town that died before it lived, that lives because it cannot die. It is a town that needs to breathe, that cries out for continuity and community, but Towaoc has suffocated on its own deficiencies. According to the Census Bureau, 1,239 Ute Mountain Utes exist, but only 887 live at Towaoc, enough to know who comes to town, in what kind of car, and whom they visit, just as in any small town. A visitor runs the risk not so much of attack but of having every movement monitored, mostly out of curiosity. Strange cars are usually followed by tribal police, who once ran a Utah television crew off the reservation. But such surveillance is not limited to the tribe; the BIA, with its office in the middle of the plaza, is also interested in who comes to Towaoc and why. Dispatches are regularly sent to the district office in Albuquerque, detailing activities of reporters especially. While suspicion of outsiders is rampant at the reservation by both Indians and bureaucrats, the attitude between them is also one of mistrust and animosity, in stark contrast to the submissive amiability that exists between the Southern Utes and their agency.

At Towaoc, the BIA, while routinely drawing up mineral leases, consolidating land holdings, pressing for an occasional government handout to renovate one of the decrepit tribal buildings, and constructing the usual tract-type housing for the Indians, functions minimally in the daily lives of the people and even less in the affairs of the tribal council. Unlike the Southern Utes, who frequently invite their superintendent, Ray de Kay, to council meetings, visit him at his house, and include him in all tribal functions, the Ute Mountain Ute superintendent, Joe Otero, is shut out of everything in a manner reminiscent of the time when the BIA at Towaoc was forced to flee for its life. Indeed, numerous threats have been made against the pudgy, innocuous-looking superintendent, who sat in his office one hot July afternoon, perspiring at his desk. There is no air conditioning at Towaoc and no fans; a slight breeze drifted in the open windows and ruffled the papers on his tidy desk, the usual government gun-metal green.

"The Utes have not looked to us as a major source of assistance," Joe Otero said, folding his well-manicured hands on his desk. Everything about him was orderly, his neatly trimmed mustache, his carefully pressed uniform, his even, white teeth, which gleamed like a television ad for toothpaste. "An organization like the bureau can only be as effective as the people will let it be."

Joe Otero, a BIA career man, had been at Towaoc four years. During that time he had tried to straighten out much of the tribe's tangled affairs, once even calling in the FBI to investigate the disappearance of funds from the tribal treasury.

"They came," he recalled, rolling his dark eyes toward the ceiling, "looked around, and told me to forget it. All the tribe said was, 'Oh well, old Henry didn't mean to steal anything. He'll pay it back sometime.' That's the attitude around here—'oh well.'" He drummed his fingers impatiently on his desk, examining his visitor closely. People were always coming to Towaoc to save the Indians, he said, and it was a hopeless task. They didn't want to be saved.

"They got all that money in 1955," the superintendent explained, "and it ruined them. A lot of people who weren't Mountain Utes claimed membership and a lot of others had a kid every year because it was a way to get money." He stopped a moment and looked out the window at a group of Ute children going by. "They have to learn to produce, not reproduce," he said bitterly. "They're like rabbits. It's the only thing they know how to do."

He turned away, adjusted his small spectacles, and continued, "Well, on top of all the land-claims money, they got oil and gas money too—about $35 million. At one time they got as much as $1,500 a year per capita, so nobody had to work. They'd drink up all their money, then come to us. Of course we tried to help them but—" he shrugged his shoulders. "It was their money, after all."

There was a rumor going around Towaoc, he said, that the FBI was coming back again, this time to discover why the per-capita payments had stopped. But Joe Otero was not aware of what was happening in the tribal office building next door; the Indians had refused to let him in and he was barred from all council meetings. "They run their ship and I run mine," he said, looking around the big, high-ceilinged room that was most of his ship at Towaoc.

Another rumor was that the children's trust agreement at the First National Bank in Denver had been canceled by the tribe, but Otero did not know about that either. "Look, they hand these kids $10,000 or more in cash when they reach eighteen," he snapped. "Certainly they blow it. They don't know how to handle money any better than their parents." The superintendent was vexed, caught in the politics of an agency that bears no responsibility to educate rising generations of Indians in money matters.

His brow was wet with perspiration, so he took out a clean, white handkerchief and wiped it. "Take their budget," he said abruptly. "It usually runs between $2.2 and $3.5 million a year but once I remember it was closer to $4 million. I was the one who

Joe Otero, BIA superintendent, Towaoc.

was supposed to approve it and when I didn't, they'd go to Wayne Aspinall [former Democratic congressman from Colorado] and he'd ram it through. So you see, they could always do as they pleased." He managed a little smile. "The BIA is not all bad. We try and do our job, but I'd say it's harder here than most places. It's not our fault they've run through all their money. We tried to tell them but they wouldn't listen."

To help them out, Joe Otero had initiated a tribal work-experience program in accordance with BIA regulations.

"We pay them the equivalent of welfare," Otero said, "but we won't pay them unless they work." At that time there were eight tribal members participating in the tribal work-experience program: One was on road maintenance, another was a janitor in the government buildings, another made sandwiches for government personnel, and another was in secretarial training in the BIA office. They all worked a full 40-hour week, since that was what the tribal council, urged by the superintendent, had decided. Their pay amounted to $.26 an hour.

"It's strictly a voluntary program," the superintendent said, "with an incentive pay of $45 a month. I want them to say, 'Why should I work for you when I can make $60 a week working for so-and-so in town?' Incentive, that's what I'm trying to build." He looked out the window toward the community center, where a group of young boys was throwing a plastic frisbee through the air; near them an old man sat on the ground drinking from a bottle inside a paper bag. Joe Otero seemed not to notice.

"Right now I'm wondering how to give them incentive to be farmers," he said. "If they get their water [from the Dolores River project] they'll have to be farmers or else lose their water rights. We've picked out a spot for them just south of here but they don't like it. They say bad spirits live there—they're great believers in bad spirits when they don't want to do something. That's why they won't live in a house when someone dies—bad spirits. Even though it's a perfectly good house, they want another one. Well, bad spirits or not, that's the only place they can farm."

The Dolores River project, scheduled to send 27,000 acre-feet of water to Towaoc for industrial, agricultural, recreational, and domestic use, will cost the Indians $150,000 a year for drinking water alone. The tribe has, for all of its history, been forced to haul thousands of gallons of drinking water from Cortez each week. Despite a recent Colorado Department of Health approval of their old spring, the Utes still refuse to drink it, claiming it makes them sick.

Joe Otero got up and closed the windows, tidied up his already tidy desk, and prepared to go home: It was exactly four fifty-nine. "Tradition," he said sadly. "There's nothing wrong with tradition. It just doesn't fit today." He slammed his desk drawer shut.

Did the superintendent think the Ute Mountain Utes were ready for "termination"? (Termination, a bureaucratic word coined by the federal government, indicates self-determination and freedom of the Indians from government control.)

Joe Otero whirled around as though stung. His expression was one of bemused dismay. "These Indians?" he asked. "They couldn't manage shit in a toilet."

2

THE MODERN WORLD is swallowing the Ute Indians whole, and the erratic natives do not seem to mind, for theirs is the way of acceptance as a tool of survival. They are losing their Indian identity, all the rich and varied characteristics that once set them apart from invading hordes of white men and their impressive array of habits, hardware, and attitudes. But we, not they, are disturbed. We *need* them to be Indians, yet now they have all but merged with the very society that exploited and subdued them shortly after the first wave of gold seekers hit Denver in 1859 and scrawled the inevitable writing on the wall. From that moment on, the Utes were destined to become what most Indians are—refugees in their own land with no dominion over it.

Throughout the course of history, strong have conquered weak, whole civilizations have fallen and others have risen to take their place. The Indians are simply pawns in the larger game of cultural chess, forfeiting old values, traditions, and lore to the king and queen of American life—consumerism and vanity. They can move nowhere, win nothing. Yet how could the Indian ever have preserved the ancient value system of his grandfather any more than the displaced Vietnamese—living in America—can cling to his rice-paddy culture? How can either resist the insidious commercialism that works its way into every waking moment of American life? While the Ute may nail a sacred buffalo head on his wall he may also hang a plastic, lighted portrait of Jesus beside it; he

OVERLEAF

Ute Mountain Ute at fall roundup, Pinecrest Ranch.

may wear his buckskin to powwows but underneath it may be a T-shirt that says *Star Wars*.

But the Indians are different than other displaced groups. They once owned the entire continent upon which we have built the most luxurious, omnivorous, and complacent society the world has ever known. And in the midst of our complacency and luxury we have created a belated guilt over our nineteenth-century genocide; to ease our nagging conscience we have awarded huge sums of money to the hapless descendants of those we wronged a century or more ago, including all three tribes of Utes—Northern, Southern, and Ute Mountain.

Since its inception in 1946, the Indian Claims Commission, now absorbed by the U. S. Court of Claims, has doled out nearly a billion dollars to the Indians in reparation for the theft of their lands. But it is an impossible situation. Not only can we not assuage the collective guilt of a nation now busy atoning for its sins in Southeast Asia, but also money cannot buy back the ancestral lands of 850,000 Native Americans; it can only destroy their self-respect and initiative. When we award sums as high as $962.5 million to Native Americans of Alaska, we are weeping not for the Indians but for ourselves.

When the Sioux finally were awarded $17.5 million plus 5 per cent interest in 1979, it was quickly pointed out that the total settlement of about $105 million would, when distributed among the 60,000 Sioux, amount to only $1,750 each, not counting the hefty percentage taken first by lawyers who have worked on the case since 1920. The probability looms that the Sioux, like all other tribes including the Utes who have divided land-claims money among their people, will simply spend the loot and destroy the precious little they had before it arrived. The United States Government did not include a course in economics within its package of blood money to the Sioux any more than it bothered to educate the Ute Mountain Utes twenty-five years ago.

By the late 1950s, when the Ute Mountain Utes were already reeling under the impact of their land-claims settlement, another bonanza arrived. This one included some $35 million for their minerals, disbursed in the form of per-capita payments; at first as high as $2,000 a year for each tribal member, it was later cut to $1,000. Some families, seeing this as a means to increased abundance, began having more and more children, or adopted orphaned Utes who were usually related to them. Others who had left the tribe years before came back and claimed membership for themselves and their families, the only requirement being one-quarter Ute Mountain Ute blood. Challenges by the tribal attorney to the validity of the claims were always dismissed by the council, who admitted everyone who sought membership at that time. This tangled state of affairs resulted in some families receiving as much as $20,000 a year, tax-free, to spend as they pleased. Even that was not the end of it.

As oil and gas money rolled in, as much as $10,000,000 in a single year, the Bureau of Indian Affairs set up an individual money account for them in Albuquerque, apart from their per-capita funds. The catch was that the Indians had to make a 500-mile round trip to get it and were usually refused by BIA personnel, who patronizingly insisted that "you Indians will only drink it up." The Utes could only get their "I Am Money," as they called it, by filing a complaint with the superintendent at To-waoc, citing a family "emergency" such as the death of a relative. One BIA official, tongue in cheek, estimated that one year there were "at least two hundred uncles who died."

Eventually the tribe, at the instigation of the BIA, set up yet another way for the people to get even more money. They called it the "10-40 accounts," which allowed members who had spent all of their per-capita funds to "borrow" against the next payment, interest-free. Hundreds of thousands of dollars flowed out of the tribal treasury into the hands of debt-ridden Utes who believed there would not be an end to the tribal jackpot. The 10-40 accounts were the frosting on the cake, and the people devoured it. During all that time, only one tribal member is known to have opened a savings account.

Ute Mountain Ute children, meanwhile, had only to wait until they turned eighteen to receive their share of a tribally run,

BIA-approved trust-fund program that gave them as much as $10,000 all at once, without supervision or restriction. On their eighteenth birthdays, Ute Mountain Ute children usually went off to Cortez or Farmington, bought shiny new cars and pickups, and when they wrecked them or the vehicles fell apart, simply replaced them until their money was all gone. In one case, an eighteen-year-old boy decided not to buy a car but purchased a cowboy hat and boots plus $3,000 worth of beer for a one-night binge that resulted in a rape and a murder. According to an official source, the combination of alcohol and cars among Towaoc's youth is lethal; in one two-year period seven Ute Mountain Utes who had received their "eighteen money" died at the wheels of their vehicles.

The promise of a windfall at the age of eighteen is one reason why few Ute Mountain Ute children are willing to stay in school; their dropout rate is 43 per cent. Only two are known to have graduated from college and less than twenty have even completed their freshman year. A 1975 provision added to the trust agreement with the First National Bank of Denver where the tribe deposited an estimated $1.35 million to be used by Ute Mountain Ute children at the age of eighteen, allows parents to raid their children's trust funds any time they wish. The provision reads that money may be withdrawn for "the benefit of the children," a handy excuse for squandering an estimated 80 per cent of the "eighteen money" long before children ever reach that age. One bank has also permitted relatives of Ute Mountain Ute children to draw thousands of dollars out of their savings accounts, leaving them depleted when the children attempted to collect at the age of eighteen. A few years ago, according to an informed source, Scott Jacket, tribal chairman, and Henry Jacket, tribal treasurer, also directed the First National Bank of Denver to pay sums as large as $5,000 out of children's trust-fund accounts to tribal members not related to the children. The bank unwittingly complied.

Inevitably, the money corrupted the people and they turned on one another, brother against brother, father against son, friend

Even children assist at fall roundup, Pinecrest Ranch.

against friend. Gradually the word leaked to the outside world that something was very, very wrong at Towaoc.

In the spring of 1977, as people moved uneasily about the reservation, caught in a web of gossip and inuendo, the FBI, armed with a search warrant, swooped down on the tribal office and confiscated all their financial records alleged to be "evidence of embezzlement, conversion, misapplication, and theft from an Indian tribal organization." An affidavit in support of the FBI warrant stated that Martha Lynch, a former tribal bookkeeper, told the FBI when she resigned earlier that spring that there was a deficit of $483,000 in the tribal account. About $200,000 of this, she swore, had been withdrawn by the entire tribal council, including Scott Jacket, the chairman, who had overdrawn $91,875; his cousin Henry Jacket, tribal vice chairman and treasurer, who owed $38,085; Thomas House, $58,871; John Knight Whyte, $3,892; Susan Lehi, $5,371; Marshall Whyte, $968; and Jack Cantsee, $950. In addition, former tribal chairman Albert Wing "owed at least $40,000" when Mrs. Lynch resigned.

The rest of the deficit was because certain tribal members had overdrawn their 10-40 accounts far beyond what their per-capita checks would cover in a year, the former bookkeeper said. The use of this credit extended mainly to friends and relatives of tribal leaders, particularly Scott and Henry Jacket, who for years had run the tribe together. Kay Jones, a former tribal secretary, claimed that "sometimes there were 50 people in there a day asking for money." Martha Lynch added, "Time after time certain individuals could come in and get a $5,000 check and old 'Joe Red Feather' had had his lights turned off and they refused to pay it." The 10-40 accounts, according to tribal figures, were $243,381 in the red.

As the FBI investigation progressed, other misadventures came to light. It was learned that the tribal council, on frequent trips to Washington, would often draw $500 each for expenses, then put all costs of their trip on credit cards. Once, while in the capital, the Indians had drunk up all the "free" bottles of liquor placed in their rooms by the hotel, a caper that cost the tribe

Julie House, senior at Cortez High School, hopes to attend college.

$2,000. Another time, a council member bought half a dozen expensive bolts of cloth to give to his girlfriends. And Scott Jacket, it was alleged, had once billed the tribe for more per-diem expenses than there were working days in the year. An ex-tribal attorney claimed, "It wasn't unusual at all for tribal council members to come in with gas charges of $400 and $500 in one month. Where did they have to go? Everything was right there."

It was alleged, moreover, that Scott Jacket had assigned a tribal work crew to pave an eight-mile stretch of road into his ranch. The chairman was also accused of accepting a kickback from a contractor who charged $125,000 to build a tribal gas station that had been estimated at $65,000. There were other allegations that Scott Jacket had bought a new truck, a new mobile home, and a $10,000 van for his daughter. It was discovered, meanwhile, that Henry Jacket's wife and sister were able to buy groceries with tribal purchase orders. "Presents" to the two tribal leaders were also discovered. Color television sets, rifles, and binoculars were offered in exchange for what one tribal member sarcastically referred to as "an audience with the Indian pope." It was done because "the Jackets expected it and would not see you if you came empty-handed, like in the old days Indians expected trinkets and beads."

Not only were charges of nepotism, bribes, and favoritism rampant, but also the two ex-tribal employees told the FBI that some council members charged hay and transportation costs for privately owned cattle to the tribe. The Ute Mountain Utes own the 20,000-acre Pinecrest Ranch near Gunnison, valued at $2 million, and lease another 14,000 acres from the Bureau of Land Management. They have a total of about 5,000 head of cattle at Pinecrest and 6 other ranches that they own, making them the largest single cattle owner in Colorado.

According to Joe Ismay, the assistant foreman for the Ute ranches, "The Indians have a good deal. The tribe owns the ranch and doesn't charge them anything for grazing their cattle. They don't have to pay taxes on the land or what it costs to haul the cattle back to Towaoc in the fall. All they pay for is vaccine and inspection fees."

Ismay said that all of the cattle except 800 "tribal" head are owned by about 60 individuals, most of whom have only 30 or 40 head. The biggest owners of tribal cattle were the chairman, Scott Jacket, and his cousin, Henry, the tribal treasurer, estimated to own more than 500 head apiece. Income from the sale of Indian cattle raised without the heavy expenses that plague other ranchers is, at today's inflated market price, about $600 per head. According to one tribal source, it costs the tribe $250 for each yearling they produce, but this cost is not deducted from the sale of cattle held each fall at Pinecrest.

Yet even the tribe's cattle operation is not free from suspicion by the Indians themselves. They once accused their longtime white foreman, Bill Ashbaugh, of selling the tribe's best bulls and substituting inferior ones. Fired by the tribe for several months, Ashbaugh was reinstated when the Indians found they could not run their ranches without him.

Shortly after the FBI seized their records, the tribe sent out letters to all members informing them that per-capita payments were being stopped. As angry Indians swarmed into tribal offices to demand their children's trust-fund money, they discovered that most of that was gone, too. "We're broke," tribal treasurer Henry Jacket announced that summer, turning away dozens of people who hammered at his door. Not long afterward, the tribe laid off half of its work force, 80 people in all, most of them part-time summer employees working for the Natural Resources Department. They had received only $1.75 an hour anyway and, according to economic development director Horace Garcia, they actually "might be better off drawing unemployment."

OVERLEAF

Dozens of Indian men and boys ride in fall roundup at
Pinecrest Ranch.

In the erupting fury at Towaoc, once-silent tribal members began to speak out. Judy Pinnecoose, a thirty-four-year-old former clerk for the BIA and mother of five children, sat in the living room of her three-bedroom house at the western edge of Towaoc.

"No accounting is ever given to us," she said angrily. "We don't know what the tribe does with the money. If we ask, they tell us it's none of our business. We never get letters from them except last month to tell us there wouldn't be any more per capita. You can go to council meetings if you're a tribal member but then if you get up and ask a question, they tell you it's none of your business and to sit down and be quiet. If Scott [Jacket] doesn't like what we say, he puts on his hat and walks out."

Political elections at Towaoc always followed a pattern, she said. The Jackets had first been elected about ten years earlier, then were turned out when an inventory showed that cameras and binoculars bought with tribal funds had turned up at Scott Jacket's house. Albert Wing was elected chairman at that point but was shortly removed for allegedly stealing. Then Marshall Whyte, regarded by most as an honest man who made loans instead of outright grants to his fellow tribesmen, was chairman for a year. But during his tenure, payments of the 10-40 accounts were cut off, and in the next election, Whyte was voted out and the Jackets were back in.

The Jackets, she contended, were always elected because the elections were rigged. "In the last election people were voting twice and three times," she said. "I saw one woman ask for an extra ballot for her brother who was going to vote absentee but later he showed up and voted. Another woman wanted a ballot for her husband who had died the year before. And a man came asking for a ballot to take to his wife but he was never married. Things like that." She attributed her own recent defeat as a candidate for the council to the crooked way the elections were run.

During ancient Indian gambling game called "handgame," players sit opposite one another, sing, play handgame drum, and guess how many fingers opponents have hidden under blankets, scarves. At Towaoc, handgames last two days, involve Utes and Navajos.

So distressed was Judy Pinnecoose over the election situation that she called in the FBI, who seized the ballot boxes. But the effort was fruitless.

According to FBI agent Bob Bishop, who had earlier raided the tribal office and seized the books, "There was no registry of tribal voters so it was impossible to tell who voted. No one signed their name when they came in to vote. All we had was a bunch of ballots with no idea who cast them."

A federal grand jury convened in Denver to consider the charges levied against the council, and the FBI recommended to the U.S. attorney that the case be tried. Their estimate revealed that at least $23 million was lost between the midfifties and 1977; another estimate by the U.S. attorney put the figure closer to $60 million, but no one knew for certain how much money the Ute Mountain Utes had actually spent, since the BIA had never demanded an accounting once the budget was approved.

In Denver, 425 miles away from Towaoc, tempers cooled as the federal grand jury did not return an indictment against any of

the council members accused of wrongdoing because it found no real evidence to do so. The election issue was not even considered, nor did the grand jury probe any of the charges against Scott Jacket. At Towaoc, tribal members refused to talk to FBI investigators, who still believed that huge sums of money had been embezzled. One Indian remarked that his people had only followed a white-inspired example. Finally, the consensus among Justice Department attorneys was that they did not want to become involved in tribal politics nor had proof been offered that the funds had been illegally appropriated. Indeed, tribal books showed that the council had always voted to pay themselves the alleged amounts they had overdrawn from their accounts, an action considered legal. It was, after all, the Indians' own money, supposedly overseen by the BIA. Justice Department attorneys further felt that to enter the case was like slapping the face of the Interior Department and accusing its stepchild, the BIA, of complacency and failure to do its job.

As the tribe reeled under the shock of its financial crisis and wondered what to do next, supernatural forces were said to be at work at Towaoc, casting spells on those who spoke out, making them sick and in some cases inducing death. For a long time, the people said, witchcraft had been used between factions vying for power, and it was a matter of "seeing who could outwitch the other." They had seen it happen only a few years before when Parley Wells, Henry Jacket's brother-in-law, fatally shot a tribal policeman who was supporting the conservative leadership of Marshall Whyte, Thomas House, and Albert Wing.

When Wells then killed himself, the people said it was because supernatural forces were at work; they could see for themselves that the Jackets had more power than the opposing faction of Whyte, House, and Wing. These political dissenters were also punished. Not long after the Parley Wells suicide, Marshall Whyte's oldest son, a member of the New Mexico State Patrol, shot himself at his home in Albuquerque. Then Albert Wing was said to have had a spell put on him, causing him to retreat from the tribe and live off in the canyon with his sheep.

With all of their own medicine men long dead, the Ute Mountain Utes had been going to Navajo witch doctors in Shiprock and Farmington for years. Even the tribal chairman was said to have his own medicine man, David Johnson, whom he once consulted about a huge bruise on his face. The next day it was said to be gone. The Indians believe that so great is the power of Scott Jacket's medicine man that they themselves can be hexed by him for crossing their tribal chairman or not re-electing him.

The Ute Mountain Utes, seeing the end of their tribal jackpot, did not know what to do. Many reported illness because of all the hexings, a spiritual crossfire that they could not escape even if they left the reservation. One woman who had fled to Pueblo, Colorado, reported that a spell had been placed on her newborn son, causing paralysis of his legs. Another Ute woman, who tried to avoid the curse by going to visit her daughter in Gallup, claimed she had developed kidney trouble. It was believed that the power of the witches was inescapable.

Amid the apprehension that pervaded the reservation that spring, a few dared to voice their opinions. Judy Pinnecoose said that people were terrified because "they think they will be hexed." Ernest House, the grandson of the last chief, Jack House, said of the hexing, "It has been going on a long time before the white people came and it's still going on. It's part of the culture. There are good parts and bad parts of the Indian culture and this is one of the bad parts."

At Towaoc, dehexing of houses of the dead is also performed by Navajo medicine men who charge as much as $1,500 for their services plus a basket of food with a gun at the bottom. To remove the spell of one Indian upon another costs $500. One Ute Mountain Ute, who complained of an intense pressure in his head as part of a hex put on him by his enemies, said he was cured when the Navajo medicine man dug in the ground and came up with a wad of hair, believed to have come from a dead relative of the hexed man. When the hair was burned, the man was supposedly cured.

But Indian belief in the supernatural did not stop there. A

tribal employee who suddenly died at his desk was considered hexed, so no one would use his office after that because "they felt a lot of pressure," according to another tribal employee who said that the desk was eventually destroyed.

An old custom of the Ute Mountain Utes has long been to take deformed or retarded children up to an outcropping of obsidian near the toe of Sleeping Ute Mountain and leave them there to die because "they were born under a spell." If the parents did not do so, it was believed that the whole family would be cursed. In the midst of the furor over the disappearance of tribal funds, a two-year-old deformed girl was taken to the mountains to die. Federal agents investigating the incident reported that her parents were advised that such an act constituted murder. The child's body, however, was never found, although a small skeleton was reportedly taken from the scene and buried.

Even the BIA has run into tribal superstition. Not far from Towaoc is a crack in the ground where a coal fire has burned for years from a seam deep within the earth. When the BIA suggested that a bulldozer cover the hole and put the fire out, the Utes became indignant. "The old folks go over there and leave offerings to the little men who live there," they said.

Most Ute Mountain Utes refuse to visit the Mancos Canyon area, claiming that evil spirits abound, left there by the Navajos. They tell about seeing a mysterious old Indian man in a blue shirt walking with a stick up and down the canyon and about hearing the voice of a woman talking in Ute and the endless barking of a spirit dog. The Utes will not remove any of the pottery sherds in the cliff dwellings, insisting that they bring bad luck. Nor will they walk on top of an ant pile, believed to be constructed on top of an old Indian grave, because they claim that causes pains in their legs and gives them chills. Whenever they picnic, they always leave food for the "little people" who live in the canyon; they refuse, however, to eat among the willows because "bad spirits are going to get you there."

By the fall of 1977 a new controversy raged at Towaoc, this one centering around the postmaster and owner of two trading posts, Byron Pyle. No sooner had the furor over the embezzlement charges died down than the fifty-six-year-old postmaster, who had operated a general-delivery service on the reservation for thirty years, was accused of using his postal authority to coerce Indians to pay debts he claimed were owed him as store owner. Tribal members charged that Pyle withheld mail containing checks addressed to them when they attempted to retrieve their mail. Most said that the practice had been going on for years and that they had simply forfeited their checks rather than argue with the postmaster, who also happened to be the man who held them in financial bondage. For most Ute Mountain Utes, unable to obtain charge accounts in Cortez, the Towaoc trading post was the only place where they could buy food, clothing, and household essentials on credit extended from one per-capita period to the next. When the Indians found themselves running short, it was either trade with Byron Pyle or go hungry.

When notified of the charges against him, the postmaster seemed unconcerned. "There is absolutely nothing wrong in what we do," Byron Pyle said, admitting that he "separated checks [from other mail] for the convenience of the people. You'd almost have to work here to know these things." He denied that he had ever withheld checks from the Indians.

Yet Lorna Lynton, a bookkeeper at the Towaoc trading post from 1969 to 1972, said that Pyle "is an Indian trader. Indian traders are notorious. He puts the pressure on them to pay their bills" by threatening to cut off their credit. They had to pay their bills when they picked up their mail, she said, or else they could not pick up their checks.

Kay Jones, who had blown the whistle on the tribal council, blew it now on Byron Pyle. During the six years she had spent as tribal secretary, she said, "all tribal checks written on payroll days were sent to the trading post by orders of Scott Jacket."

Other Ute Mountain Utes began to talk, reluctantly at first, about the Indian trader. Mike Peabody, who had gone to college for three years and was then working for the National Park Service, said that Pyle's influence even extended to Cortez, where he was a director of the First National Bank. "The Pyle family has a monopoly on that area," he said. "You cannot buy a car (if you are an Indian) without his okay. You have to do business with Pyle before you can do anything. Even though your credit is good enough, you still have to go through Pyle. He controls everything down there. Even in Durango, you go over there and try to purchase a car and they know Pyle. They say he has to okay it."

Another Ute Mountain Ute, Arthur Cuthair, foreman for the Mancos Creek project where the Indians were trying to open their own park, said that he had once been refused credit at the First National Bank in Cortez and believed it was because he would not trade at Pyle's store. "I don't trade with him because I know how crooked he is," Cuthair said. "Once I had to borrow $81 from him to make a car payment. I paid it back and the next time I was in the store, they said I still owed it. I told them I had paid it and wasn't going to pay again. I refused to pay it even when they asked a second time and after that, they didn't pester me anymore."

He was worried, he said, about the old people of the tribe who didn't understand English and paid Pyle whatever he asked. "A lot of people do pay twice," he said. "That trading post has been there quite a long time and people just take his word for it."

In an effort to outwit Pyle, some tribal members rented post-office boxes in Cortez, but even that was not foolproof. One check, sent to Towaoc by mistake, was handed over to the tribal council, which simply endorsed it to the Towaoc trading post. Those Indians whose checks managed to escape the Towaoc postmaster were reportedly denied credit at his store. Others ran into trouble at the bank.

Mildred Whyte, a Southern Ute married to Clifford Whyte, a full-blooded Ute Mountain Ute, said, "We went to the bank and wanted to borrow money for a backhoe and Mr. Pyle said he wouldn't give us a loan because we didn't do business with him at the store. We had to go over his head to get it."

It was later revealed that Byron Pyle, a director of the First National Bank of Cortez, had been paid by the bank to guarantee the Indians' notes. The bank reasoned correctly that Pyle as post-master and trader was always in a position to collect money owed the bank as well.

Judy Pinnecoose, who had earlier raised her voice against the elections, raged now against Pyle. "He didn't refuse to give me my checks when I asked, but I never knew I had a check unless I asked for it," she said. As a clerk for the BIA, her checks over an eight-year period were mailed from Denver and sometimes remained at the trading post for two weeks after she picked up her other mail. She had once complained to the postal inspection service, "If I don't call, I would never know I had a check. My checks, government and tribal, are not included with my regular mail, they are withheld. All checks are kept separate from the regular mail."

Another tribal member, thirty-seven-year-old Bonnie Hatch, said that when she attempted to retrieve a government check for more than $200, "He held my check in one hand and my credit book in the other hand. He said, 'Clear up your account.'" Intimidated by the postmaster/storeowner, Mrs. Hatch signed the check and paid Pyle about $50, which he said she owed.

However, complaints about Byron Pyle were not limited to disgruntled Indians. Felix Sparks, tribal attorney from 1968 to 1972, said, "He'd withhold their checks illegally until they paid him what was owed." But what was actually owed was also a subject for debate, since Pyle never kept an itemized ledger, his cash-register tapes were undated, and items did not carry price tags. According to Sparks, the postmaster not only withheld per-capita checks but also managed to collect much of the "eighteen" money.

"The kid would have a check for $10,000," Sparks said, "but Pyle would run a long cash-register tape totaling say, $9,600. He'd call them in, hand them the tapes, and say, 'Here, this is what you owe me.' Then he'd give them $400 of the $10,000 they had coming."

Robert White, assistant BIA superintendent at Towaoc from 1961 to 1963, said, "Most of the Indians dealt on credit with Pyle. He knew when the per-capita checks came through the mail, and if he had a doubtful creditor, there were times he personally handed that check to the creditor and got an endorsement on it. There was no question that this thing happened. You would have to talk to me long and hard to convince me it didn't."

The postal service, asked to investigate Pyle as far back as 1955, did not do so at that time, and only under intense pressure from the Indians did they decide to investigate in 1977. In Denver, U. S. Postal Inspection Service area supervisor William Chaney insisted that Pyle "had written authorizations from these people" to transfer their checks into their unpaid accounts at the trading post. "I have them right here," he said over the telephone.

However, tribal members claimed that the written authorizations were made under duress by people who still owed Pyle money and feared that they could no longer obtain credit at his store if they didn't sign them.

"Those authorizations were just passed out within the last few weeks," said newly elected council member Terry Knight.

Billy Lopez, another tribal member, said that his mail was moved to the Ute trading company for many years without his authorization and that he had signed the paper because "I want bread and butter." He said that a trading-post employee, Jay Hamilton, told him that if he didn't sign the paper he wouldn't receive credit at either reservation store.

Elizabeth Marsh, fifty-five, maintained that for years Pyle had sent her Social Security checks to the trading post without her approval, to cover her account. It was only in the midst of the controversy that she was asked to sign the authorization paper. "My mail just went to the Ute trading company," she said. "I don't know why." Despite years of problems with the postmaster, Mrs. Marsh was never contacted by postal authorities, even after a friend, Rose Paytiamo, had informed officials of her difficulties. The Indians, more convinced than ever that "the government is all on his side," believed that Byron Pyle would continue forever as their postmaster, holding their checks in the same way he always had.

Navajo women play for high stakes each year at Towaoc's Bear Dance.

"You come here, buy something, he takes your money, you don't know nothing," said one sixty-three-year-old Ute woman who cannot read or write. "You say, maybe it costs a lot, like he says, to buy things. Maybe everything is okay."

As the new conflict raged at Towaoc all that fall, business went on as usual at the trading post. For the few Indians who decided to boycott Pyle's store, it meant a forty-mile round trip to Cortez to buy food and clothing, and as many of them discovered there, merchants demanded cash. Most of the Ute Mountain Utes, while furnishing information to the newest postal investigator, a Crow Indian named Walks-Over-Ice, continued to do business with the most hated man on the reservation. One Ute man said that "somebody would put a knife in Pyle" if it weren't for the fear that Scott and Henry Jacket would "find out and put a hex on them." Another man who works for the BIA said that if hexing worked against the whites, "Byron Pyle would have been dead a long time ago."

As the postal investigation continued, it was discovered that Byron Pyle had sold the Towaoc trading post and one along the highway to the tribe the year before for $240,000. A tribal resolution passed on June 24, 1976, showed that the nearly bankrupt tribe planned to secure a $100,000 bank loan to purchase the two trading posts from Pyle and that the balance was to be taken from the tribal economic development fund.

A search of the Montezuma County tax records revealed that the two establishments were valued at $38,516 without their inventories. When the tribe purchased the stores, it agreed to pay all debts owed to Pyle in his accounts receivable, an estimated $120,000. According to Martha Lynch, "all debts to Pyle were to be wiped clean" by October 1, 1976. "That didn't happen," she said. "Tribal members still had to make payments on bills—old bills." She said that one Ute man was paying $50 to the store every two weeks, but the biggest debt of all, some $75,000 owed by the tribal chairman, had been wiped clean.

A year after the sale, as the Indians clamored to have him thrown out, Byron Pyle was still managing the trading post for the tribe and, pending the outcome of the postal investigation, was still in charge of the mail. He had, moreover, been retained for ten years as "adviser" to the tribe. One morning he sat in a small cluttered office behind the store, a benign-looking man who liked to talk of history, of how his father, Frank Pyle, had opened a trading post on Mancos Creek in 1917 and had even managed the tribe's cattle, some 3,000 head, for several years before the BIA ordered them sold during the drought of 1917–18.

"I've always tried to help the Injuns," Byron Pyle said, sorting through a pile of receipts as he talked. "My father did too. For a long time he was about the only friend they had. He'd even buy them food when they had no money and help them out as best he could. First my father and then me, we'd let them run up big bills with no hope of ever getting paid. Now everyone is saying I'm not fair when I'm just trying to collect my bills. I'm a businessman. I cannot afford to run a charity here."

He stuffed the receipts into a box and locked them in his desk. "Oh I've had to ask them to endorse their checks over to me a time or two," he said evenly, "but this is the only place where they can get credit and they know it. If I threaten to cut them off, they'll pay." He smiled and glanced out the window where an old woman was going down the road, carrying a sack of groceries.

"When the government put these people on the reservation back in the 1800s, they had good intentions," he said. "They wanted to educate them, to help them, to introduce them to the Christian religion. But it turned out to be no better than what they had. The Injuns didn't want to be helped."

Byron Pyle, with a calm expression on his face, sat back in his chair. "With per capita stopped, they'll have to go to work like everybody else," he said. "They've had it too easy with all that money coming in. They tried to start a shirt factory but the Utes won't work in it. They have the pottery but there's a big turnover. Education is the main problem here. It does them good to go to school in Cortez, where they have to mix with whites every day. Here they're too isolated. They have to know what it's like in the world. They've been sheltered and protected for a long,

long time." He seemed to ponder his words, nodding his head in agreement with himself.

One of the clerks came in then to announce that a certain man wanted to pay for $5.00 worth of groceries "with a check that'll probably bounce." Pyle, back to examining another pile of receipts, did not look up. "Tell him to pay his bill first," he said. When the clerk left the room, the trader looked up, his pencil poised in midair. "The bank won't loan them anything, so many's the time I went down to Cortez and cosigned to help them out. They have no collateral, just a pickup or car and yes, sometimes I've had to go and pick it up when they defaulted. That's business."

He got up, a big, heavy man who swayed a moment before catching his balance. "Another thing," he said, "they said I asked too much for this trading post but I told them about the blue-sky clause. It's probably only worth $100,000 but I asked $200,000 because in between is blue sky—the good will that I've managed to build up here."

He went into his post office, a small space caged off from the rest of the store, and began arguing in Ute with a man who had come to pick up his mail. Around the store everyone stopped and listened. The postmaster, growing red in the face, finally handed over a pile of letters to the man; that done, he hurried out of the cage, locked it behind him, and retreated to his office with the haste of a man who does not like to be seen.

Just before Thanksgiving, when the first snow had already fallen on Sleeping Ute Mountain, covering up the bleakness of Towaoc, Byron Pyle announced his resignation as postmaster, citing his age and physical condition. Earlier, he had been notified that his dismissal was under consideration by postal authorities. Pat Warner, Pueblo postmaster and sectional center manager, had proposed that Pyle be fired because two investigations showed that he had held checks back. Moreover, Warner said that Pyle had forwarded federal government checks addressed to tribal members to the Ute Trading Company, in violation of postal regulations.

Northern Ute singers from Fort Duchesne, Utah, play intense handgame with women opponents.

Pyle, in his letter of resignation, denied all of the postmaster's charges. Soon after, Marilyn House was named postmistress, and a neat red, white, and blue trailer was hauled in to serve as the post office across the street from her house. After more than six months of uproar, the reservation was deceptively calm as the people went about their lives the same as before, only with a new urgency now that there was no money coming in. Many sought jobs in Cortez, others applied for welfare; for most, however, bitterness settled in as deep and penetrating as the winter cold. After all the investigations, nothing had really changed. The Jackets were still in power; the expense accounts went on; the cattle were still subsidized by the tribe. If there was any wrongdoing, it was met this time with a sense of resignation. At Towaoc, everything was the same as it had been, with changes so subtle that no one really knew they were changes at all, but rather a continuation of the same old malaise.

In the two-year period following its investigation, the FBI claimed that there were no natural deaths at Towaoc. Each one reported was alcohol-related. One thirty-two-year-old woman drank herself to death in a single evening; an autopsy revealed more than 5 per cent alcohol in her blood. The young, unemployed son of a council member, described as a house painter who had no friends but talked to his paint for company, drank a quart of enamel and killed himself—the result, some said, of a hex put on his family by those currently in political power. Another twenty-year-old man who had spent two nights in the Cortez community mission trying to sober up, went back and was arrested on the reservation for drunkenness. He hanged himself in the tribal jail.

At Towaoc, where suspicion has always been part of reservation life, a new kind of hostility was extended by public employees. Darlene Bauer, the white director of the Headstart Program, when asked how many children were enrolled, snapped, "I'm not allowed to give out any information. When the tribal council wants a book, they'll hire their own writer to do it. They don't want to give information to anyone who wants to make a profit on a book."

At the food-stamp office, a secretary refused to give out information on how many Indians were receiving government assistance. "The Utes have enough trouble already," she said and walked out of the room.

At the BIA office, Joe Otero locked himself in his office and declined to talk to reporters, claiming a heavy workload. Around him, secretaries and Indian workers suddenly disappeared when questioned about the status of the tribe.

Scott and Henry Jacket were always "unavailable"; Byron Pyle soon closed the trading post and moved to town. When tribal council elections were held two new members were elected, Judy Pinnecoose and her brother, Terry Knight. They, like the rest of the council members, collected a salary of $1,000 a month plus an expense account. Tribal council meetings, previously held in Ute, were now conducted in English so that Marshall Whyte, the one dissenting voice on the council, could not understand a word. At the same time, the BIA began to dole out the tribe's $1.5 million annual budget in monthly installments.

While most Ute Mountain Utes remained silent, fearful of hexes or simply in acceptance of their fate, others voiced an opinion about the way things had turned out. Many felt that the investigation was a whitewash, that the thievery continued as great as before since the tribe had not lost its million-dollar natural-resources income, which still went into the tribal treasury to be used as the council pleased. Many spoke openly of killing Scott Jacket "some dark night"; others believed that no matter who was in power, nothing would ever be different.

Clifford Whyte, the youngest son of Councilman Marshall Whyte, who had long earned a living by operating a backhoe and haying business in addition to working for the tribe, remarked, "They're down on their knees again. They'll have to get back up." His family, unaffected by the loss of per-capita checks, had also kept their children's trust funds intact, one of the few families on the reservation to do so.

Others were not as fortunate. Another Ute Mountain Ute man who feared for his tribal job because he had earlier spoken out said, "They don't know what leadership is other than leading themselves to more money." He admitted that his children's trust funds were "nearly gone."

"We had a lot of money and we didn't use it right," said another Ute. "We didn't have the leadership and we still don't." He said he believed it was up to the people to "straighten themselves out" but confessed that "they don't know how to go about it."

Nedra Kuebler, a Ute Mountain Ute who lives in one of the new HUD houses with her son, niece, and seven grandchildren, said that she used to get money from the tribe but that now "I get $60 a month from the BIA." She had gone only to the third grade, she said, and had a part-time job doing beadwork that was sold at the pottery, a job that paid her about $12 a day if she worked regularly. "Our leaders have taken all the money," Nedra Kuebler said. "Scott, I hear, has six cars."

Marjorie Wells, Nedra's sister and another beadworker, when

asked how she felt about the lack of money, replied evenly, "The government will take care of us." She had never been to school because, according to her sister, "They couldn't find her to get her to school. We lived way on the other side of the mountain in those days." Marjorie, shy and almost childlike in demeanor, lived with her husband in a two-room house without running water. He was unemployed, so they lived on what she made as a beadworker. One of the few living Utes who still knew the ancient craft of basket making, Marjorie Wells also made baskets that she sold for $50 and $60, gathering reeds from the marshy areas along Mancos Creek. For her, the end of per capita meant simply that she would now have to turn out more beadwork and baskets than ever before.

But a sign posted at the pottery pointed out the greatest danger. It read: "Don't walk behind me, I may not lead. Don't walk in front of me, I may not follow. But walk beside me and let's be friends. Let's go to AA meeting, Monday nite 7 P.M. old building between BIA and CAP." In the aftermath of the scandal at Towaoc, the alcoholism rate is said to have doubled in a little more than a year.

Survival of the Ute Mountain Utes depends on their reaching back into a deep, old life, older than reservation pettiness and jealousy, to a time of dignity and strength long absent at Towaoc. But most have lost touch with the spiritual life and do not have a religious leader or even what passes for traditional men. The highly religious Sun Dance now is held sporadically, but only four or five Ute Mountain Ute men ever attend. Today the peyote cult has only a handful of followers, and many believe it is dying out amid the overall decay. With Navajo medicine men already accepted and established on the reservation, the Ute Mountain Utes have little left to call their own, not even legends and language, all but forgotten except by some very old men. At Southern Ute powwows, there is usually a group of singers from Towaoc, often led by a rotund Navajo preacher, the closest thing the Ute Mountain Utes have to a spiritual connection.

Ute Mountain Ute pottery employs twenty-three full-time workers; most of them average three dollars an hour.

Not far from Cortez, along Highway 160, Allan Neskahi runs what he calls "The Indian Spiritual Life Center" out of his home. But Neskahi, a blend of circuit preacher, medicine man, and revivalist, is alien to most Utes, who remember centuries of overt hostilities with the Navajos, whom most dislike and mistrust to the present day. Moreover, Navajo traditions are a far cry from their own, a fact that Neskahi dismisses, believing that tribes must somehow learn to mesh their differences and their traditions into a kind of uni-Indian religion. He views separate Indian religions as a form of denominationalism, narrow and elite.

"I spent a long time trying to find a simple way of communicating truth without having to be tied to a denomination," he said grandly. "Indian people have always been able to communicate with God without the white man's formality. They lived Christian lives for many centuries without even being baptized." He himself was an ordained Southern Baptist minister who was spared the rigors of seminary training; he was ordained after answering a set of questions put to him by officials of the Church. His religious abilities came naturally, he said, having descended from seventeen generations of medicine men on his father's side; his mother's people were all farmers.

Allan Neskahi, then suffering from boils which prevented him from sitting down, stood in the kitchen of his house, speaking in generalities about what the Ute Mountain Utes needed most. "The Utes are part of our total program," he said, launching into a discussion about how Navajos had always lived on the Ute reservation, even before the Utes came there, which appeared to entitle the Navajos to some sort of edge on their lives if not their lands. Ute Mountain Utes have long feared a Navajo takeover of their reservation, not realizing that such an invasion would require an act of Congress.

"The ties are strong between us," the minister continued, "but we don't want to use that as a crutch to put anything over on the Ute people. They come to us for help and we give it." He glanced into the living room, where his wife was counseling a Ute

Mountain Ute woman, who had come with marital problems. The two of them and their four sons ran The Indian Spiritual Life Center together, administering to troubled Indians all over North America. "Several families come to us for prayer, encouragement, to conduct funerals, and traditional Indian weddings. But the older people are torn. They know they're limited. They cope with this fast computer society. They've always lived day to day in a traditional Indian lifestyle."

He did not really know, he said, whether much of a traditional lifestyle existed at Towaoc and he did not think it was his responsibility to teach it; on the contrary, Allan Neskahi's mission appeared to be the opposite, calling to mind a sign once erected on the Navajo reservation by the Presbyterians. It read: "Tradition is the enemy of progress." If so, then progress is light years away from Towaoc.

"We don't measure success the way you whites do," Allan Neskahi said, fingering a Bible covered in white imitation leather, long ribbons between the pages he wished to remember. "Success is a lifelong thing. If I am in harmony with my family, that's success. We want to share what we know with the Utes and they share what they know and it has nothing to do with numbers but with exchanges. That's why we're not pushing for anything. This is the Indian way. Be still. Do nothing. Things will come to you." Absently, he opened the Bible to the Book of Revelation, glancing down at it out of habit, seeming to read even as he talked.

"I wish for the Mountain Utes strong leadership, a happy home, and good relationships," he said, as though delivering a sermon, the Bible before him, a symbol of what concerned him most. "If the Ute is really a spiritual Indian, he can cope with world pressure and all this trouble they're having. An Indian can cope with it easy. We did before. We had bad weather, epidemics, fires, droughts, starvation, floods, wars. Many died in the old days, too. One of our traits is not to worry about it. It's the only thing we can do." He closed the Bible and pondered the whole question.

"You can overdo relevancy and bypass truth. We are trying to bring the two together." That seemed to be the very crux of his Indian philosophy, the very opposite of Ute belief.

Abruptly, the hefty Navajo preacher excused himself in order to attend to another caller, a Ute Mountain Ute girl. He carried the Bible in his hand as he went to answer the door, formidable in his armor of synthesized religion.

In November 1979 Judy Pinnecoose was elected the first chairwoman in Ute Mountain Ute history by the six-member council, four of whom are her relatives. She vowed to put an end to nepotism, cut all unbudgeted loans to tribal members, and to invest a pending $5.8 million cash payment for oil and gas leases in economic development.

As the tribe waited for their latest windfall to pass Congress, salesmen, big-time developers, and high-echelon bureaucrats descended on Towaoc and the new chairwoman. Once again the people began to mutter about getting their share and pressured their new chairwoman to reinstate per capita.

On the reservation, nothing had really changed.

3

ON A SMALL SIDE STREET of Towaoc where a veil of dust is always in the air and an uneasy silence passes for tranquillity, two rows of flimsy houses from the fifties sit opposite one another. The houses have not worn well and now after twenty-five years they have gone to seed; inside and out the houses are filled with the stratified trash of all that time. No one ever taught the Indians the elements of orderliness, and the domestic ignorance that characterized their old life in tents and hogans remains with them still. The trash is comfortable trash, bits and pieces of affluence that have been dropped in the backyards; traces of mobility and ruined dreams are locked into dead automobiles and pickups; the molting of materialism is recognized in plastic-covered furniture left outdoors to rot or the automatic washing machine that never did get hooked up. The Ute Mountain Utes ignore their junk piles, moving among them as though they were a manifestation of internal disarray.

On one side of this street once lived Harriet Whyte and her husband, tribal councilman and former chairman Marshall Whyte, and their seven foster children, who ranged in age from four to twelve. The Whytes, in their midsixties, had already raised four children of their own and embarked upon a second family because, as Harriet Whyte once said, "These kids needed somebody and I didn't have anything else to do." The children, all relatives

OVERLEAF

Marshall Whyte, former tribal chairman, Ute Mountain Utes.

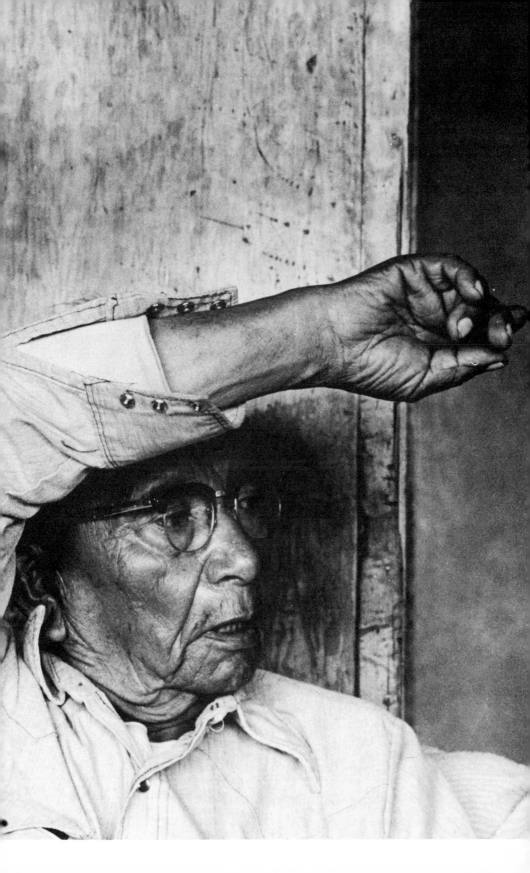

70

of the Whytes, had either been abandoned by their parents or were removed from their homes by the tribal welfare office, usually for reasons of alcoholism.

The living room of Harriet Whyte's orange-shingled house was small and cluttered with piles of clothes fresh from the dryer, well-worn toys, a discarded television set, a heap of mending, and paper bags filled with what had not been put away from a recent excursion to the grocery store. The Indian woman, accustomed to the confusion of children running in and out of the punctured screen door, was also accustomed to the shambles of her home. The look of unfinished business was always in that house and the essence of continuity also. Seated in an overstuffed chair beneath a startling portrait of the Virgin Mary, Harriet Whyte was in repose, as if on a throne from which she commanded her small and difficult empire. She wore a homemade cotton dress, her silver hair was parted in the middle and braided; she had a classic look of Indianness to her.

Marshall Whyte, who always seemed far away and troubled, sat opposite her on a chenille bedspread-covered couch, beneath a ready-made plaque bearing the unlikely Whyte family coat of arms. He smoked a cigarette with the deliberate hesitation of a man used to taking his time in all matters, even the smoking of a cigarette. His hair was thin and short, resembling a threadbare dandelion tuft.

"We were just dumb Indians, that's all we were," Harriet said. "Lived in tents, in cabins. No electricity, no plumbing. We lived up the canyon, along the mountains, all over. I lived here all my life and don't know any other place. I was born down there near Navajo Springs, just a mile or two away from here. My father came with Ignacio from the mountains, then to the desert, then here. My father was a good friend of [Chief] Ignacio. He used to tell me, 'Be strong and don't give up.'" She shook her head. "I do what my father tells me, even now." She said something in Ute to Marshall, stone-faced and unfathomable; he made no response, so she continued.

Harriet Whyte adopted seven Ute orphans after her own four children were grown.

"I've only been around here—Farmington, Shiprock, Durango. Before I die, I want to travel, see some places, but I don't know where to go. People rob you and kill you in cities and I've already seen enough open land. That's all we got here—open land. People say, you miss the mountains, the rivers, the trees? I say, all that happened a long time ago. It's finished now. This land is the only land we know."

When she smiled, her face adjusted itself to a peace inconsistent with the facts of her difficult life; old age bridged the gap between memory and expectation. Harriet sat like an Indian madonna, covered with her years.

Marshall Whyte, her husband of forty-six years, perplexed, eclipsed by life, smoked his cigarette down to a stub, then squeezed it out between his fingers, rubbing the butt along the cuff of his dull gray workman's trousers. For years, he had been something of an outcast at Towaoc because of his Paiute ancestry. This tiny band, western relatives of the Utes, lived mostly in Nevada, with a few settling in the Monument Valley area, frequently intermarrying with Navajos. Although this band was considered close to the Ute Mountain tribe and Marshall Whyte had been at Towaoc for nearly half a century, the Ute Mountain Utes never fully accepted him, and when he openly disagreed with the tribal council, they threatened to send him back to his people, none of whom were left.

Illiterate, ill at ease, and perpetually melancholy, Marshall Whyte never seemed at home among the Mountain Utes, although he had once served as chairman from 1974 to 1975 and was then in his twentieth year as councilman. When he was chairman, he had refused to follow the practice of giving away large sums of money to his friends and was quickly voted out. Most observers believe that he was continually re-elected councilman as a wedge against the ruling Scott and Henry Jacket faction, chairman and treasurer respectively, a sort of last resort if tribal corruption should leave them all without leadership. He was, in a manner of speaking, an Indian ace in the hole, but no one ever played his game. Instead, year after year, Marshall Whyte remained in the background, curiously silent, afraid to play whatever cards he had been dealt. In all matters of tribal politics, Marshall was always alone, trying to comprehend the rules of the game.

Speaking little English and with his own language largely forgotten among his own people, Marshall Whyte was a quaint old relic, a facsimile of a chief struggling to lead his people without real tools to forge his dream. There was no place for him at Towaoc nor in the terrifying world beyond; he could only remain where he was, suspended between decay and desolation, unnoticed and unanswered, a pawn pushed back and forth by two opposing factions. He was worried now about what he had recently heard at the BIA office: that there were to be some land trades and some Indian allotments sold. He sat as if in a stupor, trying to figure it out.

"I don't like the BIA," the old Indian said at last. "What they do? Take land away from us. Take everything away. Tell us what to do, where to go, what to say. They want me to resign from council. I make too much trouble, too much talk. No one but me fight them. No one but me say, 'What you do this for?' I no resign. I understand too good." It was final and unquestionable. The old man was silent, trying to put together his thoughts. The recent uproar over council embezzlement of funds had left him shaken but unscathed. According to the records, he had owed only $968, which he had later paid back in full out of a savings account where for years he had carefully deposited his per-capita checks. Nor was Marshall Whyte, since he never traded with Byron Pyle, involved in the post-office scandal. His sole concern was what was happening to reservation land.

The BIA, in an effort to consolidate the reservation, was considering selling some of the 9,458 acres of allotments near Blanding, Utah, where the Weminuche first settled in 1888; their descendants still live there, known as the White Mesa Utes, with one member in the Ute Mountain Ute tribal council. A 2,000-acre tribal tract in McElmo Canyon, about 5 miles from Cortez and ripe for development, was being offered in trade for some Bureau of Land Management acreage to the east, most of it rock.

Marshall Whyte, unable to fathom the intricacies of such negotiations, was convinced that Navajos were poised at the reservation boundaries, ready to invade. Only a few years before, in 1973, the BIA had sold four 160-acre Paiute allotments in the Monument Valley where Marshall Whyte had grown up, reason enough to suspect that nothing at all was safe.

As he sat on the couch, his eyes wide with the uncertainty that possessed him, the old Indian looked more like an ancient Chinese philosopher, trying to grasp not so much the problems at hand but an infinity of cross purposes.

"Navajos," he said slowly, unaccustomed to the English language, "they got lots of sheeps. That land [in Monument Valley], it doesn't rain there. Old Man Jim Mike, I think he's the one that sold it to Navajos for sheeps. They don't tell me about it. That's my country down there. My father buried there. All my people. They sold it but I never saw no money. I never knew what they were going to do. Now McElmo going to Navajos." Painfully, he turned to his wife, placid in her chair, her expression mirroring that of the sorrowful Virgin Mary on the wall, and voiced his concerns in his own language. His forlorn old eyes went to the bluffs far to the east, where the BLM had its land.

"He says we don't know what's going on," Harriet said finally, looking away to the bluffs also, as if to derive some reassurance from that barren stretch of rock. "He says we don't know what we're going to do. That's good land up there at McElmo. You can grow melon and corn and beans. They say trade for BLM land—that mesa out there. Nothing can grow up there. What we going to do with rocks? No sell, no trade. Keep McElmo, that's what Mr. Whyte say. It's a better place. We got to try and be farmers. Grow stuff to eat so we don't need so much money from them. We used to have a garden but when we got older, we forget about it." She shook her head sadly.

"The BIA wants to sell the land. It's true. I heard about it. Mancos Canyon is where they want us. It's hot. Nothing but sand up there. The river's not running. I won't go." With her arms folded in a gesture of defiance, Harriet pondered the whole question that loomed before her.

"I go to BIA, to Joe 'tero to find out about the land. Everybody is filling out forms, nobody listens. Joe 'tero, he says us Indians worry too much. I say what else we got to do? It's the only place we have. Joe 'tero laugh. I go home and think about it. BIA bad!"

Marshall Whyte, his feet outstretched on the gray, spotted rug, pondered the tips of his scuffed, lace-up boots, the kind used in infantry combat. His mind was on one thing only. "Navajos going to come in," he insisted, his suspicions blooming under the weight of formal discussion. "A long time ago I had a dream about it. Navajos say they lived here before we came. They fight for it. Navajos used this land for sheeps. They want it back. Where we go? What we do?" He rolled his eyes toward the ceiling and closed them.

"Everywhere you go, you see Navajos. Salt Lake. Montana. Denver. Albuquerque. They're building up. Now they say it's all government land, the land they gave us. A long time ago, the old people said when the white man gets the water, they chase you out. Now they get the water because Ute people won't farm that land up there [where the BIA wants them]. Bad spirits. Why can't we farm McElmo? No. BIA want to take it from us. Why?" The old man, his black eyes burning, was unaccustomed to so much talk. He sat, his anger consuming him, trying to find words that did not dilute his meaning.

"Ute people want to say what they're going to do," he fumbled. "Stand on their own two feet." With that, he got up and stood in the middle of the room, his own two feet planted firmly on the old rug, one toe on a coloring book, the other on Harriet's apron, which had fallen off the ironing board. Near him were the children's playthings, including a set of plastic cowboys and Indians. He stood like a statue, looking out the window, seeing nothing except his worst fears and his worst actualities, which were both the same to him.

"In the old days, we would fight, kill them, take everything back," Harriet said wearily. "Now we don't know what to do. Ute people don't want to fight. BIA take over because Ute people don't want to fight."

At the sound of her words, Marshall Whyte, his muscles tense, went to the open door and stood there, an Indian without land, with only a fragment of what he had always known still occupying his mind. "I fight," he said uncertainly, watching the children and the dogs playing in the dusty, cluttered yard. But his hands, unfurled, hung limply at his sides; in the stiffness of his wiry old body was just the merest suggestion of the resistance left in him.

But Harriet did not notice such things. Her world was not the old man's world, although her concerns were his most of the time; her world was a larger one of family and moments of household triumph. On top of the defunct television set were color pictures of her grandchildren, some of them in graduation gowns, others in school clothes; there was a picture of her son, the New Mexico state patrolman, who had recently shot himself. In that room was all of her existence, the affirmation of what her father said, the reverberation of Ignacio's futile wanderings, the recompense for a life spent with dishes that never did get done, with a house that never did get cleaned, with the more important stuff of skinned knees and homework papers. Harriet Whyte had always known her priorities, always resisted the cheap accessories of an imitation life, and took her pleasure in being what she was.

"These kids going to grow up, gone, then what am I going to do?" Harriet Whyte said as the youngest, Vincent, climbed up onto her lap, clutching a moth-eaten teddy bear. Ten years before, she had been the first woman to serve on the tribal council. "I went to Washington," she said, "got money for the kids to go to school. I told them the way it was. Need clothes. Need a bus. Need money for lunch. I couldn't get money for them here. Nobody listen. Tribal council went too but they just sat there, afraid. I told them, Great White Father brings you to Washington to impress you, just like old days. He wants you to go home with cigars and a new suit. Nobody but me speak English. Nobody but me go up to Congressman Aspinall and say, 'You forgot to help us. I'm going to sit right here till you do.'"

The tribe used to pay the Whytes $160 a month for each of their foster children but now, with tribal funds depleted, they only got $50 a month per child plus $10 a month for shoes. Harriet feared that soon it would be nothing at all.

"Tribe said, 'These are all your relatives, so we only give you $50 a month,'" she remarked. "Ends don't meet now. They're this much apart." And she extended her arms to show how far apart the ends really were. "We got good kids, though," she said as the little boy slipped off her lap in pursuit of a calico cat who darted behind the sofa. "Sometimes you can't see which way you have to stand, the back way or the front way. These kids are all going to grow up, be somebody. 'Let's save some money for the kids,' I said to the council. But it's all gone—the trust-fund money, per capita, everything."

For a moment her eyes, heavy-lidded and uncertain, filled up. Carefully, she took off her plastic-rimmed glasses and wiped them with the hem of her dress and in the process dried her eyes. She turned to say something to her husband but in one quick movement he was gone out the door, stepping past the children he no longer really saw, out into the littered yard to his silver Airstream trailer, where he spent so much time ever since his son's suicide two years before. Harriet watched him go, accustomed to his moods, his restlessness. He usually slept in the trailer and sometimes, when the weather was warm, he used to sleep in the mountains. But he had not gone to the mountains in a long time because of the strange lights that he said came on in the middle of the night. He did not know what the lights meant but took it as a sign that something was going to happen, worse than the end of all their money.

OVERLEAF

Whyte foster children and grandchildren enjoy a watermelon-seed-spitting contest in the backyard.

It was all very bad, Harriet said, worse now than the years when she was young and wore burlap dresses and rags on her feet, when she lived in a tent and ate jackrabbit stew for so long she forgot what other food tasted like. It was bad because she did not want the children to live the way she had to so long ago, with sand blowing in while she slept and her belly empty most of the time. She worried about what would happen to the children if she could not take care of them anymore or if the tribe decided to remove them because she and Marshall were too old. She worried most about losing the land though, a fear common to older Indians who do not believe that the reservation is permanent, who confuse the remote possibility of termination with the near reality of cultural destruction. Caught between the council, which refuses to help them, and the BIA, which puts conditions on everything, the Ute Mountain Utes live in perpetual uncertainty, reinforced by rumor and even wilder speculation. In the darkness of their lives, no truth is really possible.

Struggling to her feet to rescue the cat that Vincent was carrying by its tail, Harriet Whyte planted herself in the doorway as the little boy darted past. "If the money is all gone, what we do?" she asked, her face like the canyon rock, red, smooth, and durable. "Maybe they take everything away." She turned her frightened eyes to the children playing jump rope in the yard, then the solution dawned on her. "The BIA," she said, as though saved from imminent disaster, "they don't let us starve."

Across the street from Harriet's house, Mildred Whyte lives in a bigger one, a two-story frame house that is really two houses joined together, with her husband, Clifford, and her six children, who at that time ranged in age from six to sixteen. She sat at her cluttered dining-room table one warm spring afternoon waiting for the children to come home, her mind filled with an unfolding

---

Mildred Whyte, a Southern Ute, has lived at Towaoc with her husband, Clifford, for twenty years.

reel of events that connected her life to this place, this man, this destiny.

"When Clifford's brother shot himself, we went down to Albuquerque," she said calmly. "Nobody had touched him because the investigation wasn't finished yet. He was just lying there in the game room with his head off. His wife was upstairs crying. She wouldn't come down. It was up to Clifford and me to take care of it. His brains were all over the walls. It took us two days to clean it off, crying all the while we were doing it. We scraped off every little piece of brain and hair and scalp until you couldn't tell anything had happened. The rug was covered with blood and we sent it out to be cleaned. Then we painted the walls and varnished the floors. When we got done, it was like it never happened. But I was always afraid of it—that sometime she'd go in there and find the tiniest bit of brain that got stuck on some little piece of wall that we'd missed somehow. It scared me until she moved from that house and then I didn't think about it anymore."

She sighed a small sigh and ran her hands through her thick, short hair. The accident was a fact of life, accepted, unanalyzed, simply gathered up in the thread of her existence. Surrounded by grimness and unalterable statistics, Mildred Whyte had learned to make the best of things.

She was a Southern Ute, an intelligent woman of classic Indian beauty who had lived at Towaoc for twenty years. In all that time no Ute Mountain Utes had ever come to visit her because the Whytes, more than any other family on the reservation, had achieved a remarkable success. Clifford Whyte, a prepossessing man of almost disturbing handsomeness, had run a backhoe and haying business for years and was a part-time tribal employee as well, working on sewer- and gas-line maintenance. He also had about four hundred cows at Pinecrest, the Ute ranch near Gunnison, and each fall he rounded them up and sold them at the tribal sale.

Clifford Whyte owns cattle, runs backhoe business, and works for Ute Mountain Ute tribe. His wife Mildred relaxes with two of their daughters, Melanie, left, and MaDonna, right.

With only a third-grade education, Clifford Whyte, also a recovered alcoholic, had proven that "a Ute Mountain Ute can make it here," a fact that has made him the outcast of a jealous tribe. Indeed, when Clifford walks into a room, most tribal members walk out, "like I had BO or bad breath," as he once said. He has further rankled the tribe by his testing of the hunting-rights provision of the Brunot Agreement of 1873. When Whyte killed a deer without a license in 1976, he was arrested by Colorado Fish and Game officials, who brought charges against him. While the Southern Utes rose to his defense, the Ute Mountain Utes ignored him. The case was eventually decided in Clifford Whyte's favor.

The Whytes have also distinguished themselves by raising children who got good grades in school, adapted unusually well to the bigotry in Cortez, and assisted their father during haying and roundup times. On top of that, Mildred had received her GED after two strenuous years of study.

When per capita stopped, the Whytes were not affected, since they had always saved their money and Clifford had always worked; moreover, they had not touched their children's "eighteen money," so that as each one came of age, they bought a vehicle and had money left for school. Clifford Whyte, with the kind of taciturn nobility that has become synonymous with chieftains of old, has the same strength of character that enabled them to survive. Modest, unassuming, and committed to values far beyond the greediness of most of his fellow tribesmen, he remains in strife-ridden Towaoc because it has always been his home, neither involved with the degeneration of his tribe nor out to reform it. For both generations of Whytes, perhaps hardened by so much tribal strife, survival at Towaoc depends on minding one's business and forging a meaningful existence out of the chaos. The Whytes also have a strong sense of purpose and continuity, determined to carry on what is best of their disintegrating tribe no matter what the cost.

As Mildred returned from a kitchen heaped with dirty dishes

Clifford Whyte with his first grandchild, Jason, born to Clifford's son by a former marriage.

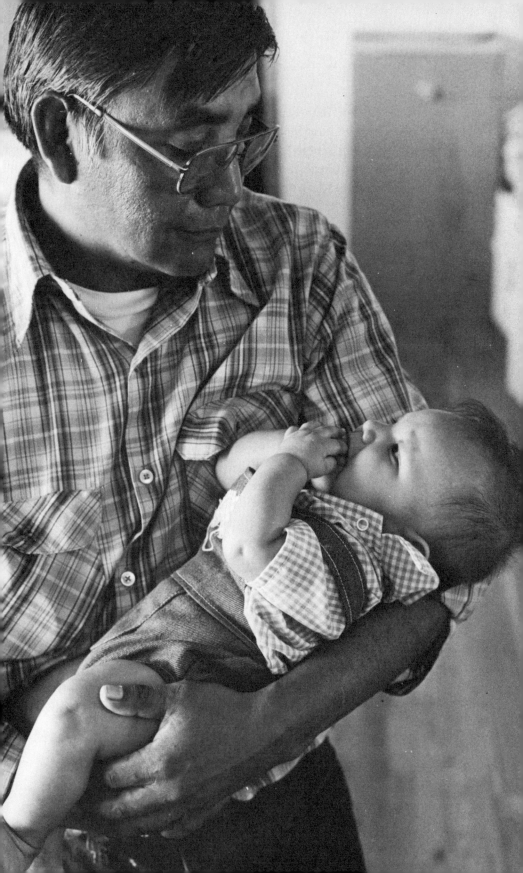

and the remains of numerous meals, stepping over soiled clothes dropped by the children and chasing away a cat who wandered across the table still covered with the morning's dishes, she was oblivious to the mess. As always, her mind was on the immediate horizons of her life, Clifford and the children, and Harriet and Marshall; she had, she said, few friends.

"When Marshall was elected chairman, it was terrible for us," she recalled. "They [the Utes] drove by our house and threw rocks. They called us names. I wouldn't let my kids go to school on the bus. I was afraid something would happen to them. A lady in town said, 'If it gets too bad, bring your kids here, even if it's the middle of the night.' I never had to do that. We just stuck it out." She opened a soda and drank it from the can. Like her mother-in-law, Mildred Whyte had a look of repose to her; a vivacious warmth and goodness emanated from deep within and gave her the only tools she had against Towaoc's viciousness.

"Marshall is used by the council," she continued. "He doesn't understand English, and the interpreter only translates part of the meetings to him. He was elected chairman by a four-to-three vote. People were trying to shift the balance of power away from the Jackets and it didn't work. Marshall favored the people not favored by the Jackets. His lack of understanding in tribal finances meant that there were no big giveaways that year. Marshall just didn't understand the procedure.

"Well, it was chaos. Marshall pretended not to understand when people would come to him and want money the same as they always did. But then certain friends of his began to get things. They were the minority, so the next year he was voted out. During the year he was chairman, he was asked to resign numerous times because certain people weren't getting enough but he always refused. In a way, it was his ignorance that saved him but I know that basically Marshall is an honest man, like Clifford is an honest man. He inherited that from Marshall. And from Harriet, this devotion to his kids."

From her dining-room window Mildred Whyte could see into backyards overgrown with weeds and strewn with debris;

some of the houses were boarded up, others stood vacant with reflections of desolation in the grimy windows. She had grown used to Towaoc in twenty years, she said, and the Ute Mountain Utes were her people; sometimes she went to Ignacio to visit her brother now that her parents were dead. At Ignacio also was a son she had not seen for many years.

"When I was sixteen, I got pregnant. I didn't want to marry the boy, though. I decided I was too young to go into it. Anyway, he was from a different family, and my parents were against it. So I had the baby and gave him to my mother to raise. I went to work and one day I met Clifford and he was right for me, so we got married and came over here. I didn't go over to see my son and he never came over here. My mother was raising him and in the Ute way it was her son, not mine, since I was already having children here. For a long time, I didn't see my mother either.

"Then when my father got sick he said, 'I think I'll go ahead and die so you can get to know your mother better.' And he did. For ten years after that, I got to know my mother. I talked to her every day. She died last year at seventy-two, the same year my son turned 18. She told me, 'He's eighteen now so I can go ahead and die.' She raised him and it kept her alive. She told me once, 'If I had it to do over again, I'd die at fifty-five or sixty. If you live past that age, you won't be happy anymore. You just get old, that's all.'"

For Mildred Whyte, reservation life meant adaptation, of discovering joy in unattended moments that held her in some sort of eternal verification; she had both peacefulness and a restless inner rhythm. Her thoughtful eyes saw past the disarray, the weakness, and the danger; she offered an indestructible spirit, and upon this she had built her close-knit family. In the honesty of Mildred Whyte was the perseverance of generations.

She laughed when her youngest child, MaDonna, a wisp of a girl with enormous searching eyes, came in from school with her books and papers, hugging the child to her.

"MaDonna was born with a No. 4 on one toe and a cross on the other," Mildred said. "It comes out when she takes a bath, like someone scratched it in. When she's sick and running a fever, a heart comes out on her head. When I was pregnant with her, I had a dream and it said: Your next child has to be the last. If you have two more, something will happen to you. One day she said to us, 'I'm going to take care of you someday. That's what I'm supposed to do.' I said, 'Oh MaDonna, you have to grow up and have your own life.' But she said, 'That's not what I'm supposed to do. I want to wait and see what happens.'"

MaDonna was followed into the house by Valerie, going on seven, a foster child who had been with the Whytes since infancy. One by one the other children came in: Donald, the oldest, who had been at band practice, then Melanie, Fawnda, Eric, and Clyde. The Whyte children had a special quality, a naturalness and ease with one another that belied the tight, suspicious world of To-waoc. Set apart on the reservation because they were outstanding, the Whytes were farther set apart because there was love and re-spect among them, a bridging of both worlds that was lost on the bitter, feuding Indians who were their neighbors and close rela-tives.

When Clifford Whyte came in for supper, there was only the briefest exchange between him and Mildred, the merest acknowl-edgment of the children sprawled out in front of the television set. Yet deep in this broad-shouldered, unsmiling man was a certain compassion that required neither words nor gestures to confirm it. Wearing a Caterpillar tractor hat, a denim jacket, Levi's, and work boots, with dirt beneath his fingernails and lines in his leath-ery face from so much time spent in the sun, Clifford Whyte looked like any other American working man who had come home to his family at night.

The only difference was the hostile tribe around him.

When Donald Whyte graduated from Cortez High School, he toured Europe for a month with the band, came back, and worked for the tribe on its Mancos Canyon project, then entered Fort

After graduation, Donald Whyte received a watch from the tribe.

Lewis College in Durango. An outgoing, kinetic young man with an easy smile and burning eyes, he was studying archaeology, in his spare time probing the cliff dwellings along Mancos Canyon, where the Ute Mountain Utes had already opened their own park. He had found many things, he said, and it gave him a clue to his people, who they were, and where they came from. In the Anasazi ruins that are part of Mesa Verde, the Indian boy had discovered the remains of a culture that had flourished for six hundred years or more, then vanished without a trace; in that unexplained mystery he saw a parallel with his own people. Each day that he uncovered a layer of earth he saw both hardship and harmony, resilience and rigidity; he saw too that these ancient people were caught and eventually destroyed by forces and circumstances they were unable to control. At Towaoc, history was repeating itself.

The more Donald Whyte dug into the past, the more he questioned the very nature of himself, his Indian origins, his Indian spirit. Unlike Indian boys of long ago, Donald Whyte had received no training from his elders, and Marshall Whyte, his grandfather, had only imparted to him the barest knowledge of his tribe; it was from Harriet that he had learned about the spirit and what his tribal responsibility was.

One bright October afternoon when he had just entered his second year at Fort Lewis, Donald Whyte drove his new Chevrolet truck along the Mancos Canyon road with his oldest sister Melanie, then home from a military school in Georgia. Because Harriet Whyte lay deathly ill in the Cortez hospital, the Whyte family had gathered from all over the country to be with her, taking turns keeping a vigil at her bedside. For Donald Whyte, who had recently turned to the Baha'i faith as a way to verify his feelings, his grandmother's illness was a test of his belief in regeneration, of Indian life coming full circle, as she had taught him.

"If Harriet dies, I pray she'll come back and teach me the old ways so I can teach my kids," he said. "We sort of pushed her out of our lives, we were all so wrapped up in sports and band practice but I know those things do not signify life to me. If Harriet dies, I have another door to the spirit."

The pickup bounced along the road, past Chimney Rock, also known as Chief Jack House Rock, past a shack where one old man lived alone with his sheep, past where Jack House had once had his hogan, now but an indistinct ring on the ground. Along that road too were Indian pictographs and petroglyphs in the rock, ancient pictures of horses, sheep, Spanish friars, birds, water signs, corn signs, and warriors; there was also modern Indian graffiti—names and crude figures—gouged into the rock by the Utes themselves as recently as 1976. In some places they had obliterated the old drawings and destroyed them, an action that nullified the myth of Indian reverence for all things.

Melanie, with her mother's dark good looks and her father's pensiveness, watched out the window at a hawk arching over a shimmering mesa to the south, where a small cliff dwelling nestled among the rocks, a ghost of a time that seemed to reach out and touch her, holding her to ideals that had not died.

"What our parents taught us is a way to survive in the white society today," Melanie said thoughtfully, her face pressed against the window as the hawk soared out of sight. "But it's not enough. The old way is the way life should be today but it's so hard to live it because people are always putting you down." At the military school, she was learning to handle a gun, march for hours in the heat, and take orders from stone-hearted drill instructors.

"It's good discipline for me and the other girls respect me but something is missing back there." She looked out across the sage-covered land where the cliffs rose against the sun and the half-hearted river meandered through the cottonwoods, golden then in autumn.

"When I'm up here, I think about Marshall," Donald said, stopping the pickup at an excavation site. "He may not come out and tell you how to live but every day he prays and sometimes his prayers come to me like a lesson from long ago. Grandpa's spirit is like the spirit of the old people who lived here. And they're here now. I can feel them everywhere."

He walked over to where he had been digging during the summer, a small kiva about ten feet deep, paused, and turned his face to the ground. He seemed to hear something coming from the perfectly round religious temple, swept clean of all its centuries of debris; the ancient adobe bricks crumbled in the sun, sharing their secrets with the young Indian boy.

Nearby, Melanie was poking around in an anthill for old beads and human bones. The Utes have long believed that ants build their piles on top of old Indian graves; indeed, Melanie held in her hand a tiny blue bead and in it seemed to find her own link with her tribe's mysterious past.

Donald Whyte examined the bead and said, "Maybe's there's an old chief buried here, in his beads and buckskin. Someday they'll dig him up and stick him in a display case so the tourists can see him. We think it's bad luck, that the spirits will be angry if the body is disturbed." With that, he carefully placed the bead back on the ant pile.

"People used to talk to animals, and animals talked to people because animals and people were alike in the old days," Melanie said, holding a pottery shard in the palm of her hand, noticing the design was like a piece she had at home. "That's what Grandma says. But our dad says you can't go around talking to animals anymore, you have to learn the white man's ways too. Donald knows that."

But Donald Whyte was not listening to her; he was bent over the earth as if in supplication. "One kiva we uncovered was fifty feet across. This one is small. Over there we found a hogan with a baby's ribs sticking out of the wall. Maybe it died in winter or maybe they couldn't get out to bury it or maybe the dogs got at it and this is all that was left. In those days, a baby had no significance."

He walked around the excavation, touching the old adobe bricks of the kiva as if to coax from them the mystery that they held. Between himself and the kiva was a certain excitement, as if centuries of sleep had suddenly produced a dream that he yearned to explore. When Donald and Melanie got back in the truck, the reality of old bricks and beads stayed with them.

The road turned sharply and began to climb out of the canyon to the top of the mesa where over the years the Indians had cut down the low forest of piñon and scrub oak so that the grass could grow better. But for all their massive efforts, the land had not responded and was covered now with sage, a luminescent gray-green bush, fragrant and cool in the late-afternoon sun. As a jackrabbit darted in front of the truck Donald said, "If people asked me if I'd rather see the Eiffel Tower or a rabbit, I'd pick the rabbit. Man can learn to build an Eiffel Tower but he can't learn what a rabbit's feelings are unless he lives with him day in and day out. That's what Grandpa says. The rabbit's ancestors tell him what it was like and so he knows what we don't know. He'll share it if we ask, but here we are hurrying away." He looked over his shoulder. "People say I'm crazy but someday I'm going to follow the rabbit around until I know him, the same as they did in the old days.

"The same is true of a deer or any other animal. They have lessons to teach us. I killed my first deer when I was seventeen because my father told me it was time—it's a rite of passage, part of being a man. After I killed it, I cut off the tender meat on either side of the spine and gave it to my grandparents. It's an old custom to give your first deer to the oldest member of your family. Harriet said when I did that, I would know what the spirit of the deer was all about.

"I guess I learned but I never told her I did. Maybe now it's too late. I think my grandmother is going to die." One small tear rested in his eye.

The two oldest Whyte children rode for a while without talking, drawing out of that immense landscape what they needed. Finally Melanie spoke up about her summer tribal job through the CETA program and how she had had to take a two-week vocational training course first.

"There were fifteen or twenty of us from Towaoc at the camp," she said. "The first day the man who ran it—a Dr. [Edward] Burger from Cortez—got up and told us we were all a bunch of lazy Indians and the reason they don't like us in Cortez is because we're nothing but drunken Indians. He said we'd never amount to anything, that all we wanted was for the government to take care of us, and that our families were no good and lazy. We all sat there and some of us tried to answer him back and I asked him what he was doing talking to us like that and he said he was trying to give us motivation. We were humiliated by that man, I don't care what he called it. Some of us talked about killing him, but what's the use of going to jail for killing just a worm?"

The face of the young Indian girl was like the face of her ancestors who had gone into the desert and out again; it was a face of youth, but it had the deeper face of experience behind it. Melanie Whyte's face had the look of generation and survival; it also had the look of expectation.

Far above Mancos Canyon, the mesatop is dry and endless; the wind blows with a searing intensity, and away in the distance, the great valleys and ridges are like a long-ago sea that has stopped, leaving permanent undulations against a ragged edge of sky. Donald and Melanie Whyte sat at the very edge of the cliff where the junipers and cedars crowd the rock, watching a golden eagle rise above the gaping canyon, caught in the last rays of sun. On the other side of the canyon was a cliff dwelling, eerie and compelling; the wind moaned, louder and louder, carrying old songs and sadness. The two, deeply moved, abandoned themselves to their history, inching closer to the abyss where it seemed perfectly plausible that they, like the eagle, would soon fly away.

"The reservation is like a sanctuary," Donald said, looking at the ruin as if he expected his ancestors to come out of it. "The world can't come in there. Sometimes when I run along the roads, back toward the mountain, I can feel the old people speak to me, the ones down there, who are still listening. They tell me that I have to go back someday and teach my people to find the good in one another again. They say it can be done even if it takes a long time." He gazed toward the ruins, waiting.

Melanie stood up, looking away to the west as the sun was going down. "I don't care what Dr. Burger thinks," she said, "we'll finish what we started, just like our parents taught us."

Fawnda Whyte was the only Indian to wear native dress at Cortez High School graduation.

The wind rose, stronger and stronger, and the ancient cliff dwelling far below was bathed in a golden light as the horizon hooked the sun and took it away; the quieting land folded the last bit of the day into itself for safekeeping. The two children got up quickly; they had stayed past sunset and now bad spirits had come out to stalk the land. They ran to the truck and got in.

Along the road, a huge owl sat stiffly, unblinkingly, caught in the headlights of the truck as it swept past; the owl spread its wings and rose, cumbersome and vexed.

Melanie gasped and turned away; Donald pressed the accelerator as if to escape the deadly message of the owl but it was too late. The owl had already marked them with his eyes. It was, they said, the sign of impending death.

When Harriet Whyte died a few months later, Donald and Melanie attended her funeral, a simple Catholic ceremony the way she had wanted it, with all of her children, grandchildren, and foster children there. Because it was so close to Easter, Marshall Whyte selected lilies, plastic ones so they would last longer, and laid them on her grave himself. Donald Whyte offered a Baha'i prayer that sounded like an Indian prayer, speaking of unity among all mankind.

After the funeral, Mildred Whyte wiped her eyes and said, "When I married Clifford, she was a mother-in-law but then she became a mother to me."

The seven foster children, bewildered and frightened, began to cook as best they could and to sweep the house and collect the things that Harriet had left behind. Then with ominous regularity, the tribal office started to make threats to Marshall Whyte, who was by then off the council, to take the children from him, and stopped their money to him entirely. The old man, stubborn in his grief, simply drew out of his savings account the money he needed to feed them.

That spring, when Fawnda Whyte was about to graduate from high school, her grandfather took $400 out of his savings account and went to the trading post in Cortez and bought her a buckskin dress. When the 273 seniors marched into the high-school gymnasium to receive their diplomas, Fawnda Whyte was the only one who refused to wear a graduation gown. While the ten other Ute Mountain Ute seniors wore their gowns, Fawnda, who planned to go to college in Santa Fe to study art, marched proudly in the buckskin dress that Marshall Whyte had bought her. She wore buckskin leggings that Harriet had beaded, too, and a feather dangling from her graduation cap.

The old man did not attend the graduation that week nor the raucous Bear Dance the following weekend when Utes from all three tribes and a preponderance of Navajos gathered to dance but mostly to gamble and play hand games. Marshall Whyte was still in mourning for his wife, still worrying about the future, still arguing with the tribe about custody of the children, only now something had gone out of him. As he stood, sorrowful and pensive on the broken porch step of his house one morning, gazing off at the mesas with his usual expression of bewilderment, he spoke of his troubles and said suddenly, "Some day I'm gonna cry." Then he seemed to realize the futility of it all and changed his plan, his lip quivering.

"This summer," he said, "I'm gonna go away someplace, start over. I'm gonna live like an Indian, Montana maybe, where I got friends."

Then, with his dream expressed, he felt better. The old man actually smiled.

THE
SOUTHERN
UTES

4

THE SKY IS ALWAYS Father, the earth is always Mother, the Indians used to say. And out of the sky bursts the Grandfather with his hot breath of life growing good crops of oats, alfalfa, wheat, and corn on small patches of irrigated land, sucking the last moisture out of fields, drying out rain pools in rimrock, encouraging old trees to grow one last time. Sometimes there is rain, marching out of a summer sky on long, dark legs; sometimes there is snow, absolving the land of its bleakness.

There is no Ute today who will say, as one Ute leader did seventy-five years ago: "We came from away over yonder to this land and we like it here. From the top of the mountains, streams are running both ways. The other side belongs to the white man. My friends came up here with me and there are not many of us left. Here in this land are our relatives and children, covered over with earth. That is what makes this land dear to us. It is not buckskin or deer's hide and we do not want to sell it or give it away."

The time of such sentiment is past, as is the time of the buffalo, and there is no one to mourn any of it. The Indians, more than a century removed from their roots, are gearing themselves for the economic, technological, and social impact of the last two decades of the twentieth century and tend to view their past as a quaint, irrelevant by-product of academic inquisition. They dismiss their rich heritage with the classic Ute rebuttal: "It happened a long time ago." What they really mean is that they are more interested in the appearances of success than they are in the facts of their miraculous survival.

The dilemma of the Utes, along with other Native Americans, is not so much whether to integrate with the white community, for that is no longer a choice, but what, if any, of their culture they want to retain. There are few among them who can recount old legends, or who can remember the stories of their grandfathers, which represented an oral tradition both historical and educational. What remains of their culture is a mongrelized version of traditions, lore, religion, and a quasilanguage that has almost lost its purity, mixed as it is with everyday English and Spanish. The Utes, like most other western tribes, are quaint old relics of a frontier that has no place for them unless they are willing to share their vast mineral reserves, on the white man's terms, as always. The Indians are symbols of innocence and valor, evidence of natural selection and survival of the fittest; they are survivors of an upheaval in social order and racial inequality. But in the process they have sacrificed all that once made them different. No one wears buckskin, lives in a tepee, hunts with a bow and arrow, or greets the sun at dawn with a prayer. Almost no one makes baskets, flutes, or weapons anymore because there are other things to do—television being the major diversion among them. And today, few Utes even wear braids, once considered to be the source of their strength, preferring instead the kinds of hairstyles worn by everyone else.

The Ute language is seldom spoken by anyone under fifty years of age, and almost no one under eighteen even understands it. A Ute language conference attended by representatives from all three tribes in 1977 expressed concern for the future of Ute as a living language, agreeing that there might not have been any Ute language instruction in school had not the Colorado legislature mandated bilingual education. Even so, there was mixed reaction in Ignacio, from the school's difficulty in finding qualified Ute teachers to the children themselves, who often seemed embarrassed at having to speak Ute in class.

"A long time ago we had only one language," said Ralph Cloud, the closest thing to an elder that the Southern Utes have. "It was the Creator's gift to us and we are obliged to pass it on. In

Essie Kent, Southern Ute, conducts Ute-language program on KSUT.

the olden days children simply grew up with it—they learned their language and traditions from parents." He shook his head sadly. "Now they don't have time. They go watch TV."

Realizing that their language was only a generation away from being lost, the Southern Ute tribal council in 1976 hired noted UCLA linguist Tom Givón to develop the first written Ute language. Givón and Southern Ute traditionalists also put together a draft dictionary of twenty-five hundred core words and finished a three-hundred-page grammar. But his efforts may be in vain, since almost no one except fellow linguists can read the grammar, and few Utes seem interested in perusing the dictionary. Such cultural apathy is not uncommon at Ignacio.

When the tribal education office once sponsored a week-long culture course covering legends, traditions, myths, prayers, old

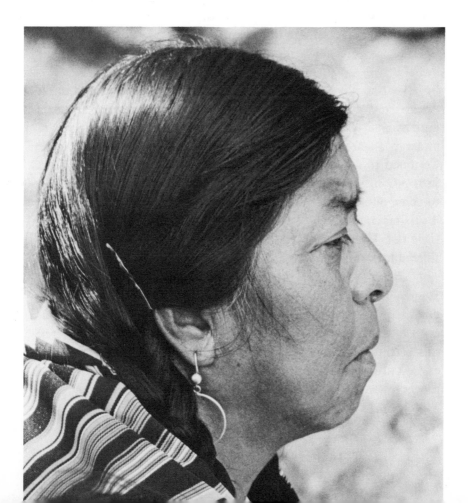

Ute dress styles, and food, less than fifty people showed up. As one young Ute put it, "Who wants to learn that junk?"

Other tribally sponsored courses, aimed at interesting young Utes, also have met with limited success. One, entitled "The History of Oppressed Peoples," taught by Dr. Tom Eckenrode of Durango's Fort Lewis College, covered Roman and medieval women, Christians, Anglo-Saxons, Hebrews, and Arabs—but no Indians. Another, on environmental concerns, presented ideas from scientists, planners, and water experts—but omitted the Indian point of view. A history course taught by Dr. Robert Delaney of Fort Lewis College, co-author of the tribe's official history, dealt with treaties, executive orders, and Acts of Congress —but no Indians. And when Tony Shearer, part-Sioux author of numerous books on Indians, tried to build a community theater for the Utes, the tribal council turned him down. "They don't need a director, they need a psychiatrist," Shearer said.

Language, legends, and Indian education are not all that have suffered at Ignacio; traditions are also going the way of the buffalo.

No one alive today, for instance, remembers what a traditional Ute wedding was like, not a religious ceremony at all but a kind of trial where the couple was asked by prospective in-laws to undergo a smoke ordeal designed to test patience and endurance. Confined to a smoke-filled tepee with just enough air to prevent suffocation, the couple remained for hours until they were asked to come out. If either of them had fainted, argued, or complained, it was taken as a sign of future weakness and a failure of the marriage test. If they emerged in harmony and silence, they were considered husband and wife.

There were other rituals, too, today largely forgotten. The Round Dance ceremony, called *mawo' qwipani*, was held to combat the spread of white-inflicted disease such as smallpox, dysentery, and gonorrhea. The medicine man, or *po'rat*, conducted this solemn ceremony, singing and fanning the people with an eagle tail-feather wand. The *po'rat* held a great supernatural power called *powa'a* and it lived inside him, a tiny being who directed the use of his power and was the one to swallow sickness and make the people whole. In healing ceremonies, the Ute shaman took certain remedies out of his medicine bundle; he had his songs, his ritual rules, and his ceremonial possessions, unique endowments offered to him alone in dream encounters between himself and the supernatural.

The last Ute shaman is said to have died twenty years ago at Towaoc and with him went *powa'a*, the reason, many older Utes believe, that today's troubles are so strong, that people die from mysterious ailments, and that strange things happen that only a shaman can ward off. Those who still believe in medicine men take their sick and dying to Gallup and Farmington, where old Navajo shamans still practice the ancient healing art.

There are no more smoke-filled tepee endurance tests, no more Round Dance ceremonies, not even the age-old custom of placing an infant's umbilical cord in an anthill to insure the health of the child. The old remedies once practiced by the medicine men have likewise been abandoned. No one goes about gathering horse's urine in a vial to be used on raised pustules, causing them to break. Flour is no longer used to curb diarrhea; skunk grease is no longer smeared on the skin to prevent chapping; sagebrush is seldom stuffed into shoes to alleviate the odor; and potatoes are not worn on the forehead to cure a headache. The modern Ute, more worldly and better educated than his parents, is also more removed from their roots as well as their remedies.

"When my grandfather was a young man," said one woman who works at the cafeteria, "he always went off alone and ran whenever my grandmother had a new baby. It was the old Ute way. When my father started having a family, he never ran. My grandfather asked him why. He said the others would laugh at him and anyway, he had work to do. I think it's funny today. If you saw an Indian run, you'd think he was out jogging. He could run for his baby and no one would ever know."

Not only traditions such as this but also Ute history remains virtually unknown outside a handful of tribal members who have managed to learn it on their own. Two books, one on the Northern Utes, the other on the Southern Utes, and published by their respective tribes, purport to relate the true Ute story, but so submissive have the Utes become that they tell their tale from the white's point of view, describing their disintegration in dull, half-apologetic prose. Because of their relative obscurity, there has been little predilection from the outside world to learn much about them either; for most people, "Ute" is a three-letter word in a crossword puzzle.

Although the nationwide movement toward Indian awareness has revived a certain amount of tribal pride at Ignacio during the past decade, there are years of indifference that prevent the seeds of Indian otherness from really taking hold. To most Southern Utes, reservation survival depends on paying lip service to a loose set of rules based on acceptance, favoritism, and silence. Utes neither criticize wrongdoing nor crusade for any kind of social change; they do not march, carry signs, nor circulate petitions. Their way is a Zen-like method of letting time solve everything, without direct interference from anyone. Yet such a hands-off attitude gives rise to apathy, and the Indians are accused of lacking convictions. Moreover, as the outside world infiltrates the reservation, the Ute is confused by the role he is expected to play, and is often called to task for his Indian ideals or the absence of them. Among a tribe sharply divided on whether to embrace the fragments of tradition or to discard them in favor of creeping modernism, today's Ute is forced to defend not so much his right to be "Indian" as his reason not to be.

The Southern Utes, more sophisticated and living closer to civilization than the other two Ute tribes, would rather learn what the white world has to offer than to probe the depths of their own rich culture. Nearly every Ute has a television set and is saturated, along with every other American, with messages of materialism, adventure, and fantasy. Moreover, they, like their white counter-

Apache dancer from Dulce, New Mexico, is frequent visitor to Southern Ute powwows.

parts, are physically mobile; except for those of advanced age, nearly every Ute over twenty-one owns a vehicle and speeds away to the cities, there to seek jobs and opportunities that the reservation does not offer. Indeed, as the better-educated Utes flee to the cities, it is the unemployed and unemployable who cling to the reservation, creating stagnation as well as a quaint vacuity that passes for aesthetic realism. A handful of Indian intellectuals has attempted to illuminate as well as to instruct, only to learn that it is an extraordinarily expensive pastime when family as well as friends turn their backs. The conscientious Ute who is able to see beyond the limited horizon of his own reservation finds it does him no good to stay around and spread his message of enlightenment; fast-growing Denver and Colorado Springs will welcome him as an oracle as well as an Indian, for the Native American mystique is far from gone as far as most Anglos are concerned. For the Indian, however, his own mystique vanished along with the buffalo.

While the white world lures and insists, with its promise of status as well as employment, the Utes themselves have offered little resistance, perhaps because their nature is basically passive, perhaps too because more than two hundred years of a shrinking land base have left them spiritually denuded. Not only have the Utes become civilized, acculturated, assimilated, and the victims of other white-invented euphemisms for tamed, but they have lost touch with old roots and old ways as well.

In the end, it is only their narrow strip of mineral-rich land, with so much of tribal life already woven into it after a century of struggle and the erosion of old values, that the Southern Utes can call their own. Even so, they do not know it the way their grandfathers did, as a source of livelihood, comfort, and spiritual renewal. A Ute seldom rides his horse or walks across his land; he drives his car or pickup everywhere he goes, considers walking fit

Tribal chairman Leonard Burch, left, and Southern Ute spiritual leader and tribal council member Eddie Box, right, offer an Indian song at opening of Southern Ute Health Center, Ignacio. Photographer is from Northern Ute newspaper.

only for athletic tourists and Indian children not old enough to drive.

No longer dependent on the land for food, shelter, or survival, the Utes are not dependent on it spiritually either. Unlike his ancestors, today's Indian does not sit mesmerized before the sunrise, nor does he talk to the trees. The purpose of open space is seldom to provide spiritual nourishment but to yield great treasures of oil, gas, and coal, enriching tribal coffers even more. The Ute, while capitalizing on his image as a downtrodden victim of nineteenth-century greed, is cast in a dual role as shrewd apologist for American business, and the result is a comic figure of Babbitt in a war bonnet that the Indian himself does not recognize.

When it is convenient for him to act the part of an Indian at dedications, ceremonials, and other tourist-attended rituals, the Ute dons his blankets or buckskin, assumes a romantic nineteenth-century posture of nobility, and leaves a convincing image in the

minds of white visitors, often including bureaucrats and legislators who are in a position to pay for the collective American guilt with bucketsful of collective American cash.

But when confronted by legions of lawyers, bankers, oil- and gas-company executives, water boards, and real-estate developers, the Ute puts on his other mask, wears a business suit, and leaves his uneasy guests to mutter about Indian duality, cunning, and corruption, all taught to them by whites in the first place. The Southern Utes, newly aware of their potential, are fast becoming adept at wheeling and dealing, shoring up their new economic advantages with double-edged rhetoric aimed at all-white audiences.

In 1972, tribal chairman Leonard Burch overcame strong local opposition to expanding the airport when he got up and said, "My name is Leonard C. Burch and I am chairman of the Southern Ute tribe. We've been here four hundred years and we believe jet service will be good for the economic development of the tribe and the area." Another time in 1977, embroiled with the federal government over President Carter's veto of vital Colorado water projects, Chairman Burch barked at the committee, "Indians are sick and tired of all the white tape. We hope you take this message back to the Great White Father in Washington so that he does not speak with a forked tongue."

Behind the whimsy is a deadly-serious strategy to enhance every economic advantage. White audiences applauded and Burch's comments made front-page news; his message hit its intended target. The airport was overwhelmingly approved and it appears that, partly due to Indian pressure, most of the vetoed water projects will be restored.

The Utes, wearing the tragedy of their past like a tattered blanket, elicit immediate sympathy among a generation brought up on Vietnam, civil rights, Zen, Hinduism, and the voices of the Apocalypse. The Indians all seem to offer a magical solution to the demons of dread and destruction; they seem to offer an antidote for what has gone wrong with the world by providing a haven for weary dropouts eager to devour their secrets for a perfect life. Idealism finds its home among the Indians, and the Utes are no exception.

Dozens of young whites, blacks, and even runaway Indians from other tribes drift in and out of Ignacio, glassy-eyed dreamers in search of Native American wisdom which, as it turns out, is a Native American myth, largely the creation of Western writers, artists, and moviemakers. Indians, in the modern vernacular, have all become "cool." Their lifestyle is mystical, a cut above the crass, burdensome realities of the white world. Thanks to the Indian awareness movement generated in the sixties, it is still "in" to be one of them.

America, bereft of heroes, has hoisted the Indian on a pedestal, dressed him in buckskin and feathers, and expects from him advice, wisdom, and spirituality in a dark age of gasoline shortages, inflation, and weak leadership—all that grips the imagination of Americans these days. No matter that the Indian was once reviled, ridiculed, and nearly exterminated; no matter that history has been unkind or that sentiment has created a neoclassic myth, the Indian is marketable and he makes us remember our errors and omissions. If only for a little while, we can ponder the loss of the great lessons he once offered and we refused.

Man has gone to the moon but no one thinks of the astronauts as heroes, but rather as highly trained, germ-free technicians. In this century, man has advanced in science, law, mathematics, and medicine, yet who would consider Edward Teller, William Douglas, Albert Einstein, and Jonas Salk heroes? John Wayne is dead and despite the claims of celebrities, rock groups, and sports stars, America no longer has a national symbol now that the bald eagle is almost extinct. Indians are not only the appropriate choice for the obverse of pennies and dollars, they are also the only heirs to a tradition older than Thanksgiving and pumpkin pie. America needs them to be Indians, but they have all but merged with the very society that exploited and subdued them over a century ago. Perhaps it is already too late, but the Utes still seem

OVERLEAF

A Southern Ute powwow.

to be grappling with one key issue—how to retain the spirit of the past while facing the wrenching challenge of the future.

An old man sat on a bench in the park opposite the BIA building in Ignacio where the road winds down the hill and crosses a bend in the Pine River. Every day he walked to the grassy, tree-lined park that held so many memories for him because it was where he used to come for his rations long ago when there were no trees or grass, just the river flowing through the quiet land. Sometimes the old man told stories to the children; sometimes he posed for pictures; mostly he just sat alone with his memories.

Even though the weather was in the seventies, the old man was dressed in a heavy plaid wool coat and a hunter's cap with ear flaps; he wore dark glasses, which kept his eyes from being seen, and when he spoke it was in halting English, a language not quite learned even then. Harry Richards at ninety-four had earned the distinction of being the oldest living Southern Ute man; he had been born on his father's farm in 1885, just seven years after the Southern Utes had accepted a handful of silver dollars as payment for six million acres of land.

"There was an old wagon road between here and Pagosa," Harry Richards said, sitting in the shade of a tree but not really noticing the land that had grown familiar to him over the years. "Once a month, they came with supplies—flour, sugar, lard, coffee sometimes. We used to line up here and wait for them to hand out food. No trees here then and no grass, just a big open field. Sometimes, in winter, we wait all day. An old wood building was over there and the government just sit and watch, wait for us to go home. It was so cold. But we build three fires to keep warm and roast meat over them. We ate good. We had to get our own meat in those days, from the mountains where our fathers used to hunt. We'd ride up in the mountains and get us a deer, sometimes an elk. No fences then. Plenty meat. The whites no like us to hunt up there but we go anyway. I run sheep up there for a while. Now nobody run sheep."

He thought about it for a while, speaking again of the government dole and the long wait, sometimes into the night.

"They think the Indians give up but we no give up. We sit and wait and pretty soon they see they have to give us something. They think maybe we starve but we no starve. We have a mouth and so we eat."

The ration system that Harry Richards spoke of lasted until 1931 when, as part of Roosevelt's overall reform, Congress ended the Indian welfare program. From then until their windfall in the fifties the Utes had to rely on the once-scorned farming in order to survive. Those twenty-five years were perhaps the most conscientious in their history, for not only did they become self-sustaining but self-respecting also; during that period the Utes won numerous state agricultural awards for crops and livestock as well as earning a reputation among fellow farmers for industriousness and honesty. The backbreaking effort to survive, creating, as one Ute man put it, "big rock Indians," also gave them self-reliance, discipline, and years of stoic self-denial. The characteristics inherent in the Utes in that quarter century were to vanish quickly later on but they left an imprint of huge sadness, like the image of a prehistoric leaf whose essential details remain forever in the stone.

The old man looked out and away to the other side of the river, to where the trees were pale with new leaves and the land was stirring with spring. Across the river was where the cemetery was, endless rows of plain white crosses, marked with the same names again and again—Cloud, Box, Taylor, Redd, Rabbit, Burch, Baker, Eagle, and Duran. The Catholics were buried on one side of the cemetery, the Protestants on the other; there was no place for just "Indians" to be. In death, as in life, they were claimed by one branch or another of Christianity. Not even Chief Ouray, who ceded so much Ute land, was spared this final indignity. First buried in a cave near Ignacio in 1880, his bones became the subject of a dispute between the Methodists and the Catholics, who dug him up in 1925 and reburied him precisely in the middle of the Protestant-Catholic dividing line.

Until he had gone into the senior citizens' home the year before, Harry Richards had lived on a farm, now run by his son. In his time he had been a carpenter, a blacksmith, interpreter, and stallkeeper; now he spent his time making crayon drawings of his early life—a tepee, a charred forest after a fire, the mountains of his youth, the animals he once chased with his bow and arrow. He had lived a long time, he said, and he could tell people what was not in the books.

"When I was six or seven," Harry Richards went on, including the sun-drenched horizon in a single sweep of his hand, "we lived out there near the wagon road. We'd hide in the trees when we heard them—the whites coming in. It took four oxen to pull it—everything strapped to the outside. Guns. Shovels. Axes. Behind them, more. They wouldn't stop for us. We were just children. But they stopped and looked at the women. All they wore was burlap in those days. A sack for a dress. Down to here." He pointed to his feet encased in buckled rubber rain boots even though it had not rained in a week. "Buckskin all gone. We were here watching the whites come in."

Except for Harrry Richards, there was not a Southern Ute alive who remembered the white invasion of the 1890s when, poised at the reservation boundary, they waited for the signal to rush in and claim what the Indians had given up. The whites had looked at the Indian women in a way that even now the old man had not forgotten. His toothless mouth formed imaginary words; his face was like weathered stone.

"Ignacio run off to Towaoc," he said finally. "Ouray already dead. Buckskin Charley say, 'Be a farmer like me.' Ah! They call him 'the Fox' but a fox no farm. Nobody know what to tell us. Now everything is changed. Everything finished. Us Indians is all through."

With that he got up abruptly and grabbed the edge of the picnic table to steady himself. "Us Ute always like horses," he said, his leathery old face turned toward the sun. "Have a lot of them. We built us a track and raced all the time. We bet a lot of money and the BIA say, 'Why you no work? Do what we say.'"

Harry Richards greets old friend Henry Stoneroad, a Pawnee employed by Ute Mountain Ute tribe.

He shrugged. "Ah!" It was the strongest expletive that Harry Richards ever used, indicating not only what he thought of the Bureau of Indian Affairs but also his assessment of the whole of United States history.

The old man, without another word, pulled down the flaps of his hunter's cap and began to walk toward town; even at ninety-four he walked at least five miles every day. Only now people noticed that it took him longer to get up the hill and that he was more stooped than ever before. But he walked unaided, with a firm but halting gait. A car stopped and he made his way over to it, speaking briefly to the young Indian man who was driving. After a moment's hesitation, Harry Richards accepted a ride but not before he looked back the way he had come, toward the river with its cloud of pale green trees.

Around Ignacio, most Utes consider Harry Richards something of a fool, not only for the stories he tells to strangers, but also for his role in the fundamentalist Pentecostal Church, where he serves as deacon and preacher at Indian funerals. Despite his age, he is not regarded as an elder, for that requires more than years, but rather

as a quaint old relic welded to a romanticized past. He is not challenged by change nor condemned for what he believes tradition is all about, a personalized blend of firsthand history and an old man's stories. It has nothing to do with Indian religion, which he, like more than half of today's Utes over the age of fifty, is able to incorporate into one version or another of Christianity. Most of them believe that if one religion is good, two is even better and, like Harry Richards who plays the morache—a notched stick—at the Bear Dance held for social purposes each spring, they attend their ceremonials with the same fervor reserved for Sunday morning in one of Ignacio's five churches.

But if Harry Richards seems obsolete to the modern Southern Ute who has his mind on a better job, a better house, and more money, he is also a mirror to a distant past that is not so much inspiration as it is a means for raising sympathy, federal dollars, and a modern Indian mystique. Harry Richards is the best PR man the Southern Utes could have, for not only is he aged and therefore venerable, but also to most visitors he appears to be the embodiment of Black Elk, Chief Joseph, and Ouray himself. No one else is nearly as old nor as directly connected to a colorful past, even though his notions of history are sketchy and often inaccurate. Like most Utes, he has never studied his tribe's past, and what he knows has been handed down by word of mouth. Thus Harry Richards, as the oldest Ute man, becomes at best his own facsimile of a warrior, mostly created by hordes of insistent tourists who come to view the Indian as a freak, expecting to find him in feathers and beads, astride a horse or living in a tepee. Few visitors to this out-of-the-way reservation recognize the true Ute dilemma—how to retain the spirit of the past while facing the wrenching challenge of the future. They would rather take pictures of Harry Richards dressed for a blizzard in May.

The Utes, like other Indians, are fighting a losing battle. Their attempts to capture what is left of traditional values are offset by more than a century of insidious pressure by the BIA to turn them into model American citizens, holding jobs and learning the power of capitalism, and drastically altering their Indian priorities in the process. Small wonder that the Navajos, caught in a bitter internecine feud on whether to exploit their land or preserve it, are nonetheless strip-mining their coal and that the Utes, with no discussion among themselves nor with the BIA on land ethics, are likewise planning to do the same. The belief that land is sacred and must be kept in pristine condition is as naïve and out-dated as the old Ute teaching that plants, animals, birds, and even rocks, clouds, and trees had spirit lives of their own, to be wisely incorporated into the daily life of the Ute. Such pantheism was long ago drummed out of the Utes by the BIA, which insisted that they give up their pagan ways and become "civilized"; no one, the United States Government most of all, ever believed that the Indians had a unique and valid philosophy all their own.

The blame for gradual tribal disintegration, translated into "assimilation" in the jargon of the times, lies squarely with the BIA, paternalistic, arrogant, and detrimental to the Indian's right to live as he chooses. While across the nation more and more Indians are calling for the BIA to be abolished, to be replaced with an independent Indian agency run by Indians, the Southern Utes remain curiously silent, perhaps because the BIA negotiates all their mineral leases for them, perhaps too because the BIA employs twenty-eight of their people, about half of the Ignacio agency. Indian leaders see the BIA as corrupt, out of Indian control, knotted in conflicts of interest, and less concerned for Indians than for the corporate giants that want to exploit Indian lands and resources. Yet the Southern Utes, unlike the Ute Mountain Utes, are locked into the agency and accept the word of their superintendent, Ray de Kay, who has been at Ignacio an unprecedented fourteen years. This balding, affable, cigar-chomping man is largely responsible for the tribe's long-term resource-development plan, the recent revision of the Southern Ute constitution, and many of the closed-door decisions that appear to be made by the Indians. De Kay and tribal chairman Leonard Burch, along with tribal attorney Sam Maynes, are seen by most Southern Utes as a *troika* of political and economic power who with a flourish of the pen can change Ute destiny forever.

The Utes, with curious ambivalence, are quick to blame the agency when anything goes wrong—such as a leak in the roof of the tribal affairs building, the loss of a federal grant, or even the wild spending of the land-claims money twenty-five years ago. On the other hand, successful joint endeavors such as $3 million worth of new tribal buildings or the Indian-operated radio station are always claimed as the miraculous achievement of the Utes themselves, with no help from anyone, including the BIA or a host of competent white employees.

At Ignacio, the BIA can point to certain achievements, such as providing summer jobs for twenty-five reservation teen-agers at a Youth Conservation Corps Camp, yet it also hinders tribal members who try to set up small businesses if they happen to work for the BIA at the same time. Thanks to an archaic rule that prohibits BIA employees from "trading with the Indians," Joe Mestas lost his small grocery store in Ignacio in 1977, six years after the BIA provided him a loan with which to start his enterprise. In 1977, as in 1971, Mestas was an employee of the BIA; however, it was not until 1977 that he was asked to sign a disclaimer promising not to trade with the Indians. After he refused to sign, Mestas was denied a second business grant and was told he must resign from his job or quit his business.

"I could have put up a sign on the door that says 'No Indians Allowed,'" Mestas said, "but that would have meant myself as well." Even more ironic is the fact that in order to get his business loan, Mestas had to sign a BIA paper promising that he would not discriminate.

Such an attitude is not uncommon in the BIA, whose goal, since its inception in 1824, has been to reform the "savages" and transform them into Christians and consumers. The bureaucracy is merely enforcing a two-hundred-year-old United States policy aimed at suppressing traditional forms of Indian government and imposing a white-defined social, political, and economic value system that bears no resemblance to what all Indians consider the Creator's life plan. The government has never, during all this time, agreed to help the Indians on their own terms but has arbitrarily and often maliciously selected a program of uniquely American individualism at odds with the centuries-old Native American definition of tribalism. Using various forms of persuasion, such as beatings, starvation, and ridicule, the Bureau of Indian Affairs has all but succeeded in destroying the great body of Indian knowledge, culture, and magnificent spiritual beliefs.

Quasi-adaptation to white standards, minus the education and experience to handle it, means for most tribes such as the Ute Mountain Utes a naïve, frivolous, and destructive tendency to spend, as the BIA looks on, all of their land-claims and minerals money as quickly and as unwisely as possible. Moreover, as Indians suddenly become aware of their tremendous mineral wealth, the Bureau, and not the tribes, is placed in the untenable position of signing away these huge resources, jeopardizing Indian lands even more. At the same time that the Indians have failed to achieve independence, largely because the United States has divested them of their lands and resources, they have been successful in perpetuating BIA domination of their lives.

Ever since the Indian Reorganization Act of 1934, often called the Indian New Deal, with its constitution authored by the BIA, virtually all tribal government decisions require the approval of the Secretary of the Interior before passing into tribal law. A resolution to spend money, sell land, select a tribal attorney, or even purchase office furniture may be rejected by the local BIA superintendent or the Secretary of the Interior. The results are often ludicrous.

Once, the Ute Mountain Ute tribal council wanted to buy a breathalyzer for use by tribal police but was first required to get the budget line item approved by the Albuquerque BIA office. Their request read, "one breathalyzer with attachments," meaning that they also wanted to buy attachments for the apparatus. But the BIA interpreted "with attachments" to mean that there were to be more pages to the memo and waited three months for the tribe to send them. When the mistake was uncovered, the BIA hastily approved the request.

Such misunderstandings are common between the BIA and its

charges, until recently called "wards" by the agency and now referred to euphemistically as "partners." While tribes cannot make any decisions that will alter their dependency status or force the BIA to accept an Indian idea of policy, the bureaucracy sets up more and more programs for the tribes as it sees fit. Thus "suggestions" by the BIA such as the distribution of land-claims money, trust funds, individual money accounts, per-capita payments, or the 10-40 accounts, are seldom rejected by tribal governments, leading to the oft-repeated criticism that tribal councils are really only puppet regimes for the BIA and the federal government, both of which seem bent on ruining the very people they are charged by law with protecting, a paternalistic concept long past its usefulness.

But the Southern Utes, more outspoken and aggressive than most tribes, have not always accepted their agents or superintendents without question and have, on many occasions, carried their complaints to Washington when they could not receive satisfaction at the local level. During the first fifty years of the Southern Ute reservation, twenty-two different agents came and went, forced out by disgruntled Indians who did not like the idea of becoming farmers or herdsmen. One, when told by the superintendent that he had to plant crops, replied evenly, "Goddamn a potato."

Both tribes of Colorado Utes were also known for their resistance to BIA boarding schools, erected both at Towaoc and Ignacio, where their children were forbidden to speak their language or to observe the old customs. Many parents hid their children from marauding BIA officials who came to take them away; others, faced with curtailment of their rations, were forced to relinquish their children to BIA supervision, only to have them die hundreds of miles from home.

Yet such resistance to the BIA has gradually faded away; except for the hostility generated toward Joe Otero at Towaoc, most Utes simply tolerate their cardboard commanders these days. Few will ever speak out against decisions made for them by the agency. Such dependency, fostered by the BIA at the same time it

Dick McKuan, Northern Ute from Fort Duchesne, Utah.

advocates a policy of termination—when all BIA services are ended—keeps the Indians perpetually off balance, like children who are given an automobile and a teddy bear at the same time.

"Termination," signed into law in 1953, "frees the Indian from the yoke of federal supervision," cutting off such long-held BIA responsibilities as trusteeship over tribal and individual lands, resources, and funds, and outlining the withdrawal of the agency from the reservation. It also leaves the Indians at the mercy of state taxation and welfare systems and sweeps them into a competitive market for which they have no training. Beyond that, termination eliminates the tribes as legal entities and in the process removes their right to claim "federal" lands never ceded to the U. S. Government by treaty, most of it in the West and rich in minerals.

As far as most Indian leaders are concerned, termination is just another devious ploy by the government to rob their people of any future claims against lands already coveted by white economic interests. Termination, they say, is simply a way for the government to escape the responsibility it assumed two hundred years ago and must continue to fulfill. In their eyes, termination is synonymous with assimilation, since once the tribe was responsible for itself it would be no different than any other group of taxpayers. Most Indians want to retain their special federal status that not only guarantees them government money and protection but also sets them apart from all other groups of Americans.

The BIA position is that they can only be, and have always been, stewards or land trustees, nothing more. Yet the Indians are inextricably tied to their lands, and whatever decision is made for the lands affects them all as well. The BIA admits that it does not want to bear responsibility for Indian lands forever and must eventually cut the umbilical cord between them and the Indians, turning them into effective land managers. But since the BIA has kept them in the dark for so long, few tribes are actually able to conduct their business themselves, and they turn to their educated white administrators for help, including their tribal attorneys, BIA personnel, and legions of federally funded experts sent in to assist them. While the BIA maintains that some tribes, particularly the Southern Utes but not the Ute Mountain Utes, are within five years of termination, in practice it invents ways to keep them tied to its apron strings. Perhaps fearing for its $850 million annual budget and the jobs of the 21,000 people it employs—about half of them with Indian ancestry—to administer to the needs of 827,000 Native Americans, the BIA continues to foster the same old dependency.

Curiously, however, the agency goes out of its way to create an illusion of partnership, citing Indian decisions to build tribal dams, roads, businesses, and factories, and to sign mineral leases, playing down their own role as instigator of all these capitalistic ventures. The truth is that the BIA negotiates all Indian mineral leases at a rate decided by the BIA, usually under pressure from energy corporations that have powerful lobbies in Washington. Contracts for tribal roads, dams, factories, and businesses are offered by tribal councils but only after the BIA has given written approval. In most cases, what appears to be the result of a tribal brainstorm to open a shirt factory, go into the cattle business, operate a bowling alley, or strip their lands for coal is actually a BIA scheme designed to give the Indians practice in becoming independent businessmen. Other projects credited to the tribe, such as the writing of their constitution, law-and-order code, and even a history book, all bear the heavy hand of the bureaucracy despite their protests to the contrary.

According to the BIA, the most successful tribes are those that have adapted well to the precepts of American business, such as the camouflage-net assembly plant being operated by the Sioux tribe and Brunswick Corporation at the Fort Totten reservation in North Dakota, or the electronics firm currently operating on the Cherokee reservation. Few tribes have businesses directly related to their heritage, for as one critic points out, there is no market for headdresses, buckskin, or tepees; moreover, few Indians today are capable of making the handiwork of their ancestors—elaborate beadwork, intricate baskets, pottery, and costumes, nor do many know how to make the traditional Indian instruments—drums and flutes. It is mainly the Navajos, still turning out exquisite silversmithing, sand paintings, and finely woven rugs, who have carried on with the best of their tribe's artistic ability and heritage.

The Ute Mountain Utes, attempting to recapture their long-lost talent for making pottery, have opened a factory at Towaoc, but much of the quality is poor, and only a handful of pieces are genuinely well designed. They have also, under BIA pressure, opened a shirt factory, but only 12 Ute Mountain Utes are among the 150 employees. The Northern Utes for some years made furniture, hand-decorated with ancient Indian symbols, but eventually went out of business because of poor management. For the Southern Utes, a short-lived beadwork co-op connected them with an illustrious beadworking background, but this received little tribal support and eventually shut down.

The BIA has never been known to encourage the pursuit of native crafts; they would rather the Indians follow a more lucrative career in resource development, no matter what it costs these Native Americans.

Ten years ago, the agency gave its blessing to the Peabody Coal Company when their bulldozers first began scraping away on the Hopi's sacred Black Mesa, a project that is estimated to bring Peabody $750 million in coal revenue during the 35 years the mine is supposed to be in operation, over 50 times more than the Hopi can expect to receive in royalties. Traditional Indians say by the time Peabody is finished, the land will be ruined, the money gone, and the BIA will be figuring other ways to use them.

The Navajo nation, with 700,000 acres of forest in Arizona and New Mexico will, at its alarming rate of BIA-set cutting, be out of trees in 20 years. And the tiny Quinault tribe of Washington, which once occupied much of the state, is now faced with utter ruin, thanks to a faulty BIA timber plan that has decimated all of its forests and salmon streams.

The BIA, when accused of trying to destroy their Indian "partner," assumes no responsibility for such blunders but fixes the blame on the tribes themselves, ambiguously insisting that Indians often do not want to do what is best for them. As then Secretary of the Interior Thomas S. Kleppe told more than two hundred Indian leaders at the White House in 1976: "Do we have an obligation to allow tribal governments to make mistakes? Self-determination says that we have that obligation to allow you to take actions which our best judgment tells us is a mistake for you. But our trust responsibility argues that we do not have the legal authority to allow you to make mistakes if we can prevent them."

Behind such patronizing nonsense is the simple fact that Native Americans are the only minority who by legislative fiat are not allowed to think for themselves and who are forbidden by law to make mistakes. The BIA, on the other hand, does not have to account for any of theirs, including the moth-eaten appearance of all Indian lands.

The BIA, anxious to speed up the assimilation process in the late nineteenth century, gave support to the General Allotment Act of 1887, a law providing that Indian reservation land, formerly held in trust for the whole tribe, should be divided into chunks called allotments. Most of these parcels were 160 acres each, and the BIA saw this as a way to force the recalcitrant Southern Utes to take up their much-despised farming. But the Indians failed to grasp the meaning of acres and allotments and had no words in their language that even came close to these euphemisms. Little wonder, then, that in 1899, after just 371 bewildered Southern Utes out of an eligible 1,307 had claimed a total of 73,000 acres of allotments, the rest of the reservation, a huge 523,079-acre empire, was thrown open to white settlement, exactly as planned by a government anxious to accommodate its own people.

Despite allotments, not all of the Indians took to farming as the BIA would have wished. Many vanished into the desert to the west, intermarried with Navajos, Apaches, and smaller tribes; others died of tuberculosis, pneumonia, and cirrhosis of the liver; still others lost the will to live and simply died.

The whites did not know what to make of it but the old Indians knew. "When an Indian and his land are separated, the heart separates also," they said. "A man cannot live with half a heart and so he dies."

It was as simple as that.

5

BY THE EARLY YEARS of the twentieth century, the old Ute life was finished. Warriors no longer warred; hunters no longer hunted; the great chiefs were no longer important. Braids were cut, buckskin traded for cotton, denim, and absurd wool greatcoats; tepees were torn down and the people made to live in hogans and flimsy shacks. Children were soon removed from parents and sent away to BIA schools, where they were dressed in uniforms, their hair shorn, their feet encased in sturdy leather shoes, their moccasins burned along with feathers and buckskin, their language and songs forbidden. When the children mysteriously died, teachers blamed it on their poor constitutions and dependence on Indian food.

The war songs were all forgotten except for the sad lament of an aged brave lasting far into the night; the war ponies were all dead, their bones left in the sun to bleach and rot back into the earth; and the stories of the great chiefs whose exploits once had given courage to a whole generation of confused and wandering people were buried along with their headdresses and buckskin when they died.

Indian women who had formerly set up camp, gathered wood, carried water, picked berries, skinned and cooked game, made garments and moccasins, done beadwork, decorated clothing, made bags and baskets, mourned the dead, scalped their enemies, and occasionally been permitted to go into battle to assist the men, and who were meant to bear four to six children and often shared their husbands with one or more women when men were scarce, now were confined to strange new homes where they were expected to cook rich and starchy foods, sew garments made of unfamiliar cloth, knit blankets made of yarn, sweep the floor with a broom, scrub clothes on boards instead of rocks, cut their hair, wear shoes, and send their children away to school. More than that, Ute women, for the first time in their lives, as the power of the men decreased, became the actual heads of households, often speaking on behalf of their husbands, who had been stripped of so much power in less than twenty-five years.

To meet the threat to their masculinity and what remained of their spiritual lives, Ute men had invented new dances in the late nineteenth century and borrowed others from neighboring tribes; the Sun Dance, derived largely from the Sioux, emerged as a source of renewal and strength for Ute men, who danced it once each year under the spiritual guidance of a Sun Dance chief chosen as the preserver of Ute religious life. But there were other ceremonies as well.

First was the Ghost Dance religion, introduced in the 1880s to the Southern Utes by one of their own members, a Weminuche who had been given, during a sojourn to the Paiutes living several hundred miles to the west, certain songs and supernatural powers. His message to his people prophesied the spiritual return of all their great leaders; he also admonished them to claim the old virtues that the leaders had left behind. At his death, Jack Wilson, a Paiute prophet of the new cult, sent a man named Yunitckwo'ov as his personal emissary to teach another version of the Ghost Dance religion to the Utes.

The traditional Ute believed that the spiritual return of the dead meant that in a trancelike state induced by the dance, the living made a visit to the dead and returned with the moral injunction to live well and follow the old Ute ways. The emphasis in the Ghost Dance was on the living and not the dead, who were simply passive onlookers.

But when Yunitckwo'ov arrived in 1914, he advised the Indians that within a year their ancestors would come from the west in bodily form; there would be a huge whirlwind and the whites would perish just as the ancestors blew in. The Utes were torn be-

Mrs. Leo Vicente, a Jicarilla Apache from Dulce, New Mexico, attends most Southern Ute Bear Dances.

tween fear of an actual ghostly visitation which, according to their own ancient belief, spelled death for the living, and doubt that such an event could actually happen.

For all of their history, the Utes had developed an outward fear of ghosts and then, as now, had many superstitions about death. Pictures of the dead were always destroyed. Haunted spots where ghosts lurked—*ihupi'arat tubuts*—were carefully avoided. Whistling at night was not permitted for fear that others would think that *ini'putc'*, the ghost, was coming. The sound of the screech owl, *otus asio*, meant that someone was soon to die; dreams of the dead meant they were coming to take the living with them.

As they were to do again more than a half century later, the Utes, in what was to become a tribal characteristic, simply ignored their self-proclaimed "spiritual leader" in 1914. When the year passed and nothing happened, Yunitckwo'ov was discredited and the Ghost Dance was suspended.

Not long after, a halfbreed named Sam Loganberry, alias Cactus Pete, arrived from Oklahoma with a bagful of peyote buttons and a strange new ritual containing certain elements of Christianity. While some of the Utes took to this new cult, others followed another peyote leader named John Peehart, an Indian who observed a purer ritual and who was considered a true teacher of the old Ute ways.

By the thirties, the peyote cult at Ignacio was fighting for survival despite the claim that it had crystallized much of the old Ute beliefs and welded them into a churchlike organization able to compete with the missionaries clamoring for the spiritual life of the people. Basically, peyote was a healing ceremony which, when coupled with a moderate dose of Christianity, was able to bridge the gap between the old religious values and the steadily encroaching American environment. In the thirties, when peyote use first began to decline, five dollars' worth of groceries were required from each participant for the peyote feast; to many, subsisting on less than thirty dollars a month, the amount seemed excessive. The shortage of money, the decline of farming, and the resistance of

the medicine men, or *po'rat*, to the ceremony, suspended peyote at Ignacio for another twenty-five years.

The thirties signaled a decline in religion at Ignacio as the peyote cult faded away. The growing appeal of hospitalization left the *po'rat* almost without function, and the Sun Dance chief publicly announced his decision to retire. Not only was the assimilation policy of the BIA to blame for the religious apathy that affected the Southern Utes, but also a criminal code, approved in 1884, that prohibited the exercise of Indian religious ceremonies. In spite of clear guarantees found in the Bill of Rights, the Indians, who were not even granted citizenship until 1924 and could not vote until 1948, were not included, and for a half century remained the victims of religious persecution. When a wave of reform swept the country in the late twenties and early thirties, liberals hailed the movement as a way to solve the "Indian problem." Actually, the eight-hundred-page Merriam Report, issued in 1928, insisted on more standardization for the Indians than ever and, in the end, what the report called "a retarded race" was swiftly manipulated into the "prevailing civilization" after all.

In 1934 Congress at last revoked the Allotment Act, in effect for nearly 40 years, enough time for the Southern Utes to have lost 33,202 acres of the 72,811 allotted to them in 1895. Before the official end of the allotment era, however, there was a mad scramble to grab what was left before the deadline passed.

One Southern Ute woman, now in her late fifties, remembers that time well. "I must have been about sixteen or so. My mother had passed on and it was her allotment I was living on, a good piece of land with water. Somebody from town drove out and said, 'Sign this piece of paper,' so I did. I didn't know I was selling the land. I thought I was just getting money for it. Of course we Utes didn't care anything about mineral rights so we signed those away, too. Now you can't, but forty or fifty years ago you could. The tribe didn't know how much it was losing at the time.

"My husband has no land either. His father signed it away before he was born. After we were married we got an assignment down there by the river. We had it for twenty years. No water, no plumbing, no electricity. I'd haul water from a stream and in winter I melted snow but my children were always clean. We had kerosene lamps and a wood stove and raised everything we needed to eat. We raised hay and sheep too—you got good money for it in those days—and my husband worked for the BIA. We were better off than most folks. We made out pretty good until all that [land claims] money hit us in the fifties. Then we got ruined along with everyone else."

Until the midfifties, the Southern Utes lived in poverty on the reservation, many of them crowded into tents, hogans, and cardboard shacks often housing two and three generations at one time. Exploited by the whites in Durango and Ignacio, who hired them for menial jobs at below-standard wages, hindered by the BIA, which felt that education in one of their regimented schools was the answer, and ignored by their own council, which spent its time wondering how to cash in on the postwar economy, the Utes, as one of them put it, "had nowhere to go, nobody to tell us what to do." Unemployment at one time reached 70 per cent, with only those Utes who remained on their farms able to eke out an existence; the suicide rate climbed; and more and more Utes fled to the cities, there to join the thousands who could not find jobs.

But unbeknownst to most Utes, two tribal leaders, Sam Burch, who eventually became chairman, and Julius Cloud, who served many years as councilman, had, along with tribal chairman Jack House of the Ute Mountain Utes, been working since 1938 to force the government to settle the land-claims suit they had brought against it. More than a half century had passed before the Indians began to realize that all of the lands taken from them in the nineteenth century were done so illegally.

Their action followed that of the Northern Utes, who in 1931 had begun to look into land claims, thanks to one Captain Raymond T. Bonnin, who spent four years of his life, without pay, digging into old records, deeds, and treaties on behalf of the Northern Utes. Although not a lawyer, Captain Bonnin persuaded the Department of the Interior to let him represent these Northern Ute bands in prosecuting such claims. In 1935, Captain Bonnin assigned his claims to the prestigious New York law firm of Hughes, Schurman, and Dwight, which in turn assigned a young attorney, Ernest L. Wilkinson, to work on them.

This task was to occupy Mr. Wilkinson for nearly twenty years, for it was not until 1950 that the United States Court of Claims awarded a judgment of nearly $32 million to the three Ute tribes, and four years after that until the money was actually paid. This sum is misleading, however, for nearly half of it went to attorneys. But as Mr. Wilkinson pointed out, more than 70 attorneys aided in the case; they traveled more than 275,000 miles by plane and train, and many more thousands by car. The attorneys for the Utes took part in at least 4,280 conferences with members of Congress and bureau chiefs and held at least 3,800 conferences among themselves. Over 1,200 long-distance telephone calls were made, more than 500 telegrams were sent or received, and 7,000 letters totaling over 10,000 pages were written. All of this, the lawyers assured the Indians, was well worth nearly $15 million in legal fees and expenses.

The Southern Ute share, after the attorneys' fees were deducted, came to $5,408,106.97, or approximately $10,000 for each man, woman, and child in a tribe accustomed to counting its money in pennies. At the same time that the claims money began to roll in during 1954, money from oil and gas leases likewise arrived, for the Southern Utes had discovered that out of 309,000 acres of reservation land they owned, 298,000 held oil, gas, and coal reserves. This oil and gas money was distributed in per-capita payments after the expense of conducting tribal affairs was met. During these early years per capita was as much as $5,000 a year, a figure that steadily dwindled until Leonard Burch, when he became chairman in 1966, discontinued the practice altogether.

But in the midfifties, the burning question was how to spend the land-claims money. The Southern Utes and the other two tribes still were wards of the BIA, and before the money was to be released, the agency required that each tribe present acceptable plans for "improving the economic and social position of their people."

The tribe, ill prepared for such a task, nonetheless managed to draft a rehabilitation program, most of it the work of John E. Baker, a man of sound economic and traditional principles who continued to serve his tribe for more than twenty-five years. Baker, working on a deadline and at times overwhelmed by the job, received, predictably, most of his input from the BIA; he had tried, unsuccessfully, to get his constituents to tell him what they wanted in the fields of education, industry, agriculture, social welfare, housing, and recreation. The plan, accepted by Congress and the BIA in 1954, was the last time the Ute people themselves were even asked to contribute ideas on how to run their affairs.

The first windfall later that year was a payment of $3,000 for each family member, to be used exclusively to buy one of the hastily built boxlike government houses, plus another $1,000 for furnishings. This catch in the disbursement of the land-claims money meant that not only were the Utes forced to buy sleazy houses chosen for them by the government whether they wanted them or not, but also that once again a paternalistic bureau had decided what was best for its children. No thought was given to what such a drastic change was going to bring nor whether it was in the Utes' best interest to be handed so much money all at one time, the ultimate in federal atonement.

For all of their seventy-five years at Ignacio, the Utes had survived on a meager cash-and-carry basis; suddenly they were involved in mortgages, credit plans, and interest rates as they began to buy new automobiles, trucks, freezers, television sets, and matched living-room furniture to go with the new houses. Insurance agents swooped down and began selling life-, health-, auto-, and house-insurance policies to people who had never given such expensive precautions a second thought. At the same time, the liquor ban was lifted in Ignacio and, almost overnight, two liquor stores and one bar opened up and began to do a booming business selling liquor to the Indians. Rural Utes, enticed by all the free money, abandoned their farms and moved to town, jobless but with the per-capita checks in their pockets, and signed up for one of the new houses, also putting their names to insurance policies and time-payments plans. One appliance salesman is said to have sold more than $20,000 worth of freezers and refrigerators to Utes without electricity before the Indians ran him out of town.

The tribal council, a well-meaning group of middle-aged men ill equipped to cope with the postwar boom, were suddenly sought out by a wave of oil and gas speculators, urging them to sign more leases on the dotted line. New offices were opened to handle all the paperwork; new secretaries appeared, nearly all of them white, as part of the *macho* image the Indian male was trying to create. New jobs in the tribal housing and development office were offered to people with limited education and little or no job experience, the rationale being that "someone has to fill them and it might as well be us."

Meanwhile, the BIA began to clamor for what it called "community development," a scheme that allowed work traditionally done by the Bureau, such as roads and plant management, to be contracted to the tribe, at a high rate, by the Bureau. The Utes, with so much money at their disposal, agreed.

The Forest Service, which had allowed the Utes free grazing on the national forests since 1906, demanded a fee to cover "operating expenses," citing the Utes' new ability to pay.

By this time the people were receiving per-capita payments as high as $750 every other month, to be spent entirely as they wished except for their children's money; 40 per cent of that was deposited in a Denver bank to be held in escrow until they reached eighteen years of age, at which time it was promptly squandered on new cars and trucks. No one worked, no one saved, no one worried about the future. The Southern Ute reservation, once a bleak settlement of hard-working, disconsolate souls, was now referred to as "Ute-topia."

Before long, however, new living-room furniture deteriorated; washing machines became clogged with debris; food spoiled in the freezers when the electricity was shut off for nonpayment of utility bills; and shiny new vehicles were abandoned in backyards when repairs were required. The Utes found themselves running to the banks to take out loans to replace vehicles, appliances, and furniture, sinking even farther into debt, drink, and depression; most of their purchases were repossessed within six months, then resold at a much higher interest rate to yet another Indian family. One estimate indicates that by 1968, fourteen years after their windfall, the average Ute family owed $17,000 against an annual income of less than $2,000. By that time per capita had virtually stopped, except for what was now called "dividends," a token payment of $100 a year distributed at Christmas.

To help pay off the family debts, Ute women took jobs in tribal offices when they could get them or were forced to work as cooks and waitresses in Ignacio; others sold beadwork and fry bread at powwows and Bear Dances; some applied for welfare. With the shift in family structure, Ute men found solace in the bottle; the alcoholism rate in the sixties reached an all-time high of one in three.

In all three Ute tribes, women have always played a predominant role, serving on tribal councils, committees, and education groups; at Fort Duchesne, Utah, Ruby Black was elected chairwoman of the Northern Ute tribe in 1976 after a number of years in tribal government. According to the Census Bureau, one out of four Ute women over the age of sixteen holds a job with an average annual pay of $1,429. But the importance of Indian women goes beyond these figures. At Ignacio, the Native American church is headed by Bertha Groves, former councilwoman; Essie Kent is acknowledged as an expert on Ute language; Annabelle Eagle, assistant tribal judge, is known for her traditional views; Anna Marie Scott heads the tribal services office; and Lillian Seibel, manager of radio station KSUT, has blasted public-school policies.

Five miles from Ignacio, another outspoken Southern Ute woman, Isabel Kent, lives with her two daughters, Cynthia, twenty-four, and Betsy, fifteen, and her eighty-seven-year-old mother, Ada Rabbit Kent. Isabel has raised three children without a husband, depending on her closely knit family, mostly a variety of cousins, nieces, nephews, and aunts who live nearby, for emotional support. For five years she has been a Community Health representative, transporting patients to and from the clinic, interpreting for the elderly, and making home visits after hospitalization. Believing that "women are winners of many things," Isabel Kent also started an Indian dance group for children five to fourteen years of age just three years ago.

While old Mrs. Kent, her snow-white hair chopped off just below her ears, sat rigidly in an overstuffed chair one warm October morning, Isabel Kent, her black hair teased into a bouffant hairdo, sat opposite her, wrapped in an old pink bathrobe. Sunlight poured through a smudged window to the east while the wind, rustling the tall, dead weeds in the fields around the house, rattled the front door, clinging precariously to one hinge. Isabel Kent stared past her mother, whose round, benign face seemed to reflect a distant history of nobler times, to the wide, open fields and the farmhouses of the whites who lived there, including in her gaze the dirt driveway, a crumbling sidewalk, her car with a flat tire, and the irrigation ditch that ran along the side of the road.

"I liked the old one better," she said, referring to the old tar-paper-covered house from the fifties that stood behind the new one from the seventies. "Everything was on one side of the kitchen—the stove, the refrigerator, the sink. Here I have to walk a mile before I get to the table. This house is only three years old but the flooring is coming up and the doors don't close good and the screens don't fit and the sidewalk's been fixed twice and has to be fixed again. I asked the tribe about it and they said, 'Go fix it yourself.' That just shut off my thoughts."

Isabel Kent fixed coffee for herself, drawing out of a barrel the water that her nephew hauled from town twice a week. The new well, dug to go with the new house, had too much mineral in it, she said. The toilet bowl had turned an ugly brown and the pipes were rusted through.

"And another thing," Isabel Kent said, looking at the walls, "I hate white. I want to put a color in here but they tell me I can't change the color until the house is paid for." She shrugged in the manner of one who has come to accept the fact of white paint,

Isabel Kent works for tribal health services, has reared three children alone.

buckling sidewalks, and water not fit to drink. "That will be thirty years from now.

"Sometimes I don't feel right here so I go over to the old house and sit," Isabel said, drinking her coffee at the table. "Grandma doesn't like this house either. It's cold and there's no light but she says where the kids will be, I'll be. Anyway, these are the best houses on the reservation. Grandma knows that."

The old woman sat silently in her chair, a fringed shawl wrapped around her shoulders, looking out the back window at the great stretch of land where she had spent nearly all her life. She spoke little English but her dark eyes were bright as she watched two hawks rising on the wind; she was a woman accustomed to watching birds and the changing life of clouds.

At the mention of her name, the old woman got up, clutched her shawl around her, and went outside without a word, pushing two cats out of the way with a small, moccasined foot. She marched across the overgrown, cluttered yard with short, deliberate steps as if she meant to return to the mountains of her ancestors. Isabel watched her go.

"Grandma was born in a tepee," she said. "I was born in an adobe house up there on the hill. Then we lived in an old BIA shed that they used for storing fence material, just a shack was all. My father was a fence rider for them but he didn't like the shed because it had a tin roof. Every time it rained it sounded like thunder, and we kids would hide in the bed. I think it was sometime in the thirties when we came down here. The first thing we had was two tents, about eight by twelve, and there were three of us in one and three of us in the other. We didn't have water or electricity or plumbing, but then, we weren't used to any so it didn't make any difference. When we got the claims money in the fifties, we built that house out back. We even had it paid for three years ago when they came and said, 'Let us build you a new house.' I thought it would be good for the girls to have a place they could have slumber parties and entertain their friends, so I said, 'Okay.' It was supposed to cost $32,000 but now I hear it's going to cost $42,000 but maybe not, I just keep signing the papers and telling them they have to fix things up and they say, 'when you pay for the house.' She rolled her eyes to the ceiling, noticing a new crack. "Pay for the house? How can I pay for the house? I paid enough already."

Like her ancestors who a century before had complained uselessly about what was happening to them, Isabel Kent voiced her concerns, then recognized the futility of it. Perhaps the house would get fixed, perhaps not. Perhaps Cynthia, at twenty-four the youngest and most dynamic director the tribal education office had ever had, could get some action. One of the first of her generation to get a college degree and planning to work on her master's, Cynthia Kent was considered the bright young star of the Southern Utes, offering encouragement to young as well as old.

"Yes," her mother said, "when Cynthia gets home, I'll ask her about it. Cynthia understands things. Me, I just feel dumb."

Isabel Kent went into her bedroom, got dressed, and went outside to look for her mother. The old woman was sitting in a dilapidated kitchen chair, her face turned up to the sun; her smooth helmet of white hair glistened in the light. Ada Rabbit Kent had the look of peace and verification about her and when her daughter spoke in Ute, Ada got up and trudged over to the old house and stood by the door, gazing out at the land before she decided to go in.

"Grandma does her beadwork in there," Isabel said. "She says in the new house, her fingers won't work. Grandma's beadwork is like the old women used to do when they lived in the mountains. It should be in a museum, but she won't sell it. She gives it to her friends and relatives. If you admire her work, she'll give it away. That's the Ute custom. We believe that if we give something away, it will abundantly come back to us. The first grow of apples we had off our tree, we gave away. The same is true of the first deer a

OVERLEAF

Ada Rabbit Kent prefers her old house to new one built in front of it.

boy kills. I remember when my son got his. He gave it to the old people and they blessed him with whatever they had to make him a strong warrior. But he's not a strong warrior now. He went and dropped out of school."

She took the seat that Grandma had given up. Her eyes went to a giant willow tree, its burst of supple branches forming an umbrella over the ground. "My father planted that forty, fifty years ago," she said. "When I sit here, I think of him and the kind of life he had. I wish I had asked him the old stories but I didn't think it was too important then. No one did. We were all told to forget. Now Grandma says she doesn't remember."

With a large sigh, Isabel got up and went looking for the old woman who was inside beading an intricate design on a pair of moccasins. They spoke briefly in Ute, and Ada Rabbit Kent shook her head and tapped her small foot on the floor. Isabel went back out but not before the old woman said firmly in English, "I no want to eat right now."

"Grandma," Isabel sighed, "she only went to third grade but she has a mind of her own. When her husband died, she was supposed to go out and die, too. It's an old Ute custom. She was supposed to go out there in the fields, lie down, and just wait for death to come.

"But we wanted her to stay and asked her to live in our house with us. If we hadn't asked her or if she had wanted to die, that's what would have happened. Grandma believes in the old ways. But what I think is, she wanted to stay around and watch the kids grow up."

Giving up on the old lady, Isabel Kent went back in the new house to see if Betsy, sleeping late on a Saturday morning, had decided to arise. The young girl was sleepily pouring cereal into a bowl and acknowledged her mother with a brief smile.

"I guess you know," Isabel said, talking over the blare of the television, "that it's a hard world for an Indian here. It always has been. I remember my grandfather, who was one of the old ones who came out of the mountains, he said it was already too late

Cynthia Kent, director of tribal education office, conducts meeting in council chambers while assistant Fritz Box looks on.

then, that tradition was not going to stay alive. And in many ways he was right because everything came at us from every side. What has survived here, like Cynthia says, is what they couldn't kill. The Sun Dance and the Bear Dance. Powwows. Some things that we still believe in like who we are and why. That's why Cynthia and I started the dance group. I thought it would be something for them to do, to keep them out of trouble.

"The kids had been thinking about this themselves. They told me that. I said, then we've got to get together and not talk about it. Dancing is my way, the Indian way, it's our way, a part of us, and only we know it. No one else has it and if we don't keep it up, it's going to fade out like our land.

"The kids are really put down in Ignacio. The schools act like they're doing them a favor to even educate them. So here was the dancing, a real chance to get at their roots and the kids went at it. We didn't have any money and everyone had to make their own costume. Some of the girls did the beadwork themselves and the mothers and grandmothers helped. One boy even designed and did his own armband. We raise money through chili suppers and the money we get for performances. The most we've ever got was seven hundred dollars for two evenings. We've been all over the state and to New Mexico and we do all the old dances—the Round Dance, the Lame Dance, War Dances, the Fast Northern Dance, and the Slow Southern Ute Dance and the Fancy with a large bustle. Now we've got about twenty kids and like I tell Cynthia and Betsy, we have to take part and do what we're supposed to."

At the kitchen table Betsy Kent had stopped eating and was watching her mother, a bemused expression of pride and shyness on the young girl's face.

"It's good to sing," Isabel Kent said, getting up as if she meant to do exactly that. "It just comes to you and you're ready to sing with them. Some say we don't know how to sing and we don't know how to dance and we don't know how to speak our language. Maybe a lot of them don't but here are twenty kids who are going out and showing the world they're Indian and they have something to say. They're not sitting in front of the TV making excuses either."

With that Betsy Kent, at fifteen one of the best dancers that Isabel had trained, got up and switched the TV to a different channel.

"Aw Mom," she said and sat down to watch cartoons.

On the door to Cynthia Kent's office in the Tribal Affairs Building, there is what is commonly called a militant Indian poster, a stylized drawing of a warrior, and in bold graphics, the message, "We are sovereign people. We prefer peace but we must remind those who would impose upon us that we were created a free people."

But that is only the introduction. In her bright corner office, Cynthia Kent has tacked other posters on the wall proclaiming, "It will be a great day when our schools get all the money they need and the Air Force has to hold a bake sale to buy a bomber"; "Select your future through education"; and "Equal rights for women now." In Ignacio, where Indians tend to be shy, noncontroversial, and often apathetic, Cynthia Kent is something of an anachronism, outspoken, tough-minded, and thoroughly in tune with the times.

She had been back at Ignacio less than two years and already she had shaken the status quo by gathering Indian women together and asking them how they felt about abortion, equal rights, battered wives, and women's liberation.

"At first they didn't want to speak up," Cynthia Kent said, between answering phone calls and questions from her Indian secretary, Luanna Herrara. "But a lot of them had faced these things, being beaten by their husbands, having abortions with no one to back them up. All at once they were asking themselves, 'Do I have rights, too?' And that's where WINGS came in—Women in Need of a Good Society." She laughed, a poised young woman who had brought a whole new definition of vitality to the tribe.

"A couple of clowns around here call it Women in Need of Guys," she went on, "and I guess we are but that's not important. We meet once a month and discuss those hot topics plus home-making, farming, education, things like that. We're trying to set up a shelter home for battered women, not just Utes, but also everyone here in Ignacio. And we want to do career counseling for the whole community. It isn't a matter of getting women out of their homes and in employment situations. I think they've gone past that stage because they know they have to work to survive. Rather, it's a matter of providing skills and opportunities so that women have more of a choice in the type of career and lifestyle they want to pursue."

She chewed on the end of her pencil, her dark eyes darting around the room; people came in and out, handing her reports, asking questions, wanting advice, and still she talked, using her hands when she wanted to make a point. A year before she had been Colorado's youngest delegate to the National Women's Conference in Houston; shortly after that she had been appointed to the Colorado Commission on Women.

"I'm a social worker, not an educator," she said, citing among her varied duties parent counseling and student advising. "I always wanted to do social work but I had no idea I'd ever be working with women's rights. My family always told me I could do anything I wanted to do, and the older Indian women said, 'You can do it, Cynthia. I never had that chance, so don't lose yours.'"

According to one Indian woman, a former classmate, Cynthia Kent had a natural asset. "She was tall and thin," she recalls. "Indians were supposed to be short and fat. I know, I was one. Everybody envied Cynthia because she grew like that, taller than everyone and standing out."

Standing out is what Cynthia Kent has always done, growing up in Isabel Kent's first house built with the land-claims money, surrounded by an extended family of aunts, uncles, cousins, and grandparents. She was always the organizer, the arbitrator, the one with boundless energy and ideas. She was also the one who wanted to learn about her Indian heritage, most of it related to her by Ada Rabbit Kent.

"My grandmother is almost ninety and she raised me," she said. "Whatever strength I have, she gave me. She's the one who made me go to college, even though she never went beyond the third grade. She said, 'The world you live in is different from the one I lived in. You have to get an education before you can do anything in your life.' And this was my grandmother who doesn't speak anything but Ute, who can't even read or write. She said, 'Go to college, Cynthia. Go far away from here.' So I went to a Baptist college where there were no Indians."

After obtaining a bachelor's degree in sociology and adolescent behavior from Carson-Newman College at Jefferson City, Tennessee, Cynthia came back to Ignacio because "I wanted to encourage the younger women just as the older ones encouraged me. I think it's sad now when I see other women who have never been encouraged to do whatever they want to do. My main goal is first to make women aware of themselves and then provide them with workshops and resources so they can go out and get a job on their own. I don't want them to come to me and say, 'Okay, Cynthia, I'm ready. Get me a job.' I want to help them with the groundwork, then leave them on their own."

Her idealism, she admitted, often met with stony silence from some of the older men of the tribe who could not accept such a broad, new role for women, even though women had held council seats and had run most of the programs of the tribe for years.

"Some of them don't understand what's happening," Cynthia said, bent over a proposed agenda for a meeting she was holding later that day. "They say, 'Who is this girl and what is she trying to do?' So far they're supportive. They [the council] give me

OVERLEAF

Dance group sponsored by Isabel and Cynthia Kent is popular among Southern Ute youngsters.

money and they listen to what I have to say but I sometimes wonder: Do they really care?"

Through the education department, Cynthia Kent was sponsoring an Indian club, a cultural-awareness program to teach children a language course as well as Native American dances. "They're supposed to have a language program at school but it's worthless. Only one child in the first grade can speak and understand Ute. Eighteen and younger, hardly anybody can speak it, or if they do, it's slang. Kids in their twenties can understand it but they refuse to speak it. You have to be over fifty to speak and understand the language." And that was part of what her grandmother had taught her. If you lost your language you "lost part of yourself, that part that says, 'I'm different.' Grandma never let me forget it. Sometimes I'd start to speak English at home and she'd get furious. 'You're turning your back on your people,' she'd say. Grandma!" Cynthia Kent shook her head and laughed. The room seemed alive with the forcefulness of her ideas; her enthusiasm was in marked contrast to the subdued atmosphere of the Tribal Affairs Building, where Indians crept around the carpeted halls and spoke in weary monotones in offices with windows that never opened.

"This year we had seventeen Indian kids graduate from high school. Eight went on to college, five to the armed services, and three to jobs," she said, making a note on a pad. "Only one stayed home. In two years, I hope to have thirty kids in college and that's a real challenge. When they come back, if they come back, you'll see new ideas and changes that haven't even been dreamed of before. The trick is going to be to keep the heritage and traditions alive without sacrificing what they've learned. I'm an optimist. I think it can be done, has to be done." She swung around in her chair, rummaged through a pile of papers, found what she was looking for, and handed it to an older Indian man who had been standing quietly by her desk; Fritz Box was a devoted admirer of the young woman and one of her stanchest allies. When he left, she said: "Maybe it's the Taylor in me. My father was a Taylor.

They're all politicians. They can get anything done. When they talk to you, you think, yes, that's what I want to do. The Taylors can convince you of anything. It's in their blood. How else could the first Taylor [a black "buffalo" soldier who came to Ignacio after the Civil War and married Kitty Cloud, a Southern Ute] have taken his wife's allotment and sold it to Anglos for [the townsite of] Ignacio? It was illegal but no one ever questioned it. Even today, a hundred years later, you ask where did Ignacio come from and no one wants to say. The Taylors have so much influence here, so much land and they are listened to and respected, well, the last thing in the world they want is for someone to say, 'What about that land your great-great-grandfather sold?' "

By then it was nearly noon and Cynthia had a luncheon meeting. She gathered up some papers and stuffed them into her briefcase along with a pamphlet on abortion and another on women in executive jobs.

"Everyone is related to everyone else, one way or another," she went on. "Just the other day a friend of mine learned who her father was—a very important man married to a woman not her mother. It took her twenty-five years to find out but she was glad because of who he is. It could have been worse. It all gets so complicated that when a Ute makes out his will, he has to specify who his real children are. The Utes have always been one family."

She put on her coat, picked up her purse and briefcase, then thought of another point.

"Religion is really a family thing, too," said Cynthia Kent, halfway out the door. "Our family aren't Sun Dancers. That's a custom of the Plains Indians, where the object is to sweat and have a vision. In the old days, we were always by a river and nobody ever sweated or thought they had to. The Sun Dance wasn't introduced to the Utes until about ninety years ago, when they were already in Ignacio. For our family, religion occurred and still does down there by the river, not out in the heat of the sun like a desert, where we can wash and be purified. I think you have to take religion seriously or else it doesn't work. I pray morning and evening—for the kids, for my work, for the tribe, but I don't go to church anymore. No time."

With that she was gone but not before she made one last remark. "Next year I'm going back to school, probably Tulane, and get my master's degree. Then I want some world experience. Someday I want to marry somebody humble but I haven't met him yet."

The sound of her laughter echoed in the sun-drenched room where everything seemed alive to her vision and her dreams. It was only later that the heavy silence of the building and the bland expression of the Indians going in and out indicated that Cynthia Kent is very much apart from the prevailing mood of the Southern Utes. In her rests consciousness and hope; in her, too, the most difficult kind of change.

6

THE SOUTHERN UTE RESERVATION is a chopped-up land, a crazy quilt of white towns, farms, and ranches studding the rolling hills and valleys that the Indians call home. Originally a solid rectangle along the Colorado-New Mexico border, 110 miles long and 15 miles wide, the reservation first became riddled with holes when the Indians accepted allotments in 1888, and what was left was thrown open to white settlement. For almost fifty years the Indians were allowed to sell their allotments, resulting in the checkerboard design that characterizes the reservation today. All of the towns that lie within its boundaries—Oxford, Falfa, Tiffany, Allison, Marvel, Pagosa Junction, and even the tribal headquarters town of Ignacio—are not occupied by the Indians but rather by a Hispanic-Anglo mix.

Most of the Southern Utes are scattered across the reservation on their allotments, living along the clear, rushing Pine River, or a mile or so from Ignacio in dreary, identical homes similar to the ones at Towaoc. In this totally Indian "second Ignacio" there is also the tribally owned Pino Nuche motel and community center, all of the new tribal buildings, the BIA dormitory for out-of-town Indian children attending school in Ignacio, some drab old government buildings, most of them abandoned, the police station, and a row of squat, shingled BIA employee houses, the elaboration of a bureaucratic attitude that has built exactly the same kind of house on every Indian reservation in the country. There is also a new senior citizens' center, the red-brick BIA headquarters, a cafeteria, a ball park, and next to that, "Ute Park," featuring a giant plaster tepee covered with graffiti on the inside and painted yellow, blue, and red on the outside. A bronze monument to the old chiefs Ouray, Shavano, Ignacio, and Severo has been erected next to the tepee, a formal tribute beside what is tacky, humorous, and utterly Indian.

The little town of Ignacio lies almost in the middle of the Southern Ute reservation, bordered to the east by the Pine River and to the west by a high sandstone ridge from which it is possible to see the whole valley and the quiet, orderly town tucked up against it. To the south, the town dribbles off into pastures owned by the Indians; to the north, along the highway, there is no geographic division between what is "town" and what is "Ute." The difference is a cultural one, an animosity among the three ethnic groups that began when John Taylor, a black Civil War veteran, sold his Indian wife's allotment to the whites for a townsite. That original 160 acres limits Ignacio's growth, for the land on all four sides belongs to the Southern Utes; it also arouses ill feelings toward the townspeople, who are still blamed for settling on that old allotment almost a century ago.

The six hundred or so white and Hispanic citizens of Ignacio seldom stray "uptown" to where the Indians are because of the tensions that automatically rise when they do so. Some of them work for the Indians, as maids, cooks, and waitresses in the motel because the Utes refuse to do such menial tasks. The Indians go "downtown" to shop and eat, preferring the excellent Mexican cuisine at Diamond Smith's cafe to the bland food offered by their own Pino Nuche restaurant. Some of them may also be found in the town's three bars, two liquor stores, and eventually at Peaceful Spirit, the Ute-run alcoholism rehabilitation center located in the middle of town.

Along the one main street there is a hardware store owned by a man named Wiseman; a bank run by a man named Whiteman; there is a post office, two gas stations, a dry-goods store, a drugstore, a drive-in restaurant, a food market, an auto-parts store, and, until it went broke several years ago, a furniture store.

"No, the Indians don't buy much from me," Benny Valencia said, a year or so before he went out of business. "They'd rather go to Durango and spend their money." He looked around his

Benny Valencia, Ignacio furniture dealer, holds old Indian photograph accidentally left in bureau drawer. He wants tribe to pay him $750 for its return.

crammed, well-lighted store to see who was coming in and who was fingering things they shouldn't be. Yes, shoplifting was a problem but you couldn't take much from a furniture store, he said, although some Indians once had tried to carry out a dresser with a mirror attached. He did not have anything against the Indians, he said, except that he didn't believe you could trust them.

"The only time they come in here is when they want to sell something," Benny Valencia said, going into his small office and coming out with a large, framed portrait of an elderly Indian couple; the picture was very old and tinted in pastel colors.

"A couple of years ago, Annabelle Eagle sold me an old chest of drawers," he said. "It wasn't worth much but I think I gave thirty dollars for it and she was satisfied. Well, a couple of weeks later, she came in and said she accidentally left this picture of her grandparents in it. It's not my business, I told her. What's left in the drawer goes with the piece. That's business, here like anywhere else. She was upset because the picture meant a lot but I told her, you should have looked in the drawer first."

He sat down on an old kitchen chair, holding the portrait in his lap. "Like I told Annabelle, if the Utes want this picture so much, let them contribute a dollar each to get it back. The way I figure it, that comes to $750, give or take a few members."

He smiled then, satisfied with the offer he had made to one of the great women of the tribe, known for her honesty, outspokenness, and traditional views toward life.

"What I can't figure is what do they want this old picture for? To hang in the council chambers? Nothing but old chairmen in there." He turned the picture around so he could see it better. "These old people weren't even anybody famous."

Up the street a block, David Pope and his wife were busy in the auto-parts store they had run in Ignacio for more than twenty years. They were devout Mormons, and what they tried to do, aside from running a good place, was to teach the Indians about themselves.

"The Indians are the lost tribe of Israel," David Pope said authoritatively, getting out his Book of Mormon. "It tells about it in here, the way they came across the ocean on rafts and landed in South America." He realized that many anthropologists didn't agree with him, but more and more evidence was being found to support the Mormons' claim.

"The Indians are curious about themselves," Mrs. Pope said, ringing up a sale, "that's why more and more are joining the church, to find out where they came from." But she had to admit that there was no real curiosity among the Southern Utes anymore, perhaps because there were so many other churches to choose from in Ignacio. In Utah, you had a different situation because the Mormon church was practically the only one around.

"No, we've never had any trouble with the Southern Utes," Mrs. Pope smiled, stepping outside to pose for a picture with her husband and their German shepherd guard dog. "But then, they know what their place is."

At the police station, Ignacio town marshal George Manzanares propped his feet up on his old green metal desk and talked about crime in Ignacio. The early-morning light spilled through a cockeyed set of venetian blinds onto the back of his head, making a sort of halo.

"We have one of the lowest crime rates in the nation," the marshal said proudly. "I've been here three years and we've only had two murders. No robberies to speak of either. Mostly, it's drunk Indians getting into fights, guys beating up their wives, and kids getting high on beer. Nothing worse than other towns this size have."

Next to the sheriff's mottled green office with its sheaf of FBI most-wanted posters tacked to the wall, its bank calendar, metal coat rack, and file cabinet, crackling police radio, and one rickety spare chair, was the fire station, which housed a thirty-year-old engine that "still runs good because we don't use it much. Stuff usually burns down first."

OVERLEAF

Mr. and Mrs. David Pope run an auto-parts store, believe Indians are lost tribe of Israel.

OPEN
HOURS
8:00 to 5:30

Come in, we're
OPEN

TIRE GAUGES · VALVES
TOOLS · COUPLERS
ACME TIRE HARDWARE
DIVISION ideal CORPORATION
Bendix
WHERE DID THE AMERICAN INDIAN COME FROM? READ THE BOOK OF MORMON
GUARD DOGS ON DUTY SURVIVORS WILL BE PROSECUTED

In order to get to Ignacio's municipal courtroom, it was necessary to go through the fire station and then through a small side door. The judge, George Armstrong, had already arrived on his weekly visit to hear misdemeanor cases, and the marshal followed him inside.

Judge Armstrong, whom the Southern Utes had dubbed "George Armstrong Custer" before firing him as their tribal judge in 1976, nonetheless still sat for the Ute Mountain Utes, the Northern Utes, Jicarilla Apaches, and Hopis, in addition to being a judge for six rural towns and maintaining a private practice.

The Southern Utes fired the judge for what one high-ranking official charged was "arbitrary and abusive treatment of tribal members." But the Ute Mountain Utes tolerate Judge Armstrong's extreme behavior in much the same way they tolerate the BIA. "Maximum George," as he is known at Towaoc, once ordered a young Ute girl taken away in handcuffs because she would not attend school. Another time, he sentenced two young Ute Mountain Ute men to jail for terms of five and six months respectively because they couldn't pay fines of $300 and $350 each.

The small Ignacio courtroom was lined with six rows of hard wooden benches on either side, its light came from a set of quivering fluorescent bulbs overhead; a bulky plywood box served as the judge's bench. While the marshal and his deputy stood respectfully against one wall, a handful of people sat in the back, hunched on the benches as, one by one, the judge called out their names. That day, there were no Indians present.

One middle-aged Hispanic man, in court to answer a careless-driving charge, when asked if he had anything to say, thought a moment, then replied, "I'm not careless. I just make a mistake."

The judge, his gaze steely but not without compassion, admonished, "What do you think careless is?" and fined him twenty-five dollars. When court was over, the judge had a cup of coffee, got into his car, and drove to his home, seventy miles away in Cortez.

Behind the court was Ignacio's jail, a cold, murky building with the heater hanging precariously from the ceiling, and water

Judge Armstrong was fired by Southern Utes.

dripping from the overhead pipes. The row of five cells were clean but empty; each cell contained a urinal, a basin, and dirty mattresses flung on metal beds. Farther down the narrow passage, illuminated by one bare bulb, was the drunk tank, a cubicle ten feet square and utterly dark.

"Oh there used to be light," George Manzanares said. "It came from the hall a little bit but then last year some guy hanged himself on the bars so I had to put plywood across." Sometimes, he said, there were as many as three men in the drunk tank overnight. "They used to let them sleep on the floor but I put a mattress down. After all, it's not supposed to be a hotel."

The marshal and his deputy, Abel Atencio, who had just bought a bar and was about to quit, each worked a twelve-hour shift and were paid $750 a month; it was hard work, the marshal said, and he liked his other job better, even though it didn't pay anything. For three years, George Manzanares had been the coach of the Ignacio Independent Boxing Club, which had twenty-seven boys in it now, Indian, Hispanic, and white.

"It's something that kids around here need," he said. "We take the clumsiness out of them, plus we teach them sportsmanship and respect for the other guy. The Indians have always been good boxers. I don't care if it's Indian or what, I sure would like to send a champion to state."

Boxing was a big part of his life, he said, and he spent at least three nights a week at it, holding his matches at the Pino Nuche community center. "The parents really come out to see these little guys fight," he said. "Maybe they only fight three minutes if they're under thirteen, but to the parents, it's like watching Muhammad Ali. The kids love trophies, the bigger the better. I think these Indian kids especially want to win one, just to prove they're as good as the white kids."

Back in his office, George Manzanares listened to his squawking radio for a few minutes, then shut it off. Nothing but the Indians talking to themselves on their CB radios, even tribal chairman Leonard Burch, whose handle was "Super Chief."

"A Ute kid would rather stay home and fool with a CB radio, drink beer, and get in trouble than go to school," the marshal said.

There has always been a high Indian absenteeism rate in the Ignacio public schools, marked by the reluctance of Ute parents to enforce attendance, encourage homework, or discipline children when they are suspended. Many Ute parents also resented the high school's 1978 policy statement, which includes among its punishments for infraction of the rules, "two swats—no exception" for students caught smoking at school. To them, physical punishment is against Ute principles, often criticized as permissiveness by angry school officials.

Other Indian parents claim there is discrimination in the schools, that "the Mexican kids beat up the Indian kids" and "the white kids think they're better, and teachers do nothing about it."

Of the 445 children who attend elementary school in Ignacio, 46 per cent are Indian and the rest are about equally divided between white and Hispanic. Armed with $128,000 from state and federal sources for its bilingual program, the school employs three Ute teachers to instruct young Indian children in their language.

Marshal George Manzanares, Ignacio, coaches amateur boxing club.

But most Indian parents think the program is a failure because classes last only fifteen minutes, the teachers are uncertified, and the children do not respect them because "they are just aides." The school recently added an "Indian resource center" but it is staffed by a Hispanic woman, Helen Lucero, and contains no books or materials that introduce Ute children to their background. The six-member school board is usually composed of whites and Hispanics, but two Southern Utes were once elected— John Baker and his brother Chris, both known for their hard-line Indian attitudes. Said John Baker after a heated exchange over the firing of a Ute teacher, "I don't have to tell you behind your backs, I can tell you to your faces: You are a bunch of bigots." Another time, when Chris Baker found himself embroiled with Joe Romero, former Ignacio mayor, school-board member, and Spanish teacher, over the inadequacies of the language program Baker stormed, "I have heard you talk, Romero, about the friends you have in the tribe but if this were the good old days we would be casting lots to see who would be tying you to the anthill."

Despite such outbursts, few Utes are willing to become involved actively in their children's education. An Indian Education Parents' Committee formed in 1976 by John Baker has only twelve members, who were once advised by the tribal council not to rock the educational boat in Ignacio but to let the school board, now composed of four Anglos and two Hispanics, decide what they thought best. Some parents threatened to start their own Ute school, mindful of the $1.25 million in federal funds that the Ignacio school system receives for 400 Indian students, a move that brought concern to the school superintendent, Russ Harrach.

"Besides the money, we'd lose curriculum breadth without those kids," he said, pointing out such "assets" as the Indian resource center and the bilingual program.

Yet with typical lack of support by the tribal council and the majority of parents, the plan for a Ute academy has fallen through.

Such apathy was one reason why Lillian Seibel, the Indian manager of Ute-operated radio station KSUT, finally decided to run for the school board. A bright, attractive woman in her midthirties, mother of two sons, and a teacher herself, Ms. Seibel, an avid supporter of bilingual, bicultural education, ran her campaign on a reform platform.

"I want to know why the Ute children read a grade below the national average and three grades below the average attained by their Anglo peers in Ignacio," she demanded. "I also want to know why students graduate from Ignacio High without mastering the basics of reading and writing. Why is tribal history not taught in school? And why doesn't the school's commitment to bilingual education extend past the second grade?" She charged that special-education classes arbitrarily included most Ute children, selected "not by test, but by surname and color." The bilingual program was, she claimed, "substandard."

Lillian Seibel, dedicated, hard-working, inquisitive, did not find the answers to her questions, nor did she find much support among Southern Ute parents. While many came out and said they agreed with her on the issues, privately they called her a "troublemaker," pointing to the fact that Lillian Seibel had a college degree and therefore thought "she's better than us." Many also resented the fact that she is married to a white man, Harold Seibel, a local contractor.

Such Ute illogic is responsible not only for Lillian Seibel's defeat in the school-board election but also for a general malaise that undermines all innovation at Ignacio. Lillian Seibel cannot be elected, reason the Utes, because she might bring about too much change; she should be elected, they also reason, because change is needed in the schools. Caught in their own dichotomy, which extends beyond education to economics, politics, and tradition, the Utes appear highly undecided, saying one thing and doing another, or often supporting two disparate views at the same time, as

OVERLEAF

Boxing matches held at Southern Ute community center attract boys from Towaoc, Ignacio, and Durango.

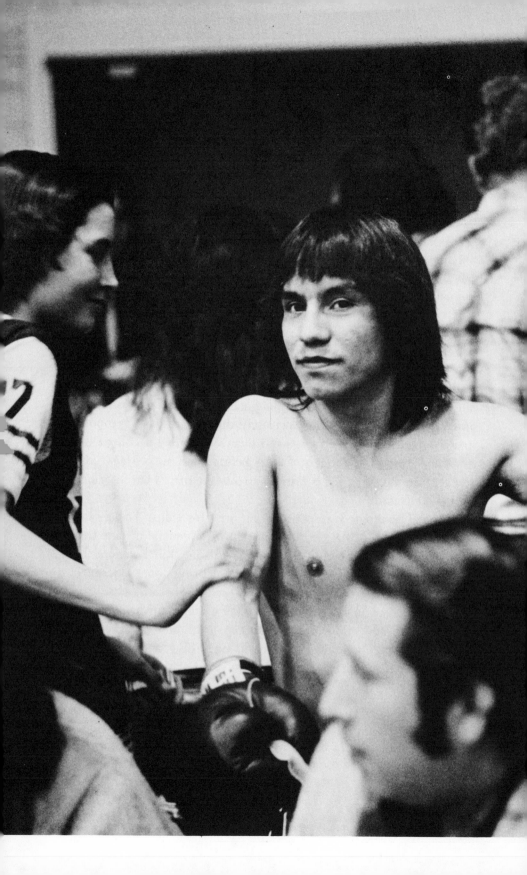

is the case with plans for coal exploitation that the Utes both support and reject.

Most of the Southern Utes' substantial annual income, $2,519,750 in 1980, a whopping 79.5 per cent increase over 1979, comes from oil and gas leases that totaled $1.5 million this year alone. The Utes receive 12½ per cent royalties on gas and oil leases negotiated for them by the BIA, the same rate the federal government charges for public lands leased for coal, gas, and oil; mineral-lease royalty rates between private individuals and companies are often higher. The Utes, through their attorney, Sam Maynes, are said to be pushing for a royalty rate increase.

In addition to its oil and gas money, the tribe also receives income from agricultural leases, fish and game permits ($110,000), Secretary of Investment Program ($300,000), in kind gas sales ($200,000), administrative overhead ($50,000), archaeological inspection fees ($5,000), and other miscellaneous income. Wise to the ways of making money, the tribe has invested $2,877,252.07 in certificates of deposit in banks in nine states, which earned interest of $200,761.42 as of July 31, 1977.

The Utes, like all Indian tribes, are exempt from paying income tax on money derived from natural or renewable resources such as agriculture, gas, oil, and coal because the land is considered federal, like national parks and forests. They would, however, have to pay taxes on anything built on the land that generates income—motel, restaurant, racetrack, all currently losing money. The tribe does not reveal how all of this tax-free income is spent, either to its own people or to the public. It is known, however, that the operating expenditures of the tribe in 1980 were $1,956,201, a figure that by no means finances the total operation of the tribe, as many tribal programs, such as social services, education, planning, law-and-order costs, court costs, and economic-development costs, are paid out of federal funds. These programs rent their offices from the tribe, and rental income for 1980 was $86,400.

Tribal losses, amounting to more than $200,000 a year, are likewise not revealed to the people because, according to one

Lillian Seibel, manager of radio station KSUT, once ran for Ignacio school board.

council member, "most people don't understand finances." Unlike the open-minded Northern Utes, who issue an annual report for all tribal members as well as make it available to tourists at the Utes' Bottle Hollow Resort, the Southern Utes are kept carefully in the dark. Few of them know that the much-touted Pino Nuche motel/restaurant/community center complex, built in 1972 with only about $10,000 of tribal funds while the federal government supplied more than $3 million, loses about $120,000 each year, a figure that the tribe subsidizes out of its operating budget. Some of this cost goes toward heating and maintaining the indoor Olympic-sized swimming pool, which operates year-round but is often without swimmers because the Indians do not like water. The Indian racetrack, Sky Ute Downs, opened in 1975 thanks to a federal grant totaling $600,000 and loses nearly $40,000 annually. It is similarly subsidized by the Utes, as is the tribally leased Shell station in Ignacio, which managed to lose $18,000 in 1977.

At the same time that the tribe receives its enormous income, it also enjoys a multitude of federal grants, which in one seven-year period totaled more than $15 million, most of it going into various construction projects; only a small amount was used to finance KSUT and its employee-training program. For a tribe with only 751 members, such a grant program seems excessive, yet the Utes have turned down federal largesse only once—when the proposed $1 million cultural center was figured to cost $150,000 a year to operate, a sum not covered by the grant. The Utes also abandoned a plan to obtain federal funds for a golf course across the highway from the motel when operating costs were discovered to be prohibitive.

The Utes' federal windfalls were mainly due to the efforts of its former economic-development director, Peggy Richards, a middle-aged Anglo woman who refers to herself as "planner." Thanks to her federal-grant experience gained through working for Johnson's War on Poverty, the OEO, and the directorship of Ignacio's community-action program, Mrs. Richards was able to guide the Southern Utes through the complicated series of maneuvers necessary to obtain federal aid. She formulated what grant the

Indians needed, then wrote the grant application, including the budget or details of expenditures within that grant. At one point she was even involved in the hiring of architects and engineers. While most Utes would agree that without Peggy Richards the reservation would be bereft of all its gleaming new buildings, many point out that even in Ute-topia, a few things have gone wrong.

When Sky Ute Downs began in 1975, it was called a "high-altitude horse-training and -conditioning center," and no horse racing was actually planned, although the original $668,000 grant provided photo-finish cameras and electric gates but no grand-stand. For the first four years, Sky Ute Downs was used mainly for horsemanship classes and all-Indian rodeos. Then the Utes, realizing that parimutuel racing was the only way that they could lure people to their mostly vacant motel twenty-five miles from Durango, applied for a second grant, totaling $780,000, to finance a grandstand, more stalls, and a jockey club.

Behind the building of the federally funded racetrack are some legitimate questions not only about the need for such an amusement park so far removed from any population center but also about the wisdom of placing it among a people who already have one of the highest alcoholism rates in the nation—now one in five (down from the '60's high of one in three), compared to the national average of one in fifteen, with a recovery rate of 1 or 2 per cent. The average age is thirty-five and dropping.

A potentially dangerous problem exists at the racetrack, for it has been built on a flood plain because, according to Mrs. Richards, "the council wanted it there." Ernst Engineering, a Durango firm that also happens to employ Mrs. Richards' husband, Paul, worked for three years as engineers on Southern Ute federally funded projects. They ran into water four feet beneath the surface at the racetrack but recommended building there nonetheless. Not long afterward, the same company did the engineering work for an apartment complex also built on the same flood plain.

When Sky Ute Downs was finally finished, construction problems began to arise. Cracks appeared, and the arches that hold

up the ceiling began to spread because the contractor had neglected to install ties at the bottom; a zigzag plumbing system
resulted in the toilets backing up each time there was a major
event at the arena. As if that were not enough, horse trainers
began to complain about everything from cold temperatures to
rocks in the arena soil until at last the Utes agreed to hire a new
manager, Ben Nighthorse, an Indian silversmith, judo expert, and
champion quarter-horse breeder.

Construction problems and complaints are familiar to the
Utes, who seem to accept them as part of the often mystifying
business of building with federal funds, just as they accept an occasional error or two. The $47,000, six-vehicle police garage, de-
signed by Durango architect Fred Stastny, was intended to house
an ambulance as well, but the bay was discovered to be too low,
and a Cortez contractor, Flaugh [pronounced Flaw] Construction,
modified it, but in the process cracked the beam while trying to
raise the roof. Cost of repair was not borne by the architect, as is
normally the case, but was paid for by the federal agency that
funded the grant in the first place.

The architect, meanwhile, went to work remodeling the
Tribal Affairs Building at a cost of $400,000, only to have the
sewer back up into the office of Peggy Richards. Refusing to fire
Stastny, as some members suggested, the council next awarded him
the contract on its new $800,000 health center, a building with
X-ray facilities but no room in which to process the film.

Even with its $1 million income and easy access to federal
grants, the Utes are far from being economic wizards. The biggest
potential of all lies in the scraggly, sage-covered foothills of their
reservation where, according to USGS estimates, close to 300 million tons of strip-mineable coal worth at least $450 million in
royalties awaits development. No sooner was the announcement
made in 1977 than more than 20 energy companies wrote to the
tribe expressing interest in leasing Ute coal, but the Utes, in typical fashion, hedged, waiting to see not only how the bidding
would go, but also how their water situation fared; for without
water the coal would remain where it was.

Tribal chairman Leonard Burch held a press conference and said that studies were under way to determine "the best way [to lease and develop the coal] for the benefit of the tribe and the area. We want the proper development of our natural resources." Insisting that "we don't want to see another coal-fired plant polluting the air up here," the chairman added, "but if it goes that route, the tribe will have its own air-quality rules and regulations." He declined to say on what standards the regulations would be based nor what the land would look like after as much as 30,000 acres are strip-mined as deep as 200 feet.

Chairman Burch emphasized to the press that "the coal will be a benefit to the tribe now and forever. The well-being of future generations of the tribe is what we are aiming for." And he added, "I don't think that strip-mining would be detrimental. We want to see it developed."

But Clem Baker, the tribe's natural-resources chief, put in a word of caution. "We are going to closely scrutinize what the companies will do to improve the reservation's environment to make sure it's put back in good order," he said grandly. "They can't put the land back in its natural shape but we will insist that the land be put back in better shape than it was previously."

Then, in what has come to pass for Ute cynicism, Baker said, "They gave us a piece of land that didn't look like much. And you wonder sometimes why the Indian nation has resentment toward the other side." He paused to let his point sink in, then said, "The way history is going, I am afraid they are going to say we Indians don't need this land either."

In Ignacio, where resentment and hostility toward the Indians have brewed for nearly a century, businessmen took a cool look at what was happening and changed their minds. Almost overnight, there was a new feeling of good will toward the Utes.

Marshal Manzanares reported fewer Indian arrests; the bank reported making more loans to Indians; the Popes took down their window sign that read, "Where did the American Indian come from? Read the Book of Mormon"; in the bars, where Utes and Hispanics had often brawled, an uneasy new peace reigned.

At the Bank of Ignacio, Executive Vice President Wayne Whiteman folded his hands neatly on his desk and said, "There is a certain amount of unemployment here [one of the highest in Colorado] that coal development would improve. In this area we are particularly interested in year-round employment. Nothing would please us more than having jobs for Indians and non-Indians alike."

Tom Wiseman, the hardware-store dealer and Ignacio city councilman who in the past had often found himself feuding with the Indians over water, adopted a new approach. "The coal will mean a lot to the Southern Utes and to the town because the Utes are an integral part of the community," he said solemnly.

It has been a well-known fact in Ignacio for years that the Utes controlled the town's water, the whites controlled the money, and the Hispanics controlled the law. Now it appeared that the balance of power was shifting toward the Utes, who had also casually mentioned in their announcement that there was enough coal in the ground to provide jobs for thirty years. There was a fervor of excitement in Ute-topia, the likes of which had not been seen for twenty-three years, when the Southern Utes received their land-claims money.

But all of the coal projections are so far on paper. The only real money the Utes have ever seen from it has been their lease with Peabody Coal, which expired in 1977 and was not renewed. That year, the Utes received only $38,905 from that one coal lease.

Their huge coal reserve, estimated to be as high as 51 billion tons altogether, has the potential of making the Southern Utes the second biggest Indian coal tribe in the nation, after the Navajos, and possibly tying with the Cheyennes. The catch is water, which the Southern Utes do not own, needed to develop their coal. They are currently exploring two options simultaneously.

The $500 million Animas-La Plata project is proposed as a multipurpose affair that would provide irrigation, and municipal and industrial water to two arid counties in southwestern Colorado, including the Southern Ute reservation. The project would be constructed by the Bureau of Reclamation, and the federal government would be repaid through a contract approved by voters in the area, an issue that has aroused as much controversy as the move to send the Utes off into Utah nearly a century ago. For years, the Southern Utes have appealed to Congress to fund this project, citing not only their own need for the water, which they cannot pay for, but also Durango's need for Ute coal if the town is to expand beyond its present size. Such support may, in the long run, compromise the tribe's own best interests.

Colorado water law, complex and often seemingly illogical, decrees that land and water are separate and that the length of an individual's tenure on the land is irrelevant to his water rights. Thus the Utes, who have been in Colorado for at least 400 years, have 305,000 acres of land, 7 rivers running through their land, and no water rights to any of them except the Pine River. The government, in its frenzy to rid Colorado of the Utes and open the way to white settlement a century ago, conveniently failed to nail down any Indian water rights in the process.

The Southern Utes have recently challenged the state water law, claiming first priority on all seven of the rivers which, if they win their suit, means that they would have their own unlimited water supply and would have no need of the Animas-La Plata project. In an effort to block such a disaster, the Southwestern Water Conservation District has filed an objection to the Indian water claims, insisting that the seven rivers are *their* water.

In a further entanglement, Gulf Oil, which owns no land in Colorado, nonetheless acquired, in 1976, 24,800 acre-feet of water at Ridges Basin, site of the major reservoir for the Animas-La Plata water project. Gulf stated in its master plan that its water rights would be used for coal development, presumably that belonging to the Utes, who may need Gulf's water if they are unsuccessful in their water-rights suit. Curiously, the matchmaker for the Utes and the energy company was a man with deep involvement in each.

The water attorney for Gulf Oil was Frank E. "Sam" Maynes, who has also been tribal attorney for the Southern Utes since 1968. While Gulf has always known that Mr. Maynes represents the Indians on *their* water cases, which have the possibility of being against Gulf's own interests, the tribe did not know that he represented Gulf until the fact was disclosed by the Durango *Herald* in 1977.

The tribe's coal-source report, which had been prepared by tribal land-use planner Ed Del Duca, was submitted to tribal chairman Leonard Burch and then, at the chairman's request, turned over to Mr. Maynes. Thus the tribal attorney, privy to Gulf's plans for its water, also became privy to the last detail of the tribe's coal reserves, a situation that many Utes feel compromises their position and some local attorneys see as a possible conflict of interest. Mr. Maynes also represents the ironically named Colorado Ute REA (no connection with the tribe), which in May 1979 announced plans to build a power plant near Kline. The only strippable coal, according to a USGS survey, belongs to the Southern Utes.

At the same time that Sam Maynes represents these entities, he also serves as attorney for Mobil Oil, a potential oil and gas lessee with the Southern Utes. A 1980 contract proposed between the tribe and Mr. Maynes would have guaranteed the attorney 10 per cent of any royalty increase in mineral leases between the Southern Utes and energy companies for oil, gas, and "other hydrocarbons and byproducts," which may include coal. The BIA refused to approve the contract. Nonetheless, tribal insiders are fearful that their mineral leases could still involve millions of dollars in legal fees for the Southern Ute tribal attorney, especially since undeveloped coal resources are worth $450 million in royalties alone. Others wonder how one attorney can impartially represent Gulf *and* Mobil *and* the Southern Ute tribe. The Grievance Committee of the Colorado Supreme Court, after investigating a complaint brought against Sam Maynes concerning his connection with Gulf, decided to take no action against him.

Meanwhile, the BIA, in an uncharacteristic move to help the wary Southern Utes, urged them to push for a gravity-flow canal across the reservation to the Southern Ute reservoir. The BIA told the tribe that pumping costs at Ridges Basin would run over $1 million a year and would require 180 million kilowatt-hours of electricity annually, enough to light up a city of 30,000. It would be far cheaper to build a gravity-flow canal, the BIA said.

The council listened politely to the BIA's advice, then mysteriously, slyly, and predictably rejected it, even passing a resolution to that effect.

"After all," one councilman said afterward, "the BIA doesn't know everything. It was them that once wanted us to be farmers."

The Utes' deprecating attitude toward the bureaucracy stems from the fact that Indians are currently in control of a huge part of the nation's natural resources. In 1975, twenty-five tribes, including all three tribes of Utes, formed CERT—the Council of Energy Resources Tribes—which owns one third of the low-sulfur coal west of the Mississippi; as much as half of the country's privately owned uranium, about 4 per cent of oil and natural gas, and substantial amounts of oil shale. Courted by a slick army of energy-company officials and politicians and enticed by a $24 million federal energy-development grant in 1980, the tribes are in the middle of a dizzy economic boom that is strangely reminiscent of the land-claims-money era.

While CERT with its non-Indian technical staff, including the former Iranian Deputy Minister of Economics and Oil, Ahmed Kooros, appears to be making its own decisions, a group of Navajo and Hopi malcontents charge that it is "a front being utilized by the multinational corporations and the U. S. Government . . . to justify the land ripoff and to disguise the corruption and the political manipulation of the resources of the indigenous people." Such warnings have gone unheeded.

History has a way of repeating itself, and most observers predict that Indian natural resources, like Indian lands of a century ago, soon will be manipulated away from these politically naïve Native Americans. The development of their only tangible assets is the key to the Indians' long-term economic survival and freedom from BIA oppression. Yet the accompanying desecration of the land is spiritually incompatible with a heritage that is becoming more and more irrelevant. The price for survival into the twenty-first century may well be the sacrifice of their land, resources, and heritage, at which point the Indian at long last will be truly "assimilated."

7

THE AMERICAN INDIAN, a noted commentator once said, is a state of mind, the product of Zane Grey, Frederic Remington, Hollywood, and more recently, Wounded Knee, Alcatraz, and the American Indian Movement (AIM). Like the overpraised, glorified cowboy, the Indian is a myth, a hero concocted for the benefit of bored and restless millions who live out their fantasies between the covers of a book or in front of a television set. And like the cowboy, the Indian has come to believe the myth himself, anxious to preserve those qualities of bravery, endurance, and self-sufficiency attributed to him that have come to make him a cult figure in recent years. But real Indians are less "Indian" than the ersatz Indians one pays to see on the screen, raising the question: What exactly is a modern-day Indian?

The reality of Colorado's Indians is too much to bear. The summer pilgrims who come to Durango, not far from the Southern Ute reservation, ride the narrow-gauge railway up to Silverton and back, expecting the western mystique to include unwarped red men speaking in monosyllables who can somehow put them in touch with old-fashioned values associated with candy stores, amusement parks, and fireworks. The public wants to be entertained, hoodwinked, and lured into a fantasyland that includes steam trains, melodrama, ghost towns, rodeos—and Indians. They would pay good money to see a Ute ride off into the purple sunset or mangle his enemies with a tomahawk, but alas, the only good Indians are live ones, and they are busy mowing the grass and buying ice-cream cones for the kids. At Ignacio the disappointed tourist will not see Geronimo but two tepees in the motel parking

OVERLEAF

Pino Nuche Pu-rá-sa Motel and Convention Center, Ignacio.

lot, a monument to some famous Ute chiefs, and colorful Indian murals painted on cinderblock walls. That's all.

The Southern Utes have long realized that their numbers were dwindling, making it difficult to preserve their image, let alone their ongoing Indian act. "Pure" Southern Utes—that is, those with 100 per cent Southern Ute blood, uncontaminated by intermarriage with any other group—are about as rare as whooping cranes. Over the years, it has been impossible to segregate Southern Utes from the rest of the world anyway, no matter how much they would have the public believe in their undiluted ancestry; like everyone else, they have married whomever they pleased —white, black, Hispanic, and Indians from other tribes. Today's Southern Ute population of 965 (751 live on the reservation) represents not a Thoroughbred stable of racehorse-quality Indians but a mixture of everything else ever since their new constitution was adopted in 1976, making it possible for tribal membership to be granted to those with only a quarter Southern Ute blood.

The Utes have never been strong in number. Indeed, at the height of their Golden Age, around 1840, there were only 4,000 of them, and that included all 7 bands. When the first census was taken of the Southern Utes, in 1890, there were just 428 left, a number that dwindled to their all-time low of 334 in 1920. After that, as more and more Southern Utes married outside the tribe, the population rose to about 650 over the next 15 years, until in 1936, alarmed at the number of "non-Utes" who were claiming membership in the tribe, the tribal council, backed by the BIA, inserted a one-half blood-membership requirement in their new constitution.

Yet the new and unrealistic blood requirement meant that once again membership began to decline as Southern Utes continued to marry outside the tribe, making them ineligible for allotments, housing, jobs, education, and health and per-capita payments. It was the pressure of these quarter-bloods on the tribe that finally brought about a new constitution in 1976, written by tribal attorney Sam Maynes for a reputed $30,000, which included

Leo Vicente, chief of Jicarilla Apaches and Geronimo's grandson, is frequent visitor to Southern Ute powwows.

printing costs. The BIA endorsed the new blood requirement, some observers believe, to assure their continued stay at Ignacio; others point out that more Indians on the rolls means more money from the federal government.

When the constitution was overwhelmingly approved in 1975, tribal membership shot up overnight from 731 to an "official" 891, a figure based on the tribe's own count with no real proof of blood except in existing records. The BIA takes the tribe's word for its membership and then makes its own list of those eligible for services. The other two Ute tribes are not recognized in the blood squabble; thus a full-blooded Ute whose father happens to be Northern Ute while his mother is a Southern Ute is considered only a half-blood. Similarly, a tribal member can be three-quarters white, black, or even Chinese, but if he has one-quarter Southern Ute blood, he is listed on tribal rolls. That the Northern Utes threw out the very people the Southern Utes now allow in—half-bloods and less—is an irony that bothers them not a whit. In their case, blood means survival, not the sharing of new-found wealth, the reason why the Northern Utes wanted to decrease their numbers so drastically in 1954.

Not long after the claims money was awarded, 1,314 full-blooded Northern Utes decided to get rid of 490 mixed-blood members—those with less than one half Ute blood. The Ute Partition Act terminated them and awarded them about 27 per cent of the tribe's assets, including $735,000 or $1,500 each; they received no mineral rights. The 490, in effect divorced by the tribe and the Bureau of Indian Affairs, which insisted that they had "attained a level of education and sophistication about equal to their non-Indian neighbors" and no longer needed the protection of the agency, formed their own group in 1961 and called it "The Affiliated Citizens of the State of Utah." Within seven years, this "level of sophistication" resulted in their losing 93 per cent of everything they had been given, including their money, stock shares, and ownership rights to the land, most of it grabbed by unscru-

Northern Ute Darrell Shavaneaux, great-grandson of Chief Shavano, attends AA meeting after release from prison.

pulous whites. In 1971, just 10 years after they united, the group disbanded and by all accounts has disappeared.

In 100 years, there could be 10,000 Southern Utes left, none of them the kind of obvious Indian that everyone expects but rather a mongrelized version bearing no resemblance to what has become idealized over the years—a red-skinned, black-hair-in-braids individual with high cheekbones, deep-set eyes, full lips, and erect bearing, not to mention his look of wisdom and nobility or his impressive beauty when dressed in Indian clothes.

The mere "Indian appearance" of an individual sets off a chain reaction of guilt, admiration, and envy in most Americans who are still apologizing for what their ancestors did to the natives. Today, the only good Indians are not dead ones but those who make themselves most visible, the new national conscience of a nation accustomed to paying its debts, albeit a century later. The Utes, along with the other 265 tribes in America, cannot afford to go out of business. Who then would teach Americans about ecology, conservation, and the deepest secrets of the wilderness? Who then, with a symbolic tear trickling down one cheek, would pose for magazine ads telling us to save our forests? The Indian as wise man is needed more than ever, to remind us not only of what we have lost but also of what we have an obligation to protect. The red man is the personification of innocence, responsibility, and the great outdoors—but only if he remains as obviously Indian as he is. A quarter-blood Indian who looks like Steve McQueen will do no good at all.

The increased membership of the Southern Ute provided an unexpected bonus—an even greater share of the $100 million Indian set-aside money in the $4 billion Public Works Employment Act of 1977. The tribe's grant of $448,130 was based on a formula that allows $1,000 for each Indian for the first 200 in population and $270 for each person over the 200 figure. The new figure of 1,119 issued by the Economic Development Office meant $77,760 more for the Indians, thanks to the revised constitution; it will also guarantee in years to come millions of dollars more in federal grants likewise based on population figures.

Should the membership of the Southern Utes begin to decline

Powwow is part of Ute tradition.

again, the tribe could, as it last did in 1935, simply "grandfather" everyone in, which means that they extend full-blooded membership to every Southern Ute then alive, quarter-bloods and all. These instant Indians, though predominantly white or Hispanic, would raise the population figures—and the federal grant monies—once more, with even greater consequences than currently exist.

The social, legal, and economic implications of the blood requirement are enormous. By Indian law, a Ute cannot will tribal property or even some of his private property to a non-Ute. What will happen when tribal members die and their nonmember survivors try to claim their property anyway? What will happen to an allotment willed to a non-Ute? Will the BIA approve the transfer, as they now must do? And what, ask full-blooded Utes anxiously, will happen when their Indian blood dribbles off into a predominantly white society? Is blood important anyway?

To save themselves and their Indian image, the Southern Utes can only "marry up"—that is, to fellow Southern Utes—creating even more problems with inbreeding. As it is now, the Utes are all interrelated and often marry second and third cousins, causing a jumble of confusing names and relationships. Add to that a high rate of divorce and illegitimacy and it becomes impossible to define families or even reliable genealogy.

As one young Ute put it, "We usually know who our mothers are, but fathers are a different matter. I know people here who list themselves as half-bloods claiming Southern Ute fathers but actually they're Apaches, Navajos, Pueblo Indians, or from the other two tribes [of Utes]. Who can prove their blood? The BIA comes in and looks at us and to them all Indians look the same, like black people. What are they going to do, run lie-detector tests? The way it is now, you could be one-eighth Southern Ute but 100 per cent Indian if the other seven eighths were each from a different tribe. But the Southern Utes would not recognize you, nor would the other seven tribes. And what the tribes don't recognize, the BIA doesn't either. You wouldn't be eligible for anything except a lot of headaches. And you wonder why our people drink? They don't know who they are anymore."

Set apart on the reservation, defined by fractions of degree of blood, an archaic concept reflecting the values of two centuries ago, the Ute actually belongs to a club as exclusive as any all-white society in America. But he cannot resign from the club because the tribe is a fixed-membership group, one that is permanent, with an irrevocable status and an unwillingness to lose or expel members. Moreover, the club is also a corporation with considerable assets guarded by an elected hierarchy fearful of any threat to its power, and that includes defining the rights of its members.

Southern Ute tribal membership, actually a disguised property right, is further defined by where the member lives. Members residing off the reservation are not eligible for BIA services, nor are they represented on the Colorado State Indian Commission. Club exclusiveness means that its members must also live within view of one another, forfeiting many of their privileges if they move away.

The club, anxious to perpetuate itself at any cost, imposes a strict set of rules on its captive members, who cannot resign, move away, or set up another club. They are forced to preserve their collective society, an imitation of a white colony, this one instigated and administered by the BIA, itself anxious to preserve the club for obvious reasons. The constitution has become one means to survival of the club, as long as the Indians are willing to adhere to it under the irrevocable terms of membership.

Many Utes believe that changing the constitution was an unwise if not fatal decision and that they would rather risk termination than to allow the quarter-bloods in. Some have openly questioned the BIA's motives, such as a thirty-eight-year-old full-blooded Southern Ute woman married to a Ute Mountain Ute. "My kids are listed as half-bloods," she said. "Unless they marry back into the tribe, my grandkids are the end of the line. The BIA duped us, saying we had to vote for the constitution if we wanted to stay a tribe. I believed them but now when I look around at all the new people coming in, it makes me sick. We are real Indians. These new ones are not. What is the BIA trying to do to us anyway?"

"Real" Indians notwithstanding, the quarter-bloods are assert-
ing their rights by running for council, applying for tribal jobs
and housing, even learning native crafts such as beadwork and
jewelry making, which they sell to tourists as "genuine Indian
made." The quarter-bloods have also taken such matters as religion, tradition, and history into their own hands and seek ways to
give their newly acquired views on the subjects; one quarter-
blood, until recently considered a Hispanic, held a class in Ignacio
to teach a mostly white audience "the Indian way of life." If
blood is thicker than water, then the new Utes are stuck with one
another, forced to maintain their new identity whether it benefits
the tribe or not. Ironically, it is these instant Utes who must now
face the unrealized burdens of tribal life with all of its demands,
limitations, and costly benefits.

The Utes, at least for the moment, are further defined by the
nature of tribalism itself, an ancient and once-revered concept
requiring the individual to subordinate himself to the tribe, never
calling attention to even his most modest personal achievements.
As the membership changes, this attitude is certain to change along
with it, bringing a whole new educated generation to the rise.
Currently, the maxim at Ignacio is that what is best for the tribe
must also be best for the individual, creating frustration among
ambitious tribal members who generally must move away from
the reservation in order to express themselves. A Ute cannot go to
the defense of another Ute unless it is for the good of the tribe,
nor can he publicly criticize the tribe, its government, or its problems, one reason why the atmosphere at Ignacio is one of con-
straint and stagnation.

A tribal member is also restricted when it comes to offering
solutions or changes in tribal government; thus those elected to
council are generally middle-of-the-road quasipoliticians committed to a don't-rock-the-boat philosophy. Reformers, usually those
who have worked outside the reservation for some period of time,
find themselves suddenly ineligible for jobs, housing, or allotments
if they have challenged the basic rules of the game.

Small wonder that most Ute elections are met with apathy,

since most voters believe that it does not matter who holds office because everything turns out the same anyway. However, an amazing 194 voters turned out for a recent council election, a hotly contested race in which most of the candidates were at odds, one of the few times when a handful of people deliberately tried to upset the status quo. Despite a great deal of heated debate, public accusations, and even one candidate's threat to take Southern Ute problems to the press, the election turned out pretty much as everyone had expected.

The biggest vote getter was a well-educated Ute, Guy Pinnecoose, who is also the highly influential employment assistance officer. He was virtually assured of election since there are few tribal members who can bypass him in their search for a reservation job. Pinnecoose, like the rest of the incumbents, did not have to provide a platform. Said he vaguely, "The most important issue is that all tribal members be served, both young and old." One priority he had was "graveling driveways for members that live off the main roads so that they have better access in winter." One hundred one people agreed with him.

Another candidate, Neil Cloud, promised: "If I am elected to the council, I will not give you the run-around. Vote for me and your troubles will be over." Cloud, with only sixty-five votes, lost to a twenty-five-year veteran of the council, John Baker, Sr., the powerful Indian politician who was responsible for drafting the Rehabilitation Program in 1954. The senior council member was more polished and self-assured than the other candidates.

"I have always believed that all of us are most important only if we believe we are worthwhile as human beings," he said. "This I keep in mind ahead of all other things. Without training and without a chance for a good learning opportunity, anyone can get lost, especially so a Southern Ute. Southern Utes should not become lost, and there are now opportunities for education and training almost without limit, which will keep this from happening."

OVERLEAF

Ute children dress up for tribal ceremonials.

Three women also ran for council that year. The most outspoken was Elberta Velasquez, a member of the Planning Commission, who demanded, "Did we not elect our tribal council to help our people or did we elect tribal council members to break us?

"Progress, our tribal council members are always telling us," she ranted. "Whose progress? I say. We have built buildings. Who is going to pay for salaries and maintenance for these buildings?" Then, in an obvious reference to tribal attorney Sam Maynes, she charged, "Too many decisions are being made by nontribal members. Can't the council think anymore for themselves?"

As if that were not enough, she took a stab at tribal mismanagement.

"Our children's trust funds are going to pot, yet we pay high salaries," she said. "Our resources we never see. Tribal council always says we have to save for the future. Whose future, if we continue to spend one million dollars on the tribal organization?"

Relentlessly attacking the council, insinuating a rigged election, Velasquez stirred too much controversy and received only thirty-nine votes. As she said later, "They were determined to keep me out. They don't want anything to change."

Bertha Groves, who had once served a term on the council, sought to run again, this time on a women's platform. She said plaintively: "I feel we need a woman among our elected council members, a woman who will feel and make humble decisions for all the womenfolk and girls, little and big, who will be women tomorrow. We need one who will think as a woman for them, knowing that we are the source, strength, and center of the tribe. We are the ones who keep the tribe going and growing. Without us women there would be no tribe. Our strength lies there among our women and our land. So I leave it up to you, my people, and my Creator, to decide if I should be elected or not."

Bertha Groves was even more suspect that Elberta Velasquez, for not only did Groves run Ignacio's Native American church and was thus considered endowed with supernatural powers, but also she had once unsuccessfully asked the council to release her from membership, saying, "I want to get off the tribal rolls and get my equity in this reservation. I'm fed up with everything here. Now I want to get out. If it can be done, maybe the council can write me off as undesirable and send me off somewhere."

The tribe did not forget such perfidy, and Bertha Groves received one less vote than Elberta Velasquez.

Thelma Kuebler, a gentle, grandmotherly woman who had already served one term on the council, sought another, promising to "reduce expenditures of tribal funds and continue to emphasize that alcoholism is a disease that should receive much attention in order to lessen the suffering of our families." She also vowed to sell the Utes' natural gas at higher rates and to push for Indian water rights. She made no promises and refrained from accusation, preferring to run on her reputation as a dedicated, hard-working council member who did not grant favors to constituents.

She was defeated, with only 47 votes cast for her name, many Utes believe because, as one Ute put it, "she has too many problems with her family." He did not elaborate.

Exactly who has the power to swing an election or how it is done remains the subject of much speculation among the Utes, who claim that there are no free elections at Ignacio, that votes are bought through drinks and promises for "favors" later on. Council members realize they have more power than anyone else in Ignacio, with the exception of the BIA, and that it is their little Indian Mafia which can revoke assignments, create jobs, award housing, and influence or control most areas of Southern Ute life.

There is also the huge inducement of salary. Council members are paid $6,000 annually plus per diem; the chairman receives $18,000 a year. Members are only required to attend one council meeting per week, lasting about all day, leaving them free for other jobs when they can get them. In addition, there is a $24,000 annual travel budget, plus credit cards, one reason why council members are always jetting off to Washington and numerous national meetings with other tribes. For most of them, unskilled at any other work, the council offers steady employment, numerous fringe benefits, and enormous prestige.

One young Ute man, a college graduate who works in Denver, put it this way: "It's simple. Nearly everyone who votes is on the tribal payroll and they want to keep their jobs. The word is passed around that if you want to stay where you are, you'd better vote for so-and-so. Is that what makes a bribe? Maybe they give them money but on council pay, I don't think anyone could afford to. It's just this day-in-and-day-out pressure; you know, you want a favor from council, so you let them know you voted for them and they give you the favor because they want to get elected next time. I don't see that it's any different from the way you whites run your politics. At least we haven't had an Ignaciogate yet.

"The reformers are really loudmouths. They have no power, no constituency. Nobody is going to take a chance on them screwing things up. So we have the same old crowd year after year perpetuating themselves and our chairman is the worst of them all."

Leonard Burch, now in his fifth three-year term on the council and in his twelfth year as chairman, was originally elected to council in 1966 after working as a realty officer for the BIA for seven years, a job he took after serving four years in the Air Force. His first bold move as chairman was to discontinue per-capita payments because he realized the assets of the tribe were rapidly being depleted. He also did not think the people used their money wisely. What convinced him to stop the handouts, he once said, was his own experience in the Air Force. When he enlisted, he ignorantly signed up for a payroll savings plan, and when his tour of duty ended, he received his savings plus interest. Unaccustomed to so much money all at once, Burch promptly squandered it on a new Edsel.

Burch, while craftily playing the part of an Indian by dancing at the Sun Dance and Bear Dance and by making speeches about "white tape" and "forked tongue," is also forced into the role of businessman, a job for which he has had no training. He is a tall, well-muscled, darkly brooding man with close-cropped hair who usually wears a polyester suit and a beaded bola tie, never any Indian garment or decoration unless it is for a ceremonial occasion. He is a board member of the Durango Chamber of Commerce, reason enough for his people to criticize him for being an "Uncle Tomahawk" or an "apple"—red on the outside and white on the inside. Some have also been known to call him a member of the "Kiwanis tribe" of Indians.

But the chairman, as most modern tribal leaders, is hopelessly caught between two incompatible systems, and he can in reality please neither. At times, facing the hugely complicated economic problems of the tribe, he hesitates to make a decision, and has come to rely on certain key whites to advise him, particularly tribal attorney Sam Maynes, who helps him write his speeches. Burch, occasionally quick-witted and possessed of great physical charm, is at his best in front of an audience, for he has learned his Indian role to perfection. When the chairman speaks, in a scratchy voice, there is scarcely a whisper. He is at once both nervous and enigmatic, seeming always on the verge of blurting wisdom; his broad-featured, troubled face never smiles or brightens, for he appears in constant unrest and indecision. But the words of Leonard Burch do not inspire or challenge; they are basically the platitudes that the white man has come to expect.

Said he to a recent graduating class at Fort Lewis College in Durango: "In the face of an incurable or terminal disease, or other disaster, the only thing that counts is faith, trust, honesty, and friendship. These are the values that will sustain the Indian, and the same holds true for everyone else. This philosophy has sustained the Indian people through centuries of attempted change, sometimes even at the point of a gun. The Indian today is not afraid to differ from the crowd if what he stands for is one of his cherished ideals or values or constitutes part of his rights."

The Utes do not believe such sentiments coming from their chairman, whom many see as basically insensitive to their most pressing needs—how to survive on a reservation divided by fear and ignorance, how to express their Indian otherness, how to acquire jobs and dignity. Burch indeed seems to lead from the closet, making few decisions by himself, and issuing even fewer guidelines for his people, who seem merely to tolerate him as their leader. The chairman, under enormous pressure from all sides, at times appears to be overwhelmed by the whites who work for him, and to have difficulty coping with mounting tensions within the tribe or with the serious questions of its future. Drawn more and more into the white man's world as one of the conditions of Southern Ute survival, Burch must also face the consequences of choosing that alternative.

The responsibility of office has already taken its toll on the tribal chairman, who, rumor has it, will not seek re-election next time.

In the spring of 1978, Leonard Burch was arrested on a drunk-driving charge and spent the night in the Farmington, New Mexico, jail. He was in town on tribal business and was driving a tribal car with his chief executive officer, Jeff Jefferson, when he, Burch, was put into protective custody. Not long afterward he suffered perhaps the greatest affront of his career when his Navajo wife, Irene, the mother of his seven children, filed a disorderly-conduct complaint against him. Tribal police, caught in the middle of a domestic quarrel, were nonetheless required by law to pick up their own chairman and take him to the Southern Ute jail. The charges were later dropped.

As if that were not enough, the beleaguered chairman must also endure frequent public attacks from his own family. Two of his sisters, Bertha Groves and Martha Myore, once stormed into a council meeting and demanded a job and housing. Bertha Groves, angry because she had been shunted from agency to agency in search of a job, was further rebuffed by the council as she made her pleas for help. Finally she turned to her brother in exasperation, "These people [the BIA] can buy me off now," she said. "I'm up for sale. That's the only thing I can understand. If I can't get help here, I'm going outside to get it. I could never get across to you, Mr. Chairman. I still can't get to you."

The chairman, stone-faced and imperturbable, merely stared

at the wall and replied cryptically, "I'm sorry you feel that way. I know that wrong decisions have been made before and we will continue to make mistakes, but as far as I'm concerned, you have never sat down with me." Brother and sister glared at one another. When she started to speak again, the chairman cut her off, as oblique as ever when addressing members of the tribe. "There are people out there who are making their own way, doing their own thing," he said abruptly. "They are satisfied. There are programs that are helping with frozen pipes and things like that. They appreciate the help. They don't come here and gripe all the time."

That ended the matter. Despite even more threats and complaints, Leonard Burch refused to yield to his sister's demands for a job, or his other sister's demands for tribal housing for her two sons. At meeting's end, the chairman even weathered the accusation that a council member, Erwin Taylor, was trying to get rid of him, encouraged by a disgruntled Bertha Groves. Implacable as ever, he ignored the charges, proceeded with business, and eventually went home.

Tribal council meetings, rambling, disorganized, and frequently interrupted by outbursts from Indians untrained in the ways of parliamentary procedure, are still the only public forum the Southern Utes have except for general meetings. At the same meeting where Bertha Groves made her feelings known, another tribal member, Annabelle Eagle, spoke indirectly of how she and her husband, Clifford, had made it on their own, without any tribal assistance. A tall, sturdy woman with direct and honest eyes, long braids, and a bearing that was coolly regal, she spoke in a strong, clear voice from handwritten notes. In appearance alone the Indian woman was commanding, a symbol of a certain strength that was once almost forgotten.

"Mr. Chairman and members of council," she said evenly, "what about the rest of the people that make it on their own?

OVERLEAF

Bertha Groves, Southern Ute peyote chief, once requested that tribal council release her from tribal membership.

What about them? Seems like certain people [a pointed reference to Bertha Groves, whom she does not like] are always coming up here and asking for help and you never hear from the rest of us that are trying our best to make a go. You never ask us how we're doing. It's always somebody who wants your help who comes up here. The rest of us who are trying to make it, we never come up here. Maybe we have problems too and yet it seems like all the big decisions regarding help always go to the ones that could make it if they tried." The chairman cleared his throat and seemed to listen.

Annabelle Eagle ignored the hostile glances of Bertha Groves and spoke firmly to the chairman, who also happens to be her cousin. He watched her without expression or interest, glancing at the clock as the lunch hour approached. The rest of the council assumed expressions of boredom, tapped their pencils on the table, and shuffled their papers around. Clearly, no one had the desire to listen to Annabelle Eagle, perhaps the only Southern Ute with enough conviction to stand up to the council and those she considers wrong. With most of her life spent in Ignacio, Annabelle Eagle had never played the game but had risked both ostracism and threat in order to speak her mind.

"I get tired of having a million-dollar budget," she went on. "I wonder where it's all going to. I wonder why my husband has to go to work every day and gets nothing out of this tribe. Why don't I get a piece of the action? That's what I say. And yet I read and hear about council members going over and getting this and that. Why don't you even think of the rest of us, the working people? Give us a chance, too. Ask us what our needs and wants are and what our thinking is. Maybe we do some thinking, too. Maybe it's not on the same line as everybody else, but after a while when you scratch for a living, you come to think a different way. All I ask is that you people set an example instead of looking out for yourselves."

She looked around at the council members sitting at the horseshoe-shaped table—Chris Baker, Guy Pinnecoose, John Baker, Sr., Joe Mestas, Eddie Box, Erwin Taylor, and Leonard Burch. All

of them appeared uncomfortable, annoyed, unmoved, and un-
movable. Over the years they had grown accustomed to criticism
from this courageous, outspoken woman who commanded respect
among a tribe that respected little. Annabelle Eagle and her family
were unlike most Southern Utes. They were not vicious, petty, or
opportunistic; they worked hard, saved their money, never drank,
and participated every year in the Sun Dance, which formed the
basis of their Indian belief. For years they had aroused jealousy
because of the way they chose to live, aloof from the tribe, at the
same time they were an active part of all that was best within it.

"Where have the elders gone?" she demanded, turning to
council member Eddie Box, who was considered an elder. "You,
Eddie Box, talk to your people. You're an elder. Where are they,
the people who are supposed to be leading us? It seems like there
are always certain families who are getting, getting, getting. What
do they give in return? I'm teaching my kids that they have to
serve this tribe, that they have to give, no matter what. We're not
so much white that we can turn our backs on the way we were
raised."

Having delivered her reprimand to Eddie Box, she next
turned to Joe Mestas, an Hispanic with a quarter Ute blood. "All
of you were raised the traditional way. You came from Indian
parents. Nobody can say, 'I'm a white man.' That's why you are
serving here, Joe Mestas. You consider yourself a Ute. Then think
the way we think." Joe Mestas looked bewildered.

When Annabelle Eagle finally sat down, there was an awk-
ward pause before the council returned to its business without so
much as a word of response. Annabelle Eagle stayed until the end,
then walked out alone; the rest of the group, embarrassed at so
much emotional display, hung back until she was safely out of the
room.

8

DOWN THE HILL AND across the open field from the Pino Nuche
motel is a row of seven identical green-roofed, white-shingled
houses, built thirty years ago for BIA employees. Along the quiet,
tree-lined street, children play games from *Star Wars* and perform
impromptu disco dances; sometimes they ride their bicycles up
and down the alley that runs behind the houses, past barking dogs
and rows of laundry hung out to dry. The yards are all fenced;
the porches are all screened; the lawns are all tended with the same
lack of enthusiasm that belongs to rented houses.

At the end of the street, in the next-to-last house, Annabelle
Eagle and her husband, Clifford, have lived for nineteen years because he has been working that long for the BIA in the Road
Maintenance Department. They have raised most of their children
in that house—Romona, called Bones, now twenty-four and married to Ronny Frost, a Southern Ute; Linda, twenty-eight, who
works for the BIA in Albuquerque; Beverly, divorced and thirty-
two, who lives there with her two children and works for the
tribal accounting office. Three others were once there—Theresa,
called Tree, who died in 1973 at the age of twenty; their son
Clifford, Jr., who was killed in an automobile accident when he
was nineteen; and Annabelle's son by a former marriage, Douglas
Remington, thirty-seven and working for the Anaconda Company
in Denver as a computer programmer.

One bright Saturday morning in May, Annabelle Eagle got
up early and began making fry bread in her small, tidy kitchen,
cooking on a gleaming white gas stove that bore a small plaque advising that it was U. S. Government property, along with the refrigerator. She did not like the house, Annabelle said, and as soon

*Native American food staple, fry bread, prepared by Annabelle
Eagle for evening powwow.*

as Clifford retired in a couple of years, she hoped to move into a new house that Beverly was building on her allotment south of town.

"They call this silk-stocking row," Annabelle said, dropping a pat of dough into the sputtering grease, "but I call it cotton-stocking row. It's a white man's house and a white man's neighborhood. We are the only Indians here. What I want is a place for Norman to have a horse and for Pooh to run around." Her two grandchildren, Theresa, sometimes called Pooh, eleven, and Norman, almost five, had been living with them for nearly four years. When Norman was small she and Douglas, then back from teaching at Alcatraz, took care of him while Beverly worked. Now that Norman was in Headstart, Annabelle had accepted a position as assistant tribal judge, a layperson's job that so far had required her to attend a judge's school and several seminars on law. She liked the new job, she said, because there was so much to learn, but what she really missed was the opportunity to speak out.

"I can't tell people what I think anymore," she said, stacking the crisp bread on a plate. "I have to be diplomatic. There are leaders and there are speakers and I don't want to be like so many of them, just speaking all the time. I think in this job I can do more good. Maybe I can show people what they've missed." Beverly, her arms full of blankets, came in the back door, followed by the children. Clifford Eagle remained outside in the car, for it was the day of the powwow and there was much to be done. Beverly spoke briefly with her mother in Ute and went back out, leaving Norman and Theresa to sample their grandmother's fry bread.

Annabelle Eagle was nearly through with her cooking; the stack was a foot high, cooling and fragrant on the kitchen table. She scraped the dough from the bowl and patted it between her hands.

"Do you know what it takes to be an Indian?" she asked suddenly. "Essence. Those old people survived even when the pressure was great because they had it. Children at the BIA school with their braids cut off and in uniforms and shoes, they survived if they had a grandfather with essence. It's your spirit, the inner life, that I'm talking about, and it's the difference between what is Indian and what is not. This revised constitution is a joke, saying you can be Indian by blood. It's not blood, it's this," and with a floured hand she patted her old cotton dress directly over her heart.

"My uncle and my grandfather taught me that. They used to say it was the one thing the white people missed, the essence, because you don't see it, you feel it, so they thought it wasn't there. My mother died when I was three and I had no sisters or aunts who were close to me, no one to teach me to be a woman. I only had what my grandfather gave me. Sometimes I think we make a mistake with our children, not giving them that. Norman and Pooh, they understand because Clifford and I have taught it to them." She sat down.

Theresa Harlan, a sweet, pensive child with a shy smile, nibbled at the fry bread, glanced at her grandmother, and slipped away to her room. Little Norman, his fine, dark hair in small braids all over his head, climbed onto Annabelle's lap with a toy truck, which he ran in a circle around the plate of bread.

"I went to the BIA boarding school from the time I was six until I was sixteen," Annabelle said, smoothing back the little boy's hair. "My grandfather and my uncle were the only family I had. They lived a mile away from school but I was never allowed to go there except for vacations and summer. They tried to kill us off. We couldn't speak the language, and if we did, they washed our mouths out with that strong lye soap. A couple of girls died from swallowing it."

She said it matter-of-factly, self-possessed as always, long shed of whatever bitterness had accumulated from her boarding-school experience.

"They cut our hair and stripped us of all our Indian things," she went on. "We didn't have much. We were very poor in those days but if we had a bracelet, a pair of moccasins, or some bead-work, we had to give it up. Three times I ran away and when they caught me, they locked me in a room and fed me bread and water for a day and a half. Sometimes we were beaten and sometimes we had to stand in a corner. We had to do everything they told us. The Navajos were there too and sometimes at night we'd sneak out in the courtyard and they'd sing their songs and we'd sing ours. In some places they beat you if they caught you singing but here they didn't care."

Norman climbed down and went out the door in search of his grandfather, carrying in his small arms a large Siamese cat named Henry. Annabelle poured herself a cup of coffee and sat down at the table again, pressing her back against a straight kitchen chair, seated out of habit so she could see down the long and narrow hall. She had found peace in that house, where memories were still in the shadows and strength materialized between familiar walls.

"On Sundays we were supposed to go to church," she said. "Us Catholic girls would go out the door and down the street toward town, then turn around and come back to where the Protestants were having church for the Navajos. There was a lot of singing there and that's what we wanted to do—sing our hearts out instead of listening to all that Catholic mumbo jumbo."

She laughed softly, a woman forged by such deep, old convictions that she seemed at once the archaic bones of reason and the new skin of painful affirmation.

"I go to Bible class every week," she said after a while. "It's conducted by the Jehovah's Witnesses and I find it contradictory to Indian belief. They say your spirit is in your blood, that's why they refuse transfusions. They believe that when you die, you're dead, that's all. They say you don't have an afterlife or a spirit that lives on, the way we Indians do. And they tell you there are different classes of people too, depending on how many new people they bring in. There's sin and the devil but the Indians don't believe in those things. Then there's Christ. We say we don't need an intermediary, that we pray directly to God, and God deals directly with us. People say they need a pope or a big church to feel God but I tell them, it's all inside you. What do you need these other things for? It makes them feel better, I guess. I go to

Bible study for the same reason. I feel better. But I don't believe it at all."

Beverly moved quietly through the door again, this time with a sack of groceries, followed by Clifford, a smooth-skinned, sinewy man in his sixties, his hair in braids, his face a blend of rare composure and the price of silent adjustment; he had the look of a man held fast to life by generation and the biding of precious time. Clifford Eagle carried a boxful of potatoes and onions and after speaking to his wife in Ute with the look of a man accustomed to the deepest communication with the least amount of words, he put the box on the table and disappeared down the hall. Beverly, unloading the groceries, received instructions from her mother on what was to be done with the meat.

"We have so much to do to get ready for tonight," Annabelle sighed, finally getting up to attend to a sinkful of dirty dishes. "We have to pick up Linda at the airport. And I have to help Bones finish the shawls. After this, we are through giving anything away." An old Ute custom is to give away possessions for years following the death of a loved one. The Eagles were still doing it four years after their daughter's death.

Clifford changed clothes and went out again; Beverly cooked; Theresa was preoccupied with a tiny kitten discovered behind the garage; and Norman rode his tricycle up and down the alley. When she finished the dishes, Annabelle went in and took a bath, braided the hair she had washed when she got up, and put on a fresh cotton dress she had made herself. Back in the kitchen, she sat in her customary chair and began to fringe a bright blue shawl, the traditional covering of Southern Ute women at powwows, an ecumenical gathering of tribes who come to sing and dance.

As if there had been no interruption, Annabelle went on. "I'm doing my part telling it to my grandchildren," she said. "I was taught that it was better to read about Indian life from a book like *Hiawatha* than to learn it from your heart. You try and think back, what was that story but it's so far back and there's no one to ask. What was it like? Who were the leaders? What happened to

*Eagle grandchildren include Norman and Theresa Harlan, above,
and Sadie Frost, right, first full-blooded Southern Ute baby
born since 1974.*

us in those days? We have these history books but what they say is a white man's view. They would have you believe that we wanted our lands to be taken, that we allowed our children to go to BIA schools, that we were all weak and cowardly. It couldn't have been that way. That's what my grandfather said."

When Norman came in crying with a small scratch on one knee, Annabelle whispered to him in Ute. He nodded, wiped away his tears, and ran back out.

"To us, it's important that these children learn Ute, so we speak it whenever we can. Clifford has always been that way because that's what his father taught him, the importance of language and traditions. You don't see many Ute men believing the way he does. You should talk to him sometime because what he says is true. Clifford never went to college but he's the best-educated man I know.

"When he was young, Clifford was favored the way he favors Norman now, taking him out and teaching him things so he'll grow up strong. Douglas does the same thing when he's home, he looks after Norman like he was his own. It's the Ute way. You'd never know it the way the tribe is now, but in the old days, men were not ashamed to be tender with their children. They loved them in a way you don't see much anymore except with men like Clifford and Douglas. It's bred into them, this way they have, like the old days when boys were given every comfort because it was up to them to provide and defend. It was the mother's job not to frustrate him so his spirit wouldn't be frightened. It was her job to teach a boy gentleness and at the same time toughness. You can't be weak on the inside and on the outside strong. You have to be merciful too. A young boy today is like a wild thing with no soul because his parents aren't teaching him. It takes a while to learn strength but the kids think they can get it from watching TV, this toughness like a policeman. With that kind of learning you are only half a life. What I think is that everyone is reduced to a family—a man, a woman, and children. That's all there is in the end. That's another thing the BIA did: They tried to destroy the family."

Later that afternoon, when Clifford, Beverly, and the children had gone out to pick up Linda at the airport, Annabelle Eagle sat on the sofa, fringing a turquoise shawl, the last one she had to do. She had been weeks getting everything ready for the powwow, now she was almost through. She sat undisturbed and thoughtful, her full-blooded features illuminated by a streak of light coming through a narrow window. The old house groaned as if from the weight of her concerns; not even the impersonality of a rented government house subdued the vitality within it.

"It's women who really run this tribe," she said firmly. "You will never hear a man speak out the way we women do. In the early fifties when they got the claims money, women came out of their homes and began to serve on committees for education, housing, social services, care for the elderly, day care, and employment. They began to have more and more authority, like Anna Marie Scott, who has been over there at the tribal-services office for twenty-five years. They couldn't get a man to do it, so she did. The men all took menial jobs—they never were good at decisions anyway. All of a sudden, women had money for their homes and they wanted to know how to make them look nice. They didn't have to accept rations anymore or be told by their husbands [to] do this, do that. They went out and did things themselves. It was a freedom to them and besides, they were getting things done. The men didn't like it but Ute women have always been strong.

"In the old days, women marched first, in front of the men with shields made of several thicknesses of animal skin. Some people say they went first because if they got killed it wouldn't make any difference, they were just women, but I've always believed they went first because they were the bravest. So when the women started going out into the world, doing this and that, the men couldn't stop them. The women had always done what they pleased. When the reservation was first set up and the men couldn't go out and be warriors anymore and couldn't even hunt, it was the women who held the families together. They stood up to the government as much as they could. The men would have gone crazy except for what the women did.

"At least, that's what my grandmother said."

In the living room above the fireplace hung a large oil painting of her deceased daughter Tree, dressed in a dark-blue crushed-velvet blouse, wearing her finest beadwork and turquoise jewelry. Her sleek black hair was parted in the middle, braided and tied at the ends with strips of fur; in her small and delicate hands she held a white eagle plume. But it was neither the dress nor the beauty of the girl that gave the portrait its disquietingly lifelike look; it was the expression of some secret deep within her. The portrait was finished just a few months after the girl's untimely death and presented to the Eagles by Santa Fe artist Vera Drysdale, who chose not to sell it. The portrait stood out in the spare, impersonal room, stripped of all its furniture the day that Tree Eagle died. There was no other indication of an Indian home except for Norman's small tom-tom in a corner and the sound of Indian music coming softly from a tape recorder. Now that it was spring, the Eagles had begun to play the Sun Dance songs; the music mellowed the house and gave a benediction to what was ordinary and plain.

The Indian woman stared at the painting and said softly, "When my daughter died, I lost everything. There was no pain left. We gave everything away. All our furniture and clothes. Pots and pans and dishes. Curtains and rugs. The television set, even our beds. The jewelry and the beadwork that she's wearing we buried with her. Someone from another tribe came with a bag of rice and put it in her casket. They said, 'She'll need it on her journey.' All of us cut our hair. It's the custom. When the house was empty, people started to bring us things and leave them at the door. Blankets. Tables. Chairs. Even money. When someone close to you dies, you realize how unimportant possessions are. They only clutter up your mind. You should be thinking, 'What am I going to do with this life? How am I going to pass it on?' Not, 'What can I get? How much can I use?'" Her head dropped down; her eyes closed and for a moment that expanded to become all time, the woman was alone with her daughter. The radiance of the painting engulfed the room.

"Ever since then," Annabelle Eagle said at last, "we've given things away at powwows. Blankets. Shawls and beadwork that I've done. We give it to people who knew her, who were her friends. That's the custom, too. And tonight is finally the end of it. Clifford and I, Beverly, Linda, Bones, even Norman and Pooh, we'll stand up and give what we have away." She glanced down at her work; she had not added a single fringe in a little more than an hour. "After that, we'll just continue to leave tobacco at her grave. The spirits are hungry for tobacco. It's the Indian way."

Automatically, her strong, brown fingers began to knot the thread.

"She was not like anyone else, everyone said that. She knew. She had this spirit I was telling you about, only more so. She wanted to live the old way. She wanted to teach people, to show them things. That's why she danced the Sun Dance that year. It was a sacrifice. It was for the people of this tribe, to help them be Indians again. Many have told me since, our lives have changed because of her. And I believe them."

With that, Annabelle Eagle got up and walked into another room, then came back with a small clipping. It read: "In memory of our daughter, Theresa Anne (Tree) Eagle, who left us a year ago. You are with us still when we greet the morning sun and hear the silence broken by the singing song of the birds. When we hear the drums beat and the songs sung by our people, you are there. And when the evening shadows creep over the land, we will meet again." It was Annabelle Eagle's final tribute to her daughter.

On a warm spring evening a week or so after the powwow, Clifford Eagle sat on the back stoop of his house, smoking a cigarette and watching the crimson sky to the west change into purples and mauves; the night was sweet with the scent of damp grass and earth. Above him, a nighthawk wheeled against a cloud shaped like an enormous buffalo head; the old man studied the bird, the night, and the buffalo. He was not given to words, and that night as he waited for Annabelle and the children to return from town, he was as silent as ever. Then, when all that remained in the western sky was the palest streak of light and the first stars began to come out, he spoke quietly and slowly of the things that were on his mind.

"We have no elders here, none that teach anymore, so many things are different, even our prayers," he said. "We have now something from the Sioux, something from the Shoshone, something from the Navajo who used to be our enemy, even something from the Bible, so that there is reference to Jesus in what used to be Indian prayers. In the old days, the elders would not have allowed it. Now everything is different. Many changes here."

By the light of the street lamp, the Indian's face was like sculpture but with a richer, deeper meaning behind; he had an old man's disciplined face of wisdom but there was the fearless ingenuity of a young boy's face also.

Clifford Eagle preferred silence, for there was much to be learned within it. His words seemed not so much speech as the configuration of a well-used mind.

"In the old days too the Sun Dance never lasted four days, it lasted three," he said. "With four days you just sit around on the first day and it takes your energy away. In the old days we danced all night but now we sleep from one to four. My grandfather used to say that unless you danced the whole three days, night and day, the meaning of the Sun Dance would not come to you.

"We follow the Sun Dance all summer long, sometimes to Idaho or White Rocks or over to Towaoc if they're having one. Sometimes I dance or sometimes Douglas, Bones, or Linda. There is always one of us there. We're a Sun Dance family, so there always has to be one of us to carry it on.

"If you're on the inside [of the Sun Dance circle] you're not thinking about the outside. You go in there with your mind empty so that whatever happens to you is because it has a way to come in. You want to have a vision but you don't ask for it. It comes to you if your mind is ready and your spirit is a certain way. If you are chosen for a vision, you don't ask to have it explained. In another dance you find out why. You don't go in to find an answer to your problems or to be an important person. You have to leave all that outside. You have to be open to whatever comes.

"When Sun Dance time is over in the fall, you become very full. It is this fullness that stays with you all year long until the next Sun Dance time. For us it starts in May when we play the Sun Dance songs (on the tape recorder) to remind ourselves of what is coming soon. For us, the Sun Dance is the holiest of times. When the white man says, 'You Utes can't have any religion because you only practice it once a year,' we don't say anything. You can't talk to these people about the way it is. I don't go up to a man and talk to him. He would not understand my mind. He would give me the wrong advice. That's why we Indians keep to ourselves. We talk to our wives about what we have seen in there. But that's all."

Clifford Eagle smoked his cigarette down to the stub, then tossed it into the alley, watching the small red glow until it finally went out. He sighed deeply and stretched his legs, wondering what had kept his wife so long. Turning his face in the direction of town in order to see her coming, he said, "When I'm working around here I get tired. But when I'm cutting trees for the shade house [at the Sun Dance] it's not work. I sweat and get thirsty but I don't mind it. This is what used to be—the Indian man always built a shade house for his family."

He glanced over his shoulder at the outline of his white-shingled house, illuminated by the street lamp. "I don't like living in this house," Clifford Eagle said. "It's too good. I'd rather live in a shack with a dirt floor and be able to get away from all this. I retire in a few years and that's what I want to do—live in a shack and build a shade house. Then I'll be free as a bird."

He stood up and peered down the alley at a set of headlights that stopped at another house. He hesitated for a moment, thinking to go inside, then changed his mind and sat back down, saying nothing until he had smoked another cigarette.

"I can't hunt anymore," the Indian man said quietly. "I have a .30-.30 that my father gave me. I went out last year and shot a deer. He fell and I went up to him and he just got up and ran away. I followed him for a half hour but there was no blood and I gave up. The same thing happened with an elk. I shot him six times but he never fell—he just stood there looking at me and turned and walked away. I wanted to kill an eagle too—for the feathers—but I had a dream telling me not to. Maybe if I move away from this house, the hunting will come back to me. I want to kill a deer once more. In the old days, it would be a bad sign for a man not to be able to kill. If I dance the Sun Dance again, maybe I will know why this has happened to me. But I have not had the dream about it yet."

He fell silent, not smoking or moving, yet there was movement in his stillness. The wind came up out of the field below and made a song in the big old elms beside the house; the wind was from the west, the direction of the buffalo. In the silence the sounds of the crickets and the bullfrogs rose higher and higher on the wind until their song and the song of the wind were the same: It was the song of an old warrior come home.

Clifford and Annabelle Eagle, in their wisdom and their suffering, living by conviction and disdaining the mean and the trivial, transcend what is most seriously wrong among the Southern Ute tribe. It is they, moreover, who hold the seeds of regeneration among a group of people whose fate, at best, seems uncertain. Genesis and not genocide is what they symbolize, and along with a handful of others, they offer it to their disconsolate people, subtly, unfailingly, and without reward.

The Eagles recognize what is already there, the essence of Annabelle Eagle's grandfather, a slender thread that unites the people even now in a way that their land cannot and will not. This thread results from the vestiges of a unified consciousness spun out of long-ago experiences, legends, and way of life.

The unified consciousness of the Utes, or what is left of it, draws as much from experience, superstition, myth, and legend as from the ancient lessons of grandfathers, medicine men, and from the fullness of nature most of all. According to this principle, the present life is but the sum of all other Ute lives that have preceded them, rich and indestructible because what was not good was long ago eliminated, a spiritual version of survival of the fittest. Even now, traditional Utes believe they have been given certain powers from the animals with whom they lived for untold centuries, powers passed on to them through intensive observation.

From the buffalo the Ute acquired protection and leadership, and to this day this creature remains the center of all Ute symbolism, spiritual and material. When they say, "the buffalo will come again," they do not mean that the West will once more be filled with millions of the shaggy beasts, but that the spirit the Indians had when buffalo were plentiful will come again. Before that happens, they say, the world will drastically change, a hint at the Armageddon that most Indians believe will befall everyone else but themselves.

Such simplistic faith stems from a time when the Indian nations of the land managed at worst to fight one another for hunting territory, at best to ally themselves for a common good, to prevent the invasion of the white man. The buffalo, for Plains Indians as well as Utes, was the source of strength and dominion and served as a symbol of their greatness. In the practical sense, it was this one animal who provided everything—tepee covers, buffalo robes, sinew thread, bowstrings, horn glue, skin bags, moccasins, and meat.

The Utes say that when they were forced out of the mountains, the spirit of the buffalo came with them and enabled them to endure the pain and dishonor of the past 120 years. With them too came the spirit of the deer, and from him they learned agility;

OVERLEAF

Clifford and Annabelle Eagle in their shade house made of cottonwood branches. Tree in center is cedar.

from the eagle they learned courage; from the coyote they learned cunning; from the fish they learned the meaning of freedom while confined; from the beaver they learned efficiency; and from the bear they acquired wisdom and healing powers. Even the lowly ant had a lesson, for it was he who taught them industriousness.

Even trees and rocks held a meaning, so did earth and sky, although it was sky that held a deeper meaning because of its mystery. The whole life effort of the Utes was to be in harmony with all living things, who shared with them a common Creator, and each provided a valuable lesson. The Utes did not pray to the birds and animals for possession of their great gifts but spent their lives studying every animal habit, applying these learned characteristics to their own lives.

Above all was the Great Spirit, a bisexual deity associated with the sun, whose power created all life. Every day they arose before dawn and stood facing east, to greet the sun and ask its blessing, scooping up its warmth with their hands and pouring it over their bodies from head to toe. This ritual is still performed at Sun Dances by at least a hundred members of the tribe.

In Ute religion, there was neither heaven nor hell but the Happy Hunting Ground, where all Utes eventually went, whether they were good or bad. To them, there was no such thing as sin, redemption, penance, or damnation; there was likewise no Judgment Day presided over by a wrathful God capable of sending them into the everlasting fires of hell or to the pleasant haze of heaven. The Ute basically judged himself and had his punishment meted out, in the case of transgression of tribal laws, by the elders or by his own family members. Once paid, his debt vanished from any sort of earthly or heavenly roster of wrongdoing; the Great Spirit was wholly benevolent, incapable of revenge or carrying a long-term grudge.

Beneath the Great Spirit were other lesser deities: a God of War; a God of Peace; a God of Floods; a God of Thunder and Lightning; and a God of Blood, who heals the sick. These gods saw to every need and emergency, and Ute shamans invoked them by offering prayers and a sacrifice; nothing more was needed, and the gods in time obliged.

If the Indians failed to respond to such doctrines as the Holy Trinity or the cult of the Virgin Mary it was because the concept of three gods in one was incomprehensible, since all was god and all was holy. The notion of the son of God having a virgin mother was even more unlikely. When confronted with these ideas by Spanish friars early in the eighteenth century, the Utes did not argue; they simply allowed themselves to be baptized because they usually acquired horses as reward for supposedly accepting Christianity.

The Indians continued to believe in the Great Spirit, the animals, and all the lesser gods; they believed, moreover, that man was essentially good, as all of nature was good, for man was coequal with his natural world, sharing responsibility with it. Nature was the supreme gift and man could only be its modifier.

To the newly arrived European refugees, with a dearth of philosophical roots such as these, the Indian offered his wisdom and was refused on the ground that it was pagan, false, and utterly incompatible with the strange, new European religion. The taming of the new American land meant taming Indian religion as well, for it could not be allowed to compete with Christianity which, along with the lust for land, provided a double-edged sword that brought the Indians down. Armed with Bibles and baptism, the whites launched five hundred years of spiritual aggression, forcing their own rigid values upon a primitive people who had practiced one of the most successful religions of all time.

Along the Rio Grande, hundreds of Pueblo Indians were put to death for refusing to accept Christianity; hundreds more simply superimposed Christianity on their Indian religion in order to survive. Other tribes—Navajo, Hopi, Sioux, Cheyenne, Kiowa, and Arapaho—were forbidden to practice sacred dances and rituals, but many continued to do so anyway. Such repeated contact with the very touchstone of their existence kept them from forfeiting their Indian otherness entirely.

For the Utes and the Plains Indians, separation from their homeland meant severance of deep religious roots as well, a fate that has gradually extinguished all but token naturalism in their lives. Now, far removed from their spiritual source except for infrequent walks in the mountains, the Utes live with the memory of nature and express themselves not through experience but through an inherited point of view.

The Utes do not go to the mountains anymore because all of the land is fenced and accounted for; instead of being teachers for the Utes, the mountains are now someone else's territory, defined as national forests, parks, and wilderness areas. Moreover, the age-old affinity for streams and rocks and trees, for animals and birds, for the seasons' comings and goings, and for the splendor of each new day, is now but a memory held mainly by the old because the young have not been exposed to it. Most of the young Utes, with cars, pickup trucks, and CB radios, race through the mountains to get to Denver or Albuquerque, scarcely noticing the shape of clouds or the magnificence of the snowclad peaks. They are little different than their white counterparts, oblivious to grace and beauty, and always on the run. Their Indian blood guarantees them nothing except tribal membership. For a few, however, blood still means something else entirely.

Dean Taylor stepped out of the control room at KSUT, the Ute-owned radio station in Ignacio, a record in one hand and a glass of milk in the other. His hair was in long, dark braids, and he wore tight-fitting blue jeans and a white T-shirt with a picture of a giraffe stretched across his chest. It was his twenty-fourth birthday and Lillian Seibel, the Southern Ute woman who runs the station, had brought him a cake with candles. He blew them out, and the staff—Lillian and her two Ute assistants, Dawn Santistevin and Evelyn Hudea—sang "Happy Birthday" to him. When they were all seated on folding chairs, balancing their cake plates on their laps, someone asked Dean about his work as a teacher's aide at the Indian Center in San Francisco, a job he had held for more than a year before coming back to Ignacio to work at the radio station.

"I was a tutor in heritage," Dean Taylor said, his smooth, unfinished face reflecting a certain peacefulness as yet untempered

Dean Taylor, radio announcer, KSUT, was once a "tutor in heritage."

by Ignacio's harsh realities. "I tried to give them a sense of identity. A lot of them were just kids, mixed-bloods mostly, who had lost their reservations. I told them it didn't matter, that if you have Indian blood in you, then it would give you a strong feeling within yourself. I took them to powwows. I told them they should not be on drugs or alcohol. Look, every one of you is given a chance, I'd say, so go ahead and be Indians in the right way. Sometimes they'd just look at me like they didn't believe it. Then sometimes one of them would say, 'Well, I think you're right.'" He smiled slowly. "I had to come back here, though, because it's where I was raised and where I want to stay."

Dean Taylor finished his cake, then helped himself to another piece while the women cleaned up. In another minute he would be on the air, this time with a news broadcast. Impassioned, vulnerable, with zealous conviction radiating from his face, the young man seemed not so much anachronistic as he did naïve.

"I guess the inner self is like an eagle," Dean Taylor said grandly, pausing by the door to the control room. "It spreads out and out and out." Not long after, Dean Taylor was arrested for theft and sentenced to one year in a reformatory. While on probation at Ignacio in 1979, he disappeared and has not been heard from since.

The spiritual issue is really at the heart of Ute existence. Without it, they cannot survive or even exist as the people they like to think they are. With renewed spirituality, the Utes could at least have a chance to defend themselves against what they fear most—eradication of all the old values, thanks to the revised constitution, the encroachment of the modern world, and their own inability to act against the threat to their survival. But there are no real spiritual leaders at Ignacio anymore, no way for the Utes to gather strength and push on. Their unified consciousness needs valid interpretation and expression through the teachings of wise men and leaders whom they respect and trust.

In the old days, spiritual leaders provided comfort, inspiration, and, best of all, a cohesive body of traditional thought to which the Indians could turn again and again, resolving their conflicts through age-old beliefs. The old Ute ways were held in sacred trust by the elders, who never presumed to tamper with tradition or to offer their own version of what had been handed down. Between them and their people was a bond of loyalty, faith, and credibility.

Further, the task of the elders was to oversee the spiritual life of each Ute male, to give advice on matters of conduct and principle, and to settle religious disputes. An elder was not merely an aged man, for few of the old ever became elders, but rather the holiest and wisest among them, chosen for his virtue, leadership abilities, and knowledge of sacred matters.

Traditionally, the chief elder or spiritual leader was also the Sun Dance chief, an honor greater than that of chief of the tribe. The powers of the Sun Dance chief were mighty; it was up to him to decide who was worthy enough to dance after each participant, always a male, had had a dream about it. The Sun Dance chief also was charged with upholding the integrity of the dance, allowing only traditional prayers, clothing, and ritual during the three-day ceremony. The Sun Dance chief was a low-profile figure who went about his spiritual business quietly and humbly, never calling attention to himself, his words, or his great deeds. In his old age, the Sun Dance chief had the privilege of naming his own successor, generally a man who had trained with him for twenty or thirty years and who was, by the time of the chief's retirement, considered worthy of the honor.

When the last Sun Dance chief of the Southern Utes died in 1941, he had not named a successor, and the dance, which had already declined in the thirties, was abandoned for thirteen years. During that time, tribal elders remained curiously silent, offered little in the way of leadership, and provided almost no spiritual guidance. Most Southern Utes went to Sun Dances at the Ute Mountain Ute or Northern Ute tribes, wondering what would happen to their own sacred dance since the matter of a spiritual leader seemed to have faded away.

In 1954, the Southern Utes found to their amazement that not only did they have sudden wealth but sudden religious life as well when a new Sun Dance chief and religious leader appeared, a situation all the more surprising since tribal elders had not selected him. Eventually, the Southern Utes found that many changes were to be made in their Sun Dance, from new prayers and procedure to the alarming new practice of allowing women to dance. Other innovations took place too as the spiritual leader accepted speaking engagements all across the country, opened amusement centers, conducted new rituals such as the sweat-lodge ceremony, and finally got himself elected to the tribal council after a stint as tribal public-relations director.

The man who had apparently nominated himself to the sacred position of spiritual leader was no stranger to the Southern Utes, although he had been away for some years. He had not been known as a deeply religious man either until his return to the tribe at almost the exact moment of their wrenching shift in economic status.

His name was Eddie Box.

9

WHEN EDDIE BOX WAS growing up in Ignacio during the thirties, he was known as "a boy who sleeps with the bears," meaning that he was one who kept to himself, apart from the rest of his people in the tradition of the legendary bear. His early years were not spent in preparation for his later spiritual life; according to people who grew up with him, the elders gave him no special notice or sign.

"There would be a Sun Dance," said one man who went to school with him, "but I don't remember Eddie there." Then he added the characteristic Ute phrase of noncommitment and evasion: "Of course, it was a long time ago."

"He was always quiet," said a woman who is his second cousin. "I don't remember much about him except he never smiled. He was too serious even then. There was something on his mind, but like the rest of us, I guess he was wondering what he was going to eat. It was during the thirties, you know, when everyone forgot about us. There were times when all we had for dinner was coffee and bread. If there wasn't a lot of bread, we drank a lot of coffee to fill us up. Eddie must have been nine or ten at the time."

Shortly after the war broke out in 1941, Eddie Box enlisted in the Navy and served through five Pacific invasions. When he got out, he lived in California for several years with his wife, Dorothy, a Southern Ute who had been in the Women's Army Corps. Eventually he came back to Durango, where he worked first as a machinist, then as an asbestos salesman. Once he even had a rock band, wore his hair short, and belonged to the Catholic Church. In his later years, he did not want to be reminded of any of it.

"That was a long time ago," Eddie Box said late one winter afternoon, seated in the dark, cluttered living room of his little pink house at the edge of Ignacio, where he and his wife once had a curio shop. On one wall was a buffalo head, on another was an Indian painting done by his younger son, Jim. There were a few books on the shelves, among them the Bible, *Black Elk Speaks*, and the Book of Mormon.

Eddie Box seemed far away, trying to find the words to tell what had happened to him after the spirit came to him in 1954 and urged him to return to his people after more than a ten-year absence. It was, he decided, the work of the Great Spirit who had simply moved through him, urging him toward the position he now held, calling himself Red Ute.

"The One-Above," Eddie Box said solemnly, pointing a finger toward the ceiling. "He decides everything. You have to listen to him and do what he tells you. You must be humble and not call attention to yourself. You have to listen to the elders." He rolled his woeful eyes toward the group of eight or ten who had gathered around him. There was one Northern Ute, two Southern Utes, and one Navajo; the rest were white. They sat on the blanket-covered furniture or on the curled-up edge of the rug; no one spoke for fear of breaking Eddie Box's reverie.

Leaning forward in a small overstuffed chair with one of its legs braced up with a brick, Eddie Box frowned and spoke, scarcely moving his lips. "I wanted to make something of myself," he admitted. "I hated schedules. I hated the white man's world."

With a small-wristed hand, he brushed back his saucer-shaped bangs, which had fallen over one eye; his braids, tied at the ends with leather strips, were nearly in his lap. On one forearm he wore a tattoo—an anchor and the letters "U.S.N."—United States Navy.

Around the room, the small group, all of whom were slated to attend the sweat-lodge ceremony the next day, nodded their heads in hushed agreement. Some of them moved closer to the man, now in his midfifties, who aroused so much controversy outside of that room. Others pushed back into the shadows, closer to the wall, and appeared to reflect on his words.

"In the old days when we lived in a tepee, it was for a very good reason," Eddie Box said. "It was made of an incomplete circle with an opening to the east. In the morning we always rose with the morning star and there were still spirits moving about from the night. Before dawn the spirits would come in the opening and visit us. It was a time of complete harmony then just as the sun was coming up. We stood outside and asked a blessing from the sun and no one moved until the sun had passed the horizon. The sun was round, our house was round, as the earth is round and the sky is round above us. Nothing in nature is square. It's unnatural.

"Now this house of mine has no power because it has corners to it. In here, I cannot make contact with the spirits anymore. You become the way you build. If it's square like this house, you become that way, closed to everything. There is no square opening to the mind. In a square house, you cannot learn anything. You stumble when you come to a corner. It's always dark inside because there is no opening to the sky as with a tepee." His living room, with one window facing south, was growing dim in the late afternoon as the winter sun cast a pale, silvery light through the pane.

"I think I should not live here anymore," Eddie Box said absently, his round face drawn up in an expression of melancholy. "I should live as I was told."

His eyes, forever sad, went to the window where the traffic was zooming down the main street toward Ignacio. A mile away he could see the big sign and the sprawling buildings of the Pino Nuche complex; he could see, too, nearly all of the new buildings that had gone up over the past few years.

While Eddie Box droned on, Betty Box, his daughter-in-law, came quietly through the front door carrying an armload of clean laundry. Ever since Dorothy Box died several years before, Betty had been coming from her own house on top of the hill to take care of Eddie, cooking his meals and cleaning the house. She also helped him with the sweat ceremony and the Bear Dance, the way his wife had, accepting her role with a sense of pride and achievement. As Dorothy Box's surrogate, she had risen in the eyes of those Southern Utes who were Eddie Box's followers and who overlooked the fact that she was three fourths Hispanic and one fourth Navajo. In charge of adult activities at the community center, Betty Box teemed with ideas for projects and displayed such energy that even the older Utes who had once grumbled about an "outsider" taking over so much of tribal life now admitted that without her driving ambition, the community center would be dark most nights.

But it was not her job that aroused so much jealousy among the Southern Utes but rather her unswerving loyalty to Eddie Box and her manic protection of him, which often formed a wedge between the spiritual leader and his pilgrims, mostly whites, who were trying to catch a few minutes of his time. Indeed, it was said in Ignacio that if you wanted to see Eddie Box, you had to get on Betty's good side first and that she had developed a knack for screening out those who might tend to discredit or annoy him. Married since the age of seventeen to Eddie's older son, Eddie, Jr., a tribal policeman, she was then twenty-seven and had three children; Edward, nine; Matthew, seven; and Melanie, four. Although the children strongly resembled their father, there was something of their mother's luminescent good looks about them. She was poised, slim, pretty, with evenly spaced teeth, a high forehead, and long, dark hair. As she grew older, she was looking more and more Indian, acquiring an indirect gaze along with her braids and reddish skin.

"I'm what they call an unclaimed Navajo," Betty Box said, plugging in the percolator in the kitchen. The breakfast dishes were still in the sink, so she began to scrape and wash them. "My father was a sheepherder, part Navajo, and my mother worked in a tomato factory. She was Spanish. If you weren't obviously Indian, the tribe didn't want you. The Navajo kids were raised to think you had to be 100 per cent Navajo in order to belong so they would shut you out if you had even a quarter Spanish blood. But then the Spanish kids didn't like the Navajos either and they would beat them up and call them names. The only ones who were interested in your Indian blood was the BIA, and they'd go

Betty Box greets Southern Ute girls at Bear Dance, Towaoc.

around checking to make sure you had enough to qualify for their programs. It was like Army recruitment and I'm sure everyone had a quota. You know, get ten half-Indian or quarter-Indian kids a month and send them off to school. When I was seven or eight, that's what happened. I didn't want to go and my parents wanted me home, but we had no choice. The BIA came and took me away. And of course the purpose of the school was to make you forget your Indian blood that you had to have in order to get in." She glanced up at the children who had followed her in and were now going off to the bedroom to watch television. "It was crazy, it really was."

She wiped her hands on a dish towel and went to the cupboard and got out a set of cups, which were cracked and of various kinds. "I don't care how much Indian blood I have," she said. "I know that spiritually I'm a Ute. I know people around here who are full-bloods but they might as well be white. I don't want the kids to be anything but Indian and that's what Dad says too. They have their braids and they go to Sweat and in a couple of years, Edward will dance in the Sun Dance. I want them to understand what they have to do when they get older and all this pressure is put on them to be white. Sweat helps them to understand that. The reason for Sweat is that you want to be cleansed and strengthened so you can take it. There is so much sickness in everyday life. You just want to get it out before it poisons your whole body. But like Dad says, Sweat is a trial, not a test. A test is final. You live or die. A trial—well, you just find out what you can bear but it's really not the heat."

She smiled mysteriously, aware of her secret and with no desire to reveal any more. It was the way Eddie Box had taught her: to be at once quixotic and direct. With dark-eyed, mischievous Melanie on her lap, Betty smoothed back some wisps of stray hair that had come loose from her tiny braids. "They didn't used to allow braids in school," she said. "Even with all the Indians there, they just wanted everybody to look the same. We had to sign some sort of paper saying we invented God to get them to allow it."

The two boys tiptoed into the room and stood beside her; they were shy, serious children with pensive, mysterious faces that, like their grandfather's, seldom broke into smiles. The two boys, under the religious guidance of their grandfather, were different from the other Southern Ute children, set apart not only by their braids but also by an awareness of the two worlds in which they lived. Theirs was an infinity of opposites; sooner or later they would have to choose.

"Edward says he wants to play sports in junior high," his mother said. "To do that, he has to cut off his braids. At least that's what the school says. But I'm going to pray about it so he won't have to. You can pray for those people to understand. Dad says so. He says that if you think negative, it pulls you down so I only think, Edward won't have to cut his braids in junior high."

In the living room, Eddie Box was still talking in a low monotone. "It starts with the little ones here," he said, patting Matthew's head as the boy came over and stood by his chair, glancing suspiciously at the small group. "People who are teaching young kids about language are teaching them about their roots. Take the word 'sky.' Sky is sky, nothing else. In the Ute language we call it *ta-koop-pa*. The word itself explains it. It means it's there, lofty, a cover for the earth. Somebody far beyond the universe has put it there and you respect it. The teachers of English simply repeat words. They require more words to understand the first word. For us, it is just sky—*tuqú-payá*. Beyond that is God's territory. It's sacred and holy. And all of that meaning is contained in the one word, *tuqú-payá*. But you in English would need a hundred more words to describe the same thing. Language is supposed to guide you. It's a parallel with the spiritual life."

For a moment, his head down and his eyes closed, Eddie Box seemed to be praying. Then like one awakened from a dream, he shook his head and announced dramatically, "The spirit of Sweat is summed up in a word we have—*u-tum-mus-saw-ve*," he said. "It means perceive it, be humble, take it, you know what it's for. Now the most important thing is: Don't let it pass. There are three rules to this word. One is understand, open your heart. Two is when it comes, you must be ready. And three, by all means, do not let it pass.

"If you say this word backward it means, if you don't accept this spirit at a time when you're supposed to, it will ricochet. It will pass from your life."

Betty Box, a new softness to her face, sat on the arm of the couch. Like most Indian women, she said nothing when in the presence of a man. She sat there listening, like everyone, to Eddie Box's notions of the sweat ceremony and his insistence that next morning everyone would be purified. He spoke of the sacredness of it, of how it was always used in the old days before a treaty or a war party went out. The Sweat was the most sacred medicine of all, ranked before all fasts and important ceremonials. What Eddie Box did not say was that the Sweat had never been a Ute ceremony until he himself introduced it. The Sweat had belonged to the Plains Indians, particularly the Crow and the Sioux. Before the middle of the twentieth century, few Utes had even heard of it.

As the sun went down, the room grew dim but Eddie Box did not turn on a single light. The room was strangely peaceful in the twilight, silent except for Eddie Box's monotonous voice, soothing yet disturbing. He got up suddenly and took an instrument down from the wall and held it toward the window to catch the very last light of day on its smooth, dark wood.

"Here is a red-cedar flute," he said dispiritedly, pointing the flute toward the sky. "I made it with a song but if you listen for my song, you won't hear the words because the song is all through me. I'm going to give this flute to an Indian boy but he has to be worthy. I will make one for your son, but not your daughter. Instruments are always played by a man, never a woman. The drum, the flute, these are the songs of a man." He turned on a light.

Eddie Box, like all Indian men, was of the opinion that Ute rituals should be closed to women, that they could not be elders nor smoke the sacred pipe, and that they should be limited to wife-mother roles. Only once had he allowed women into the Sun Dance, an action that had fatal consequences. Women came to the Sweat, however, because he had always permitted it, ignoring the

Northern Ute Darrell Shavaneaux and his wife Kathy in Eddie Box's living room.

Plains Indian tradition that prohibited men from participating in the Sweat with women.

The people in the room had been there for several hours and they had hardly moved or spoken; it was as though they had fallen into a trance. As Eddie Box put the flute back on the wall, a Northern Ute named Darrell Shavaneaux roused himself and said, "I just got out of the pen. Three and a half years on an assault charge. A white man came up and called me a name. I wanted to teach him a lesson so I beat him up pretty bad."

Tall, well muscled, with a tense energy on the brink of explosion, it was easy to see how the Indian had won the fight. At Fort Duchesne on the Northern Ute reservation, Darrell Shavaneaux had once been a Golden Gloves boxer and had even made it to Denver for the finals. He should have become a professional boxer, he said. That way he would have stayed out of trouble.

"I blame it on the Mormons," he said bitterly, his pock-marked face drawn up in a scowl. The great-grandson of the famous Ute chief Shavano, Shavaneaux had grown up in Utah surrounded by Mormons. "They tried to tell us we were the lost tribe of Israel and they said, 'Before long, you'll be white like us. You'll be Mormon first and Indian second.' Some of my people said that was the way to be if you wanted to get along, but you see how I never believed them."

He had come to Ignacio to start a new life, working part-time for the radio station and on Monday nights conducting the AA meetings at Peaceful Spirit, the Ute Rehabilitation Center. "I went that way for a long time," he said. "I was about fifteen years old and I said, 'What's the use?' And I took my first drink. That's what a lot of Indians say, 'What's the use?' So they drink and kill somebody."

"They told me I was drunk and no good and I believed them. They said I wouldn't amount to anything and I said, 'I guess you're right.' So I was drunk and no good for six or seven years and nothing happened. I wasn't going anywhere. I straightened myself up after I got out of the pen. I went to AA and left the Northern Ute reservation. I came to Sweat. I'm all right now but sometimes I wonder, why should it be so easy to believe when they tell you you're no good. We were not proud to be Indian in those days. It was something to be ashamed of. The Mormons understood this and they capitalized on it. They'd hold out their arms and say, 'Look, soon you'll be as white as us.' And they believed that our color would just gradually fade away. I used to look at my own skin and think, 'Why should I do this? I don't want to be a Mormon or a white man. I want to be what my grandfather told me it was all right to be.' But it took a long while to believe it."

Having said too much, Darrell Shavaneaux fell silent, sinking back into the shadows under the buffalo head. His wife, Kathy, a Shoshone-Bannock, remained in exactly the same position she had occupied for the previous hour, her face impassive, staring out of the window at the street. Eddie Box, subdued and weary, cupped his face in one hand, lost in his own thoughts, neither listening nor speaking to anyone.

By this time, with most of the afternoon spent in the sanctified atmosphere of Eddie Box's house, the air was worn out with significance. The guests had stayed too long and they shifted uneasily, shy, uncertain, imprisoned by the suggestion of relevance and meaning. All of them had come, not out of curiosity, but from a genuine need to find their religious roots; for both Indians and whites, the meeting with Eddie Box was meant to teach and redefine.

But their spiritual leader, Red Ute, seemed to be falling asleep. As Betty Box got up and began to pass around cups of steaming-hot coffee, one of the guests spoke up and asked Eddie Box to explain the meaning of the Bear Dance.

Like Carlos Casteneda's medicine man Don Juan, Eddie Box also enjoyed his teacher role and he could spend hours rattling off impressive-sounding thoughts. But unlike this well-publicized hero, Eddie Box expected nothing of his students and in fact grew bored whenever they spoke. Now he furrowed his brow and gazed off into the gloom, his face serious and almost sad under the austere responsibility of spiritual enlightenment. He began slowly,

"Bear Dance is a rebirth, an awakening of the spirit. It's a time of awareness. You come to learn from the past in order to arrive at the present with an understanding of the harmony of things." He looked up. He was the center of attention once again.

"A long time ago, the animals were our teachers," he continued. "The bear taught us knowledge of the herbs—144 of them, one for each part of the body but the principal one was the yarrow plant. The bear used these herbs on himself, curing heart trouble, pain in the stomach, and headache, so he was able to continue this dance, year after year, for a thousand years or more. He was able to bring people together, to teach them to live in harmony all year long, not just at Bear Dance time.

"The Creator used the bear to teach the Ute strength and wisdom and survival because no matter how many times he was shot at, the bear had the power to cure himself through herbs. Even with arrows sticking in him from every direction, the bear went on. When the Utes finally learned their lessons from the bear, they were closer to Him, to the One-Above."

Again, he pointed his finger toward the sky, solemnly lifting his eyes as if to give a benediction. The room was hushed and dim except for the soft whimpering of a year-old baby boy. Quietly, Betty Box passed sandwiches around, and managed to make it an act of supplication.

"Long ago when people were having a Bear Dance, they'd take a log and cut it out and cover it with rawhide—deer or elk or buffalo," he said, this time dragging out his old hide-covered drum and striking a single blow with his drumstick. "The hollow sound of it would imitate the bear. We don't use hide now because it's not too important. It could be done but it wouldn't have the same meaning as in the old days."

He beat the drum slowly, giving emphasis where he wanted it; the notes reverberated throughout the room. The effect was as he wanted it, eerie and heavy with history learned better without facts to dilute its weight.

Traditional Bear Dance has long been a way for young people to meet; girl always asks boy to dance.

"Now we use a box covered with corrugated tin," he said. "We try to bring out the effect of that harmony so the dancers feel a rhythm in their whole bodies. They just want to get out there and dance. Humans are supposed to have rhythm, just like the animals. They were created that way. The inner rhythm is brought out in the Bear Dance. That's why we dance together in a line. We don't go opposite, we go along with it. The harmony is rolling and we are rolling with it. It is given to us to get back in rhythm every spring when it's Bear Dance time."

With that, he sounded one last note on the drum, then put it to one side of his chair.

"You see," Eddie Box continued importantly, "we are all created with a rhythm. The sea has a rhythm. The clouds have a rhythm. The birds have a rhythm in their wings. Even the plants have a rhythm as they sway and grow in the wind. The rhythm is really a song.

"And there are the unseen words in these songs that every part of nature has, even rocks and trees. Whenever you dance, it comes to you what the song is. The song itself takes the form of a spirit. It's the song that says during the Sun Dance, 'When I am sung in the afternoon, think of me and I'll bring you water.'"

By then the room was unbearably heavy, and a chill crept through it. As two or three people stood up to go, Eddie Box rose and turned on more lights. Everyone blinked. Saturated with so much of Eddie Box's thoughts, no one could speak. As he made his way to open the door, he offered, "This is what the elders have taught me. A general knowledge of things."

The sweat lodge was built in the backyard of Eddie Box's house beneath a couple of old cottonwood trees, leafless now in March. The oval-shaped lodge was made of canvas, stretched over a frame of willow saplings, held down by ropes and cement blocks. There was a flap for a door and it faced east, as was the custom; to the right of it was a buffalo skull with sage stuffed in the cavities of

---

Bear Dance singers play a morache—a notched wooden stick—by running a pipe over it. "Drum" is a box covered with corrugated tin.

eyes and mouth and on the top of its head. Near one corner of the house, a galvanized tub held more sage, and the people picked up bunches of it, as one by one, they went in, barefoot, clad only in bathrobes, carrying the towels that Betty Box had passed out. The morning was gray, cold with an unsettling wind blowing out of the north; a low line of dark clouds hugged the horizon to the east. Overhead a crow screeched and flapped its wings.

Eddie Box was still in the house as the small group gathered and went in, careful to pass to the south of the bleached-out buffalo skull, past the lone eagle feather and the clay peace pipe that rested on a little mound of earth. West of the lodge, a deep pit held a pile of hot rocks the size of basketballs. At dawn Eddie Box had come out and built a fire of juniper and piñon and when it burned down to red-hot coals, he had put the rocks in. His son, Eddie, Jr., turned them carefully with a shovel; his face bore an expression of brooding reverence. His hair was cut short, perhaps out of deference to his policeman's job. Beside him were Matthew and Edward, who, as solemn as ever, stood and watched the rocks

turn red; the brothers were contained and unnaturally still in the cold. It was irresistible four-year-old Melanie who scampered about, clad in corduroy pants and a sweatshirt that bore the legend: "Custer Had It Coming."

Inside the lodge, the light was ghostly pale, coming only from the open flap, and it did not reach the back of the lodge a few yards away. The arched roof was padded with blankets and towels to absorb the heat better, while the dirt floor was covered with straw, sweet grass, and sage. In the center, the sacred fireplace had twelve bricks neatly arranged within it; these were the bricks for the rocks that represented eternal Mother Earth. A four-pronged stick was inserted in the earth and on it were tied four ribbons: red for earth and longevity; white for winter and purity; blue for sky and water; and yellow for sunlight and the dawning of a new day.

The people sat cross-legged in a circle on top of the straw, rubbing themselves with sweet grass and sage; the Indians prayed silently while the whites watched them curiously, not knowing what to do. A white man named Tim McMahon sat near the back with his Navajo wife, May, and young son, Tommy, who whimpered now and then. White-haired, patient Sunshine Smith, a Southern Ute who was once married to Diamond Smith, a white man who ran the best Mexican cafe in Ignacio, sat stiffly on the ground, arthritis raging within her joints, as it had done for many years. She opened her robe and rubbed herself with sage, her lips moving, her eyes closed. Next to her was Darrell Shavaneaux with a subdued weariness about him; he rubbed himself with sage, his eyes blurred so that he looked unfocused. Near him was his wife, Kathy, her enormous, sad eyes fixed on the fireplace; her expression revealed boredom, tension, uncertainty. Suddenly she dropped to her knees and faced the pit, oblivious to the people in front of her as she crowded against their backs. Betty Box came in with Melanie and seated herself to the right of the door; it was a signal of some sort, for the flap was quickly closed and the lodge plunged into utter darkness.

When all was quiet, Eddie Box stooped low to get through

the flap, said something in Ute to his son, and began, "Grandfather, Great Spirit, you have always been and before you no one has ever been. There is no one to pray to but you. This is my prayer, hear me!" He began to chant in Ute as Eddie, Jr., came with the rocks on the shovel, four of them at first, which Eddie Box grasped one by one with two Y-shaped sticks and placed in the pit. When the remaining stones were placed in the pit in the same manner, a hide container of water and a wooden cup were passed inside. As the flap closed, darkness gripped the lodge and the heat became immediately intense.

Eddie Box began to pray again, first in English, welcoming the bathers and telling them to seek the Great One-Above and to pray to Him. Then he spoke in Ute, mentioning everyone by name, praying for each of them to be cleansed, forgiven, so that they could start life anew. He said it all reverently, in his low monotone, then he poured four cups of water on the stones. Hot steam filled the darkened interior and someone gasped. The temperature was perhaps 150 degrees.

Then Eddie Box, who was, according to ritual, the water chief, opened the flap and a jug of water was passed; everyone drank thirstily and soaked their bunches of sage. When the flap was closed for the second time, there was again a prayer and the passing of the clay pipe, which was filled with tobacco and lighted. Once before, Eddie Box had told about a white man who took part in a pipe ceremony, normally reserved only for Indians and in the most sacred of places, but the pipe would not stay lighted.

"It was a sign," Eddie Box had said then, "and the white man saw it and said, 'I realize how corrupt I really am. The Indian way is the right way. From now on, I will follow Him, the Great One-Above.'" But the pipe did not go out as Eddie Box passed it; that would happen nearly three years later, when many other things had occurred. Now there was just a prayer as each participant smoked and offered the pipe to the next person.

When the pipe had been passed throughout the circle, Eddie Box handed it through the flap to his son. When it was closed a third time, he poured seven cups of water on the stones, praying again for purity, using sweat, the most sacred medicine of all.

All was sweat. All bodies melted and became liquid heat. Sweat overflowed mouths and eyes and filled the parched throats hotter than smoke, searing, burning all the way down until it exploded against hot, empty stomachs, contracted, rose, was forced down again. No one was conscious of a body, only sweat that was fire, yet there was neither hot nor cold, light nor dark, only the absence of those things. There was no vision because all was vision, all was color, the red, blue, white, yellow of the ribbons, rising and falling like waves, grinding away like an ocean, like time that was not time, merely a vast, empty place deep inside, which was the gaping mouth of the buffalo.

Then the flap was opened for the fourth time and the water passed and the sage soaked again, yet there was not the sensation of a wet, cool herb anymore, and the smell of the sage was gone. This time when the flap was closed, Eddie Box poured on the stones many cupsful of water, called "million wishes." He cried out for the sacred eagle and called out the name of eagle, which was the Indian name of his grandson Edward. All was heat and dark and there was no earth floor nor was there the half dome of the lodge; all was like the sky and floating, released in fire, consumed by fire and yet not fire, for the sensation of heat was replaced by an implosion of a cold, black space, a void like sleep, like death, with a strange white light following, becoming brighter and brighter, a million suns exploding.

The sweat-lodge ceremony, alien to Southern Ute belief and observed by fewer than thirty of its members, is nonetheless a way for people to come in contact with what eludes them most, the unified consciousness or thread of their ancestors. With few alternatives available and with no elder challenging Eddie Box's position or his doctrine, the Indians are forced to accept him because no one else even comes close to offering an alternative to what most of them believe is only a poor imitation of their original religion. Indeed, so much time has passed since the Southern Utes actually had a spiritual leader that what remains of the old religion lies buried in the hearts of older members, the very ones who scorn Box the most, yet do nothing to curtail his power. Many fear to cross him, claiming that despite his quasimedicine-man techniques, he does have the power to cast spells, invoke spirits, and even bring death to his enemies. The majority of Southern Utes go along with him, some out of fear, some out of belief, but most because they feel he is better than nothing at all. Even a traditionalist like Clifford Eagle participates in Eddie Box's Sun Dances because he believes in the essential purity of the dance itself; he does, however, go in a day late to show his disapproval of Eddie's four-day schedule.

Without Eddie Box there probably would be no Bear Dance or Sun Dance either, for it is he who gets the money, recruits the singers, and issues posters that attract huge crowds, unheard of in the days before his reign. But even at the friendly, social Bear Dance, Box has instituted change, installing electric lights around the outdoor circle made of freshly cut aspen trees and putting in a public-address system; he is also said to conduct a predance prayer ceremony that is not Ute. In the old days, Ute women used to prepare a huge feast when the two-day dance was finished, inviting all of the neighboring tribes and guests. Now, because the numbers are so great, the task has fallen to Diamond Smith, who got the job soon after he married Sunshine Cloud, a Southern Ute. His recipe for Bear Dance stew:

400 lbs. beef
200 lbs. potatoes
50 lbs. onions
50 lbs. carrots
50 lbs. celery
1 lb. salt to taste

Simmer 6 hours in 75-gallon pot over cedar fire. Serves 1,500.

OVERLEAF

Eddie Box, left, has added outdoor lights, loudspeakers as part of Bear Dance innovations.

Southern Utes object not only to Eddie Box's tampering with tradition but also to his frequent public appearances at everything from a White House prayer breakfast to the dedication of a Durango amusement park.

Summoned to dance at snow-starved Vail in December 1976, Eddie Box, his grandsons, and a handful of other Southern Utes arrived at the ski resort the same day as President Gerald Ford, who took off for the slopes just as Box, wearing buckskin and his "sacred blanket" over his winter clothes, a fur cap on his head, spread his arms and murmured, "We cannot say whether it will be successful but if we all get together and think alike, it's very possible He will have mercy. We pray to the supreme being that causes our moisture. It all depends on a power beyond us."

Unlike his appearance in Vail in 1973, which coincidentally produced two feet of snow within three days, Eddie Box's incantations were not answered until a week later, when six inches of snow came down.

Eddie Box, a council member since 1964, even carries his religion into council chambers, frequently conducting a pipe ceremony within its plastered confines. Most of the council members participate, with the notable exceptions of senior member John Baker, who has always refrained from what he considers a liberty with a sacred ceremony, his brother Chris, and quarter-blood Joe Mestas. Seldom offering concrete solutions to tribal problems, Box depends instead on religious rhetoric to calm his constituents.

Said he when Bertha Groves applied for tribal assistance, "I think it's going through my mind that we have energy here that can be used through Mrs. Groves. We know that certain people have lots to give to our people, and Mrs. Groves is one of those people. I'm not talking to her as an individual, I'm just saying that it's possible that it may be. I'm not saying one way or the other that the techniques that are being used are good or bad or whatever. All I'm saying is that here we have an energy with one person and she asked for assistance. What I say is, why can't the energy of the whole thing work together to help one person?"

Energy or no, the main criticism of Eddie Box is that he is too vocal, too visible, too free-wheeling in his rituals. He is denounced for his self-styled preaching, his bending of religious rules, his seemingly endless travels as Ignacio's official spiritual leader (although he claims only to be a "traditionalist").

One Ute woman believes that Eddie Box is merely an opportunist. "No one wants to get up there and make speeches," she said. "We have a bunch of cowards for men. They want Eddie Box to do it because it saves them the trouble. He wants to do it because now all at once he can be important, whether people like him or not."

Yet another Ute woman said: "I remember when he came back from the Navy. He was ashamed of being Indian. They must have done something to him out there. He was ashamed of the color of his skin. He put us down for a long time, then one day we heard he was starting up the Sun Dance. My mother told me, 'Don't believe this man. He's a white man now.' She told me not to go to any of the dances here but it was all right to go at To-waoc. So I went to the Bear Dance there after she died and I thought of her. But I don't go to Ignacio anymore because I get a strange pain when I do. It's a warning, that much I know."

A traditional Southern Ute man who seldom speaks up described Eddie Box thus: "A spiritual leader does not have to announce himself that way. It is an honor that the elders give after many years of learning. We have no elders here—none that teach anymore. So Eddie Box had no one to learn from and besides he was gone a long time in the service and here and there."

Box, mindful of the resentment against him, claims it is because of his previous life away from the reservation. When he came back, a "born-again Indian," as it were, the people were not impressed. Acceptance in Ignacio requires lifelong residency; returning prodigal sons are always suspect, for they have been contaminated by a world that few Utes seldom experience. Born-again Indians are not unconditionally welcomed back into the fold but are subject to lifelong scrutiny, doubt, and suspicion.

"I remember when he wore a white shirt and tie and had a

rock 'n' roll band," a former council member said. "His son used to play the drums. After a while, Eddie started putting on his Indian clothes to get more people to come. He saw his opportunity and came back here. He says he's an elder but he can't be—he has two older brothers and anyway, he proclaimed himself. You can't do that. It's something that's passed down without any fuss. He's not even at the Bear Dance this year. He's off in Georgia giving an invocation at a meeting of tribal chairmen."

But Box's troubles go deeper than mere criticism. Because of his controversial spiritual role, Eddie Box is blamed for tribal deaths and bad luck, even for the drought that has plagued the Southwest for several years. A forty-four-year-old Ute housewife said, "The people are getting upset with him changing things to suit himself. They look at this drought and say it's because we're not following the old ways. We're listening to Eddie Box. Ralph Cloud says the drought's because of the rocks they brought back from the moon, that the Creator never intended foreign substances to be here. But most of us say Eddie Box has something to do with it. The whole earth is disturbed now; there are droughts and floods and earthquakes everywhere, and people are not the same. This is what is happening to us and the whole world is feeling it, thanks to Eddie Box."

Most Utes believe that Box's trouble began not in 1954, the year that he decided to come back, but in 1973, when, defying all Ute tradition, he allowed five Indian women to dance. The Utes were stunned; never within memory of the oldest of them had women ever been allowed to participate in the Sun Dance. To them, it was heresy. But the five—Ute Mountain Ute Judy Pinnecoose, Southern Utes Theresa Eagle and Bertha Groves, and two women from the Northern Ute tribe—all solemnly prepared themselves according to tradition and danced four days along with two dozen men.

Two months later, strange things began to happen.

Theresa Eagle, known as "Tree" to her friends, died in a Durango hospital from a sudden illness never really diagnosed; she died after seeing the sacred Ute water bird in her IV tube.

Regina Box and infant son James, five months before her death.

Not long after Tree Eagle died, Eddie Box's wife, Dorothy, died, stricken in her office at the Tribal Affairs Building. Then Leonard Burch's aunt, who had raised him, died, followed by the death of Ralph Cloud's wife. Then another man's wife died and the man himself lost a leg in an accident. Each of those people was connected with the Sun Dance the year that Eddie Box let the women dance.

But there was more to it than that.

According to one of the older tribal members, Eddie Box made an offering of human flesh on the sacred tree that stands in the middle of the Sun Dance circle. The flesh came from the thigh of one of the women who danced and she allowed Eddie Box to offer it for the good of the tribe, convinced by him that it was a sacred act.

The older Indian said: "To us, to offer flesh is a sacrilege. Only the devil would do it. So now the people are saying, 'It will be on us.' They wonder who will be next. The only way to stop it is to throw Eddie Box out. But I don't know who is going to do it. The council is afraid of him. And the people are, too. They think he's a fraud, that he's gone too far, but they also know he has a power over them. Each man you see dancing in the Sun Dance is aware of it and he's dancing for the good of the tribe, to break the spell of Eddie Box. And he's dancing for himself, too, to be purified and made strong enough to fight this thing."

Even that was not the end of what was happening to Eddie Box.

In the fall of 1976, Jim Box, his younger son, came home drunk late one night, and after an argument with his twenty-two-year-old wife, Regina, shot her in the head, killing her instantly. She was a Shoshone-Bannock, a popular young woman who had been teaching Indian dancing to the Utes. She was also the mother of a six-month-old boy, James.

Jim Box was indicted by a federal grand jury in Denver and was charged with voluntary manslaughter, to which he pleaded innocent. He faced a maximum one-thousand-dollar fine, a three-

Jim Box, center, plays at Bear Dance shortly before he killed his wife.

year prison sentence, or both. But because Box was a first offender the charges were reduced to involuntary manslaughter and he pleaded guilty after spending five months in jail awaiting a hearing. He was given five years' probation.

When Jim Box returned to Ignacio in the spring of 1977 and tried to take up his old life, the Southern Utes began to mete out justice in their own way. Quietly, subtly, and completely, they began to shut Jim Box out of their daily lives. In the only town he had ever known, among people who had watched him grow up, there was hardly a person who accepted him anymore. They appeared to take no sides even though they believed that Regina Box had been murdered; they simply went about their lives as if nothing had ever happened and Jim Box did not exist.

But by then another force was also at work. According to the Utes, the Shoshone-Bannocks, angered by the death of one of their tribal members, decided to seek revenge and put a curse on Eddie Box. As if he did not have enough trouble already, the spir-

itual leader would have to meet the Shoshone-Bannocks medicine with his own medicine in order to break the curse.

The people waited to see what would happen, wondering whose medicine was stronger, the Utes' or the Shoshone-Bannocks'. Would even more dreadful things happen to Eddie Box and his family, or would there finally be an end to it? Within the reservation, gossip and superstition raged.

"A few years ago," one woman said, "Jim Box wrote a play about a young man on his way home who gets into trouble and dies. My daughter was going to be in it but I told her no. We Utes are superstitious about death. We don't like to talk about it or make fun of it. If a child starts to cry, pretending someone will die, it's bad luck. Or if you start walking backward, your mother will die.

"So I wouldn't allow my daughter to be in it. There was an old lady in a shawl who was in it. She didn't say anything, she just sat there. The next year she died. Jim Box was in it and the next year his mother died. Last year he shot his wife in the head and she died.

"Now he goes around like nothing happened. He and Eddie are trying to raise the baby alone but Eddie has him most of the time. After a thing like that, you're supposed to be quiet, out of respect for the dead. But he goes around so everyone will see him. He announces at all the powwows and what I hear is, Eddie is going to let him into the tepee during the Ute-Comanche signing. If that's what happens, there is going to be more trouble yet. You cannot allow a murderer to participate in tribal events."

The Ute-Comanche Peace Treaty signing on July 24, 1977, was one part circus, one part hype, and one part history. The brainchild of Eddie Box, who wanted "a Class A powwow," the treaty was the re-enactment of a nineteenth-century treaty—never signed—between the two tribes, who had been at war with one another for a century or more.

As three television networks, two wire services, plus an assortment of newspaper, radio, magazine, and free-lance reporters and photographers converged on Ignacio along with a crowd of three thousand people, the Utes and Comanches staged their pow-wows, dances, and parades for four sleepless, beastly hot, tension-filled days.

Behind the scenes, Eddie Box aroused the ire of his people when first he appointed Jim Box cochairman of the powwow, and then when he insisted that his son be allowed in the tepee for the treaty signing and the sacred-pipe ceremony, a privilege granted only to council members from both tribes. Following Eddie Box's announcement at a heated meeting in council chambers, Leonard Burch defiantly added Anthony Burch, his brother, and Julius Cloud, a respected elder. Then council member Guy Pinnecoose, angered at the inclusion of Jim Box, insisted that his own eight-year-old son Marvin accompany him into the tepee. The cere-mony, held while television cameras whirred outside, photog-raphers shoved for a better view, and an expectant crowd surged, broke even farther with tradition when the pipe was passed *across* the tepee entrance, in violation of both Comanche and Ute tradi-tion. As was expected, Jim Box put his signature on the treaty scroll, an action that one Ute said "brings shame to the whole tribe"; Jim Box also brought a nontribal member friend into the tepee, to the resentment of most Southern Utes.

Eddie Box again found himself in the center of a bitter dis-pute at the dedication of the new health center in October 1978. After the ribbon cutting he stepped forward and announced that the next event, the pipe ceremony, would be held on the grass, again a violation of Ute tradition.

"It's not enough to cut this ribbon," he said. "We have to remind ourselves that our strength comes from the One-Above. We are here to reaffirm ourselves today and to do His will. This

OVERLEAF

At sacred-pipe ceremony, held at dedication of new health center, pipe is smoked by group of men including Indians, whites, and Hispanics as Northern Ute photographer records event for tribal newspaper.

pipe ceremony is to insure that our spirits as well as our bodies are involved in this health clinic. I asked for chairs to be put here so some of our elderly members could sit down but they reminded me that the pipe ceremony is always held sitting on Mother Earth so we will sit over there on the grass. Now some have asked me if women can participate in this ceremony now that we have women's liberation. I can only answer that it has always been for the men to conduct these ceremonies and I apologize to the women for not being included. Men are men and women are women. I invite our other tribesmen—Northern Utes and Ute Mountain Utes—to join us for the pipe ceremony."

With that he went over and sat in front of the building, waiting for his grandson to hand him the pipe. But among the twenty men seated on the grass were several whites and Hispanics and even the BIA superintendent from Towaoc, Joe Otero, known for his bitterly antagonistic attitude toward the Indians.

The Utes were shocked and angry. Several of them left; others talked among themselves as the bizarre ceremony unfolded.

One Ute man, a relative of Box's, said later, "In the old days a boy went into the mountains, and the medicine man dug a pit for him to sit in for three or four days. If he was old enough to smoke the pipe, he would be given that. He would stay in this hole without food or water until he had a vision. The pipe was always used in a sacred manner, in an inner circle by certain men of the tribe, never outsiders. My grandfather used to say you have to be equal to it—it's an honor. When Eddie Box passed the pipe, there were whites and Chicanos there. And they were seated on the grass in front of the clinic with people watching and taking pictures. No wonder the pipe kept going out and Eddie even choked on it. It was a sign that he had done the wrong thing. In the old days if it happened, a man would have to purify himself." He shook his head sadly. "Eddie Box thinks he's God."

Eddie Box lights pipe as grandson Matthew looks on (above); then passes it to tribal chairman Leonard Burch, who offers prayer before smoking (below).

Conspicuously absent from the dedication of the health center was Jim Box, who had not been seen for nearly three months. He was, people said, being punished for his behavior at the Ute-Comanche signing the year before. And they grumbled about how Eddie had let him into the Sun Dance despite the advice of certain elders who feared what the action would bring.

In the summer of 1978 Jim Box danced four days in his father's Sun Dance, enduring the heat and the pain for the sake of what was between him and his conscience. Then, on the day he was finished, the parole officers came to pick him up. He had, they said, gone back to drinking again, in violation of his parole. Allowed to rest for one day, Jim Box was then taken to a rehabilitation center in Texas where he was committed for alcohol abuse.

By that time, the people's sympathy was all with Jim Box's little son James, then almost three, a beautiful child with enormous, searching eyes. He went to live with Betty and Eddie Box, Jr., and began to follow his grandfather around, appearing at pow-wows and dances dressed in a little buckskin outfit, his fine black hair in braids. He had, the people said, the spark and determination that his father once had when he signed his paintings "Spirit Horse." James had the good, strong, classic features of a Southern Ute too, but he had his mother's eyes.

10

LONG AGO WHEN BUFFALO covered the plains and the land
stretched from river to river, unbroken except for rocky bluffs
and isolated stands of cottonwood trees, the Indians moved across
it like waves, rising and falling with the wind, shaped to earth and
sky. In those days the grasses were deep and golden, game was
abundant, and the whites had not yet interfered with a life so old
that it seemed eternal, lost in the unseen power that directed and
preserved it. In song and ritual, the Indians rejoiced, gave thanks,
and through suffering and testing, assured the continued
beneficence of the Great Spirit, the One-Above. Vision quests,
self-mutilation, and fasting were the common means for warriors
to attain that special state of grace necessary for purification of
their spirits.

Above all these rituals was the spectacular Sun Dance, a tribal
ceremonial event, re-enacted but once a year and considered the
holiest of all, the ultimate expression of sacrifice and purification.
It was practiced for years by the Arapaho, Arikara, Assiniboine,
Cheyenne, Crow, Gros Ventre, Hidatsa, Sioux, Plains Cree, Plains
Ojibway, Sarsi, Omaha, Ponca, Shoshone, Kiowa, Blackfeet, and
late in the nineteenth century, by the Utes.

The means by which the Utes learned the dance remains
unclear; one version is that they copied it from the Shoshone; another is that on a raid on the Kiowas in the midnineteenth century
they acquired not only the dance but also one of the nine sacred
Sun Dance dolls, said to be still in the possession of a Southern Ute
family. Whatever the source, the Utes have practiced the Sun
Dance intermittently for almost a century, foregoing the self-tor-
ture aspects of skewering their chests with leather thongs attached

to the center pole. For them it was enough to fast and dance for three days and three nights, at a time when the moon was fullest and the sun was hottest. During that time, the men of the tribe danced to gain power to cure through being cured themselves; they danced after they had had a vision and related it to the Sun Dance chief or shaman, the holiest of their holy men.

The Plains Indians have not practiced their Sun Dance for a half century or more; their old lands, now farmed, paved, and strewn with bustling towns and cities, reflect no glory and no shame. In the breadbasket of America, where farmers drive air-conditioned tractors across the carefully tended land, shaped neither to earth nor sky but trying merely to survive, the memory of the Sun Dance has risen on the wind and blown away; the hallowed ground of the Indians is planted now in corn. And those long-ago tribes whose songs expressed their joy, their sorrow, and their highest hopes, are scattered, extinct, or far removed from drums, flutes, and whistles.

The Sun Dance, a leftover ritual from a simpler time, finds expression now chiefly among the Shoshones, the Sioux (who still pierce their chests with thongs), and the three tribes of Utes, a fragment of hope and fulfillment among a people desperate to hold on. Performed by fewer than a dozen Southern Ute families, the Sun Dance is an anachronism in today's world, held amid tribal dissent, looming assimilation, and ever-increasing pessimism.

That perhaps is the reason why they need it.

Not far from Ignacio a steady stream of cars and pickup trucks moved east along a dirt road late one afternoon in July, turned off at a sign that said "Sun Dance," stopped and were checked by tribal police, then went on to a broad, open field where the grass had turned brown and dry. Three tepees stood out in the sun-baked meadows; between them were two dozen shade houses, low, oblong, and covered with fresh, green cottonwood branches. The shade houses and the tepees formed a huge circle in the field, in

Ute Mountain Ute singer, Blanding, Utah.

the middle of which was the Sun Dance lodge, made of cotton-wood and juniper branches. The Indians walked back and forth across the field, skirting the Sun Dance lodge, visiting from camp to camp, talking quietly, carrying things into their shade houses and the tents beside them. The Sun Dance was about to begin.

The tepee to the west belonged to Eddie Box and was painted with fanciful pictures of deer and buffalo; another, to the east, was plain and belonged to Bertha Groves, the peyote woman and Eddie Box's spiritual rival. In front of the tents, shade houses, and tepees were parked cars, trucks, and campers in a thick pall of dust; beside them children played idly in the dirt, pensive and re-strained. The sober mood of their parents was contagious.

The camps settled down as the sun set in a burst of pink and mauve, touching the clouds that formed over the distant moun-tains to the west. The pungent odor of sage rose on the cooling air and mingled with the sweet smell of piñon fires over which the In-dians were cooking their evening meals, the last food that some of them would have for four days. The Sun Dance participants were all with their families, eating and drinking, preparing themselves in various ways for the sacred old ritual. Nearly two hundred In-dians—most of them Utes—waited and said little. Some smoked, some chopped wood, others sat before the glowing fires or stood apart, gazing up at the sky. No one spoke of the Sun Dance or its meaning, for that was the white man's way, to discuss and explain. For the Indians it was enough to watch and feel, to be one with the dancers in spirit, remembering a time when their ancestors came to dance and inflict torture upon themselves in fulfillment of promises made to the sun. The entire tribe came in those days, to fast and pray for the sick, seeking also the strength and wisdom needed for the rest of the year.

Inside his shade house, Clifford Eagle finished the last of his supper and smoked a cigarette. He said nothing but watched his five-year-old grandson, Norman Harlan, playing with some visit-ing Indian children. There were three other Ute men at the table, singers from the Northern Ute tribe, who were camping with the Eagles. The three would go shortly into the sacred circle, but

Clifford Eagle, to show his disapproval of the four-day dance, increased from the traditional three, would not enter until the following day. At the back of the shade house, Annabelle Eagle finished the dishes, hung up the towel to dry, and disappeared into her tent. Outside, Douglas Remington, Annabelle's son by her first husband, was unloading the car, carrying bedding and water jugs into the shade house, where a low murmur of voices broke the quietness of twilight. A big, broad-shouldered man, Douglas had a degree from the University of Colorado, had taught at Alcatraz, worked at KSUT, and now was working in Denver. In his spare time he campaigned for the Democratic Party, marched against the nuclear facility at Rocky Flats, and even worked for the National Organization for Women. That July, as in other years, Douglas Remington dropped whatever he was doing and came back to his family at Sun Dance time.

"The Sun Dance is the only thing I believe in," he said, leaning against the car, his nephew held in his arms so the small boy could see better. There was activity in the direction of the Sun Dance lodge. "I play so many roles but I don't play a role as a Ute, because I am a Ute. Our family has always danced because we're a Sun Dance family. Clifford's wasn't. The first time he ever danced was the year after Tree died. She was a Sun Dancer, so are Bones and Linda. So am I sometimes. I'm planning to go to Idaho next month and dance. Annabelle never did because there always has to be someone on the outside, to bring you things, clean sheets and clothing, and later on, fresh leaves and sage. Annabelle does that. She's the one who's there for the rest of us."

With that, he and Norman slipped away into the twilight, held in the headlights of the cars that had come out from town and were lined up in front of the sacred circle, waiting for the dancers to appear. The smell of piñon fires drifted over the land, and above the low murmur of voices came the soft, pliant cry of a

OVERLEAF

Tepee and shade house at Southern Ute Sun Dance, Ignacio.

whistle held on a single note. Heat lightning flashed across the in-
digo sky, and thunder rolled lazily behind it. Theresa Harlan came
out of the shade house and asked her mother, "Is thunder really
angels rolling around in barrels?"

Beverly Harlan, her dark eyes laughing, did not answer her
but whispered to her friend, a Ute Mountain Ute, "What I heard
was that it's the devil making love to his sweetheart."

The Ute children were impatient; they climbed on the hoods
of the cars and began to sing a song in Ute, learned from a language class they had been attending that summer. "What is this
song, an old Ute war chant?" someone asked. They laughed. "It's
'Ten Little Indians,'" they said.

There was only a dim smudge of light to the west now; the
moon was a quarter full and hung low, cupping the clouds that
raced toward it. All at once a single drum beat sounded, muffled
and forlorn; the whistle blew again, and voices spoke in Ute. Then
without warning the dancers emerged from their camps and walked
quickly toward the lodge in groups of two and three; they were
wrapped entirely from head to toe in white sheets, ghostly in the
pale moonlight. As they neared the sacred circle, Eddie Box cried
out to them in Ute.

Fifteen dancers wrapped in sheets, caught in the stunning
lights of the cars and pickups, moved like mummies single file
after Eddie Box, his solemn face upturned toward the nighttime
sky as he blew on his eagle-bone whistle, making a noise that the
Indians believe is always heard by the Great Spirit. The Sun
Dance chief marched triumphantly, his shoulders thrown back,
the edge of his sheet dragging the ground. Each dancer blew on an
eagle-bone whistle; each held a sacred eagle plume in either hand
as they circled the Sun Dance lodge four times, once for each day
they were going to dance. The ghostly parade, on completion of
its final circle, turned and went through the opening of the lodge,
which faced east; across its wide entrance was bunched a huge,
heavy piece of canvas on a wire. On the cool night air rose the
strains of a Ute prayer, uttered by someone in the circle.

The dancers went inside, one man at a time, moving quietly

in the darkness to their chosen places against the back of the lodge, pressed against fresh branches of cottonwood and cedar. By the pale gleam of moonlight the gigantic buffalo head on top of the center pole seemed ominous and from another time entirely. It loomed stark and eerie against the inky blue sky, dotted now with stars and the neat, clean quarter slice of moon. An ancient ritual of purification had begun; between dancers and buffalo there already seemed a strange, unearthly power.

Half of the circle was occupied by the dancers; the other half was for the people and for the singers who were seated around an enormous drum. It played softly as the Indians filed slowly in, spreading blankets on the ground. Insistently, the drum beat the same note again and again, regular as a heartbeat; the sound filled the enclosure and quietly and demandingly awakened the earth.

In the dimness the people sat, some covered with shawls and blankets, others in heavy jackets; even in July the nights were always cool at an altitude of six thousand feet. Outlined in the gloom was a pile of sticks in the shape of a tepee placed at the entrance to the circle; one man stepped out of the shadows, bent, and struck a match. In the sudden illumination the buffalo head came to life, glassy-eyed and gaping down at the dancers from its perch on top of the center pole, a sacred cottonwood called the Tree of Life. Stripped of its bark and embedded in the sacred earth of the sacred circle, the tree was tall and straight, chosen for its symmetry and for the fork at the top, on which the head and some of the hide of the buffalo rested. The back of the carcass was stuffed with sweet grass as an offering to assure the animals abundant grass the following year; on either side of it, attached to the fork of the tree, were ribbons of the four sacred colors of the Sun Dance—red, white, black, and yellow, one for each of the races, Eddie Box once said. These colors were always together to show that all men are brothers underneath, he claimed. But traditional Indians insisted that the sacred colors were nothing of the sort. Red always meant earth; white was for purity, yellow stood for enlightenment, and black was the unknown night. The base of the tree was painted red and black and around it were placed offerings of tobacco and sage, left there by the families of the dancers for the spirits in order that some special favor be granted.

The dancers, illuminated by the light from the fire, were naked to the waist. Some wore beads, others were painted with the sacred colors of the ceremonial, all were dressed in colorful long skirts with beaded waistbands; their feet were bare, as is the custom, for they must always be in contact with the sacred earth. The fifteen men stood motionless; their torsos, some hard, some flabby, gleamed in the firelight. They waited expectantly as Eddie Box paused at his spot in the middle of his dancers; to his left was tribal chairman Leonard Burch, suddenly more Indian than he had ever appeared in his office. Near him was Harold Silva, a twenty-nine-year-old Southern Ute, participating in his second Sun Dance.

Eddie Box stepped to the center pole and told everyone to sit on the ground, to "come in contact with Mother Earth." Then he sang four sacred songs, the ones, according to one of the dancers, that the men sing to themselves while dancing. It had never been done in front of the people until that night, but few seemed to understand what had happened except for two dancers who suddenly tensed as though shot.

The songs finished, Eddie Box stood reverently beneath the beady gaze of the buffalo, staring up at it as though he could hear it speak, blowing the eagle-bone whistle, an eagle feather in either hand. Because he is the Sun Dance chief, he was the first to move forward in a kind of strut, up to the pole and back, his eyes always on the buffalo, his movements slow and deliberate. When he was back against the boughs, another dancer moved out in the same way, then another and another. Some shuffled clumsily, others moved lightly on their toes; some bent their shoulders toward the pole, others were ramrod straight. All of them held their heads high; their eyes never wandered from the darkly brooding buffalo head. After a while they appeared hypnotized as they moved steadily back and forth, their legs like pistons, their arms waving, their faces with the most profound expressions of humility and frenzy.

Ute Mountain Ute women play handgame, Towaoc.

The drumming and singing became furious; the sticks of the drummers lashed the hide of the drum, and the energy of the dance exploded, the energy entered the dancers and enriched the breath that escaped through their whistles. All was energy, for all was power. All was continuous, in the sacred circle of the dance and the sacred circle of the drum; all was continuous in the circle above the sky and the circle below the earth.

The moon rested at last in the fork of the tree on the buffalo's horns. With the moon in this position, the first group of singers left and another took its place. The canvas curtain was drawn across the opening, sealing in the feeble warmth of the fire smoldering at its edge; the fire cast a glow around the circle, infusing it with importance and mystery. The old ritual, older than the oldest man, older than the town, the treaties, and perhaps even older than the tribe, took root in that circle, blessed by fire and moonlight.

The singing and dancing lasted almost all night. Most of the people eventually left; others, the families of the dancers, dozed on the ground next to the singers, curled up on blankets and sleeping bags. As the singers urged them up, the dancers, tense, particular, stately, rose and began their shuffle back and forth, confined to the narrow path between their positions and the tree, a path eventually to be worn into a rut before the dance was through. Every movement of hand and foot had some significance and there was a prayer in the action itself, understood by the dancers' women, who sat on the ground all night and did not sleep. When a song was finished and the drum rested, the women sang a sort of "amen" together, a personal offering of encouragement and salutation in the night.

There was sleep but it was wakeful sleep, with the drumming and singing lasting until long after the moon had set. By four o'clock in the morning the world was silent except for the lowing of a cow, the chirp of crickets, and within the circle, a Ute who had remembered his prayers. In the gray light of predawn, the drum began again, softly at first, then in the earth language that it possesses.

The sacred fire had burned all night, and before dawn, the

ashes were carefully gathered and the canvas curtain was pulled back. Around the circle, the people who had spent the night were stirring sleepily, hurrying to rise and walk through the lingering coolness of the night. The crickets still sang, small bats scurried against the approaching light, and a chorus of frogs still croaked in the nearby marsh along the river. As the night watchers left, others came silently, reverently through the opening facing east, to the sacred circle, and stood there shivering, faces turned toward the flaming horizon. The dancers, asleep for several hours, got up from their sleeping bags and huddled beneath the Tree of Life. Their whistles became a shrill, insistent greeting to the sun about to begin its journey into the sky. The drum was a crescendo, the heart of the earth bursting toward the sun, to be consumed and purified. Earth to sun. Sun to earth. People to sun. Sun to people. We welcome you, the giver of all life, the power behind all growth, the father of the universe. In joy and expectation, in thanksgiving and reverence, we greet you, mighty sun. We ask your blessing, your goodness to shine upon us and all our people now born and those who are yet to come. Hear us!

The power that came from its night in the Lower World was now ready to possess the Upper World. The power was manifest in the thin arc of brilliance lying on top of the mountains to the east, the thin arc expanding to the incessant din of the whistles until it became whole. The dancers and the people stared steadily at the sun until it had popped all the way up in the sky, a giant, blinding ball of fire. By then the whistles were so shrill, so filled with the joyousness of the new day, so intense with the efforts of the dancers emptying themselves of passion that the sacred circle vibrated and was lifted by the relentless pounding of the drum out of the earth circle into the sky circle, where it joined the sun.

The people, wrapped in blankets, and the dancers, wrapped in sheets, parted their cocoons in one great encompassing gesture, arms extended toward the sun. The warmth, power, and mystery of the sun were contained within those arms, drawn back against the body; the sun washed over the face and the beating heart. The people helped themselves. The generosity of the sun was theirs for this day; they walked in grace for they had remembered to greet the sun at dawn, as they had always done in the old days and now did but once a year.

One by one, the people lined up for a blessing by Eddie Box and Leonard Burch, severe in countenance yet soft in their posture toward the people who had come to be blessed with an eagle wing, holding the sacred earth and the sacred herbs as they did so, standing barefoot, in touch with Mother Earth and Father Sun. Eddie Box had the appearance of a holy man as he pressed the eagle wing against their bodies with a firm, quick gesture that had behind it both faith and exhibitionism. A woman who had cancer felt the bad spirits drawn out by the eagle wing, and consolation dwelled where pain used to be.

Screwing up his face, Eddie Box held the eagle wing up to the sky, first to the east, where the sun was then a dazzling white orb, then to the south, the west, and the north; he was giving thanks to the four directions, asking for the power to cure the sick to be given to him by the Great Spirit. Leonard Burch, perhaps wishing to impress his people with a traditional gesture, did the same, blessing a group of Utes who came especially to seek him out in a way that none of them would have done in his role as tribal chairman. Here it was different. Leonard Burch was neither adversary nor autocrat; he was an intermediary and they accepted him as such. A look of austere contentment was on his face, absent at other times. The leader had succeeded in making an impression on the people.

From the small, hushed crowd an old man stepped, a Taos Indian who had his grandson with him, a boy about seven years old. The old man faced the boy to the east, directly into the sun, then stooped and gathered a handful of earth from the base of the Tree of Life. Some of it he pressed into the child's hands, the rest he rubbed on the boy's entire body, from head to toe, offering a prayer as he did so. The grandfather did not need Eddie Box's medicine; he had medicine of his own.

Then the Northern Ute medicine man stood with Eddie Box and Leonard Burch; the medicine man, too, had his own medicine,

Ute Mountain Ute girl, Blanding, Utah.

the eagle wing, the herbs, and a fresh pile of leaves on which he stood four small children, blessing them.

When the medicine men were through, the people came forth shyly, some to touch the sacred tree and to pick up pieces of earth around its base. An old woman in a shawl who had seen many Sun Dances in her time gathered up the earth, then stood facing east, letting the earth pass through her gnarled old hands to the ground.

Among the Indians—some Utes, some Pueblo, some Apaches, and some Shoshones—surged an old and powerful belief, a unified consciousness that transcended the realities of their lives. There it was, felt rather than seen, and honored most of all. The strength of the Southern Utes, in considerable doubt for many years, flowed out from them, embracing the world. Their ancestors tiptoed in.

The first day had begun. Within the lodge, still cool and sweet-smelling, the dancers lay back down on their sleeping bags and mats. Some of them smoked, a practice once forbidden in the Sun Dance of old when nothing touched their mouths for three straight days. The people left to have breakfast and to clean up their camps. Even the drums were quiet as the sun rose, the dancers rested, and the Indians moved from camp to camp, visiting one another. The dancers who had filed in first were on the north side, where there was no shade; the north side was the hard side, chosen by the most dedicated dancers as evidence of their desire to become purified. On the north side were Eddie Box, Leonard Burch, Harold Silva, and before the day was over, Clifford Eagle. The spell of Eddie Box seemed remote and improbable, the curse said to be on him and his family even more unlikely as Betty Box came with fresh green leaves that Eddie put all over his body while lying down. She, along with the other women attending the dancers, had also brought fresh sheets and towels. Now ritual had replaced rumor; purification held sway over pettiness, and in the blazing heat of the circle, time and bitterness were suspended. Eddie Box as spiritual leader, Sun Dance chief, or whatever else he decided to call himself, had brought the people together.

By midmorning the drumming began again. A single powerful stroke brought down by one of the six singers seated around the drum announced that the ceremonial had resumed. Then came the songs, monotonous, simple rhythms as sacred as the dance itself, for they have been given by the spirits to the present singers or to someone who has handed them down. The people came through the opening and sat down, this time on fresh reeds that had been placed there; the men went to the north side of the circle where the sun was hottest, while the women remained on the south in the shade with the singers.

That first day, the dancers held back a certain energy, perhaps because there were still three more days to go, anchored in the merciless sun beating down out of a hard blue sky. The circle was like a furnace, growing more and more intense as the sun climbed. The singers, assailing the drum, coaxed, prodded, and dragged the dancers to their feet; slowly they began their shuffle, sixteen pairs of feet in an ancient, plodding rhythm. The buffalo stared down at them, and in his impenetrable gaze was the conviction of generation that those Indian men all sought from him; the buffalo was holy and taught them his lessons in the heat and dust, drawing the dancers into his deep mystery. The buffalo had a lesson behind his bulging eyes and in the medicine bundle at the top of the sacred pole.

When nighttime came, the ceremony took place as it had the night before, begun with the lighting of the fire made of four sticks laid down east and west and four more north and south. The only change was in the dancers' costumes. They all wore different skirts; some wore eagle-claw necklaces, others the skin of a weasel around their necks. The dancers, infused with new energy now that the sun had gone down, stood on their toes, enticed by the buffalo; their movements were sensuous, prolonged, oblivious. Again and again they came closer and closer to the pole, not actually touching it, for it was sacred, the ultimate in grace. The

OVERLEAF

Jacalyn Tom, Ute Mountain Ute.

body of each man, now nearly emptied of food and water, newly craved the spirit. The moon, as usual, was in the fork of the tree.

By the third day, the dancers had smeared themselves with ocher, the Indian version of sunscreen applied to escape the deadly rays of the sun. There were sheets between them now, fastened to thin willow trees that the families had brought, being careful to strip away the bark first. The willows provided scant shade, for the sun was remorseless; there had not been clouds for three days nor any hint of rain.

The dancers, parched, baked, and covered with dust, were the color of the earth, their bodies were like the earth, cracked with pain and exhaustion. One wondered how they stood the heat, how they survived the thirst as their bodies cried out for water, and were made to forget water through the sheer effort of the dance.

One time a dancer had said: "You burn on the inside. You're so dry that when you take a breath, it's fire. But you don't think of that. You can't be distracted by the crowd or by the people around you. You know what you're in there for and that makes you strong. You think you can't go on, that you'll die with every step you take, making your path between the pole and your place in the circle. But you keep going. You cannot show weakness by giving up before it's time.

"Your body stores a lot of water and a lot of food. You draw on that for four days and use it up so that what is not pure comes out. You sweat it out and there's nothing finally, only your body as empty as you can make it. When you fall, if you do fall, the spirit has come down and touched you and you become full of that. You need no food, no water after that."

Eddie Box, smeared with ocher and his face painted to show he was in a sacred condition, wore a mink pelt around his neck, and a long red skirt, to show his position as Sun Dance chief. He walked wearily to the pole where bunches of sweet grass and wheat had been laid at the base, then he called to one of the singers, a Northern Ute who wore a crucifix around his neck. The man got up and went out of the circle and came back with a wheelbarrowful of mud, which he carefully patted into a little mound around the base of the tree. Someone gasped. The dancers, who had not tasted water for three days, stared at the cool mud and seemed to recoil. It was against all the rules for any kind of moisture to be brought into the sacred circle; the day before, even a man wearing a Coors beer T-shirt had been turned away. In the little crowd assembled, a murmur arose. Eddie Box caught the eye of a woman complaining angrily about the mud. When he spoke to her in Ute, she shook her head and left.

The third day is always the hardest day, the day that the old dance ended. These men, exhausted, dehydrated, had another twenty-four grueling hours to go. They lay listlessly on their pallets, leaves pressed against their bodies, the sheets on three sides forming cubicles to give them privacy. A breeze stirred the dust and whipped it into their shelters. They were beyond feeling by that time, into the deepest part of the dance.

A group of Southern Ute men arrived carrying bunches of sweet grass, reeds, and purple wildflowers, which they presented to Eddie Box. Standing at the base of the mud-packed pole, he offered them to the sun, looking directly into it without blinking, then offered them to the four directions. He danced alone with the flowers and lay down finally, distributing a little bunch of flowers to each of the men.

The dancers pressed the flowers to their faces, cool, faintly moist, fragrant. They rested with the flowers, then one by one they rose and began to dance with the flowers, to the memory of flowers and living things. The flowers seemed to give them strength to carry on.

Leonard Burch danced slowly, methodically, his powerful shoulders thrown back, his strong arms gripping the eagle plumes and the flowers at the same time, his feet the color of the sacred earth. He had worn a path from his place to the pole, deep and bold, hollowed out by countless steps. He danced on the third day with a new exuberance, released from discomfort, free to know the secrets of the pole.

Clifford Eagle, who was only in his second day, danced with

more reserve than the others; at sixty-three he was the oldest man there. His movements were slow and tentative, sincere and well directed. His sad, compassionate eyes remained fixed on the pole; he blew his whistle with particular vehemence, as if he expected the spirits to hear him better.

But Harold Silva seemed to be saving himself for later on. He rested most of the morning, and when he got up finally to dance, he bore the painful look of plowed ground. He took longer than the others to make his path to the pole and back, and each time he did, he swayed with a listless resignation that even drooped his shoulders and forced him down to his bed on the hard, hot ground.

That last night, when about a hundred people had crowded into the circle, the singers sang especially loud, the dancers danced especially hard; the women who sang "amen" did it especially fervently. On the last night, everyone was excited and filled with expectation; the songs were more prolonged, lasting twenty and thirty minutes as the dancers pushed themselves harder than they ever had, in more of a trancelike state than before. Suddenly it became obvious that Harold Silva was about to fall, a sign that the spirit had touched him and that he had received his curing power. The other dancers respectfully drew back; the singers belted out the deepest, loudest songs they could, and the people stirred and got to their feet, aware of the holy importance of the moment. Harold Silva, blowing his whistle with little short gasps, rushed up and touched the sacred tree with his hands, again and again, harder and harder, as if he meant to batter himself against it. The earth shook with the fury of the drum, the songs broke the air, and the whole circle was tense with excitement. Perhaps twenty minutes passed in nonstop uproar. Harold Silva's path became shorter and shorter, his breath came in anguished gasps as he struck the tree repeatedly, then all at once he fell to the ground, unconscious. The singing and the drumming ceased. Eddie Box came forward with two dancers, who gently picked him up and carried him off

Ute Mountain Ute, Towaoc.

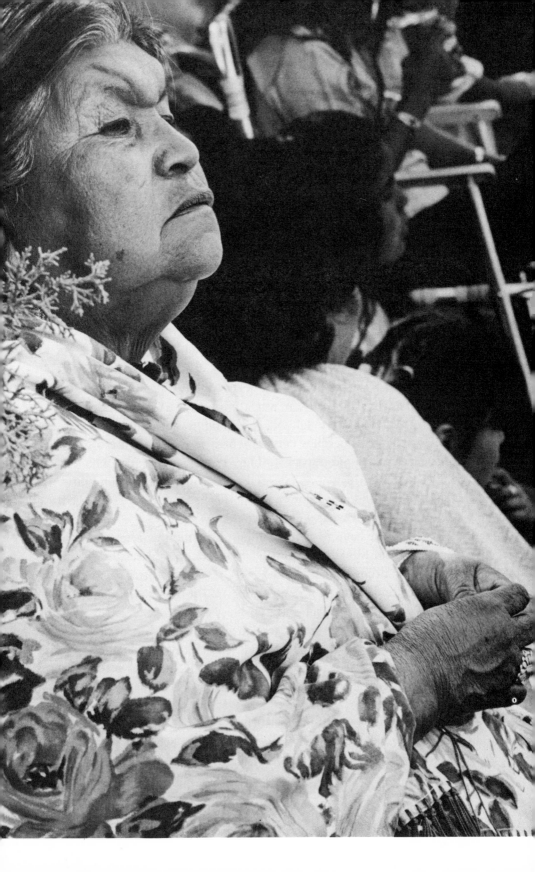

to his shelter. The dance resumed but the meaning was all gone; Harold Silva had taken it with him, a bestowal of grace that was like a visitation of angels or the appearance of the Holy Spirit. Harold Silva was in a sacred condition, according to the teachings of the Sun Dance.

But later, some of the people were uneasy. A few of them said privately that it was not a true fall, that he had fallen for the benefit of the people watching. When a dancer falls, they said, you feel something because you know that he has done this for you. The spirit has come to him for you. When Harold Silva fell, one woman said that she felt a cold wind rush through the circle. She said that something would happen to Harold Silva before the year was through.

Even Clifford Eagle was disturbed by what had happened. A few weeks after the Sun Dance he said, "In the old days, you never touched the pole the way Harold Silva did. You always stood back from it because it was a holy object. My grandfather used to say, 'You only fall once. Falling is not something you choose—it happens because you are worthy of it. To fall is a great honor and our people respect it. They respect the dancer who has achieved it.' But this young man fell twice, once last year and now again. It's up to him to know why he did it, but I have never seen it before. I wonder what will happen because of it."

He did not have to wonder long. Two months after the Sun Dance, Harold Silva died from what the doctors described as an overdose of drugs. But the Southern Utes knew better. Those of them who understood the Sun Dance said it was something else. When you violate the rules of the most sacred dance of all, bad medicine will follow. First it was the year that women were allowed to dance and Eddie Box made an offering of flesh, then it was the year of Harold Silva's fall, the presence of mud at the base of the pole, and the sacred songs that Eddie Box sang aloud. Bad medicine had followed each transgression.

In Ignacio, everything had changed. The Indians believed that the curse remained with them, unbroken even by the fierce dancing of the men at the Sun Dance, by then violated in its meaning also. The people went their way, convinced that even more terrible things were to follow. If purity and regeneration were still to be found, it was in the quiet dignity of Annabelle Eagle one bright fall morning as she visited her daughter Tree's grave, prayed, and left a pouch of tobacco at the headstone. That simple, touching ritual conveyed more than Eddie Box's words or dances.

"She lives," she said.